International Strategies for American Investors

International Strategies for

AMERICAN INVESTORS

John P. Dessauer

PRENTICE HALL PRESS • New York

Published by Prentice Hall Press
A Division of Simon & Schuster, Inc.
Gulf + Western Building
One Gulf + Western Plaza
New York, NY 10023

Library of Congress Cataloging-in-Publication Data

Dessauer, John P., 1936–
International strategies for American investors.

Includes index.
1. Investments, American. I. Title.
HG4538.D48 1986 332.6′7373 86-17026
ISBN 0-13-652793-0

Designed by Irv Perkins Associates

Manufactured in the United States of America

10 9 8 7 6 5 4 3

Contents

Chapter 1

The Crash of 1990

IT PROBABLY ALL BEGAN with the election of Ronald Reagan as president of the United States. The impact on society, financial markets, and the fortunes of all Americans is already evident. Powerful, far-reaching forces are moving the United States and world financial markets in new directions. There has been a complete reversal of trends.

In the 1960s during the terms of John F. Kennedy and Lyndon Johnson, the United States *assumed* that its position as the richest nation in the world was guaranteed. We put a man on the moon, created the space shuttle, spent hundreds of billions of dollars fighting in Vietnam, and launched an all-out war against poverty. We acted as if we had found the secret to everlasting wealth.

In the 1970s the United States ran up against its limits. We withdrew from Vietnam and watched in horror as the number of poor and homeless Americans increased, and spending on social services rose to record high levels. In 1986 the explosion of the space shuttle *Challenger* cast doubts on our ability to spend wisely in science. Our failure was followed by widely advertised Soviet space shot successes.

The United States changed. From a self-assured, arrogant nation of incredibly rich people we became more introspective, quiet, and open to criticism. Our attitudes shifted from certainty about our nation's financial future first to a feeling of national doubt that we would make it at all and then to a realistic, confident search for answers.

Events have shaped our attitudes. Rebuilding our economy has become the number one challenge. Poverty at home, difficulties abroad, and even science are likely to lag far behind finance and economics as national interests in the coming decade. The financial markets have already begun to reflect the changes. Stocks are up and interest rates are down. Pessimism is giving way to new optimism.

You might think that a new optimism, rising stock and bond markets, falling oil prices, and lower interest rates would make financial life easier for everyone. That is not the situation. Millions of investors missed the bull stock market when it began in 1982 and stood on the sidelines waiting for a plunge even as the Dow Jones Industrial Average rose first above 1,500 and then above 1,900. They held on to "safe" investments such as high-yielding government bonds and felt smugly confident. Their income, after all, was supposed to be secure. The best economists in the nation forecast higher interest rates right to the end of 1985.

When the stock market soared and yields on bonds plunged, there was joy in some corners and bitterness in others. Suddenly a new truth emerged. Government bonds, for example, were exposed as not so safe after all.

In 1976 U.S. government bonds paid between 8 percent and 9 percent. By early 1986 the impossible had happened; yields on government bonds had fallen back to the levels of 1976. Holders of government bonds were losers. Between 1976 and 1986 inflation had cut the value of a dollar in half. To be even you had to double both your income and your capital. Government bonds failed that test. Their value and their income were the same in 1986 as they had been ten years earlier. An investor with $100,000 in U.S.

government bonds bought in 1976 enjoyed an income of $9,000 a year. In 1986 the income level was nearly the same, but just to be even with inflation an investor needed $18,000. Venturing into government bonds when yields were much higher did help for a while. But, as those bonds came due, the holders found their income falling. Only those who were nimble enough to buy bonds when yields were at their peak managed to come away with a capital gain large enough to offset the eroding effects of inflation.

The punishment dealt to investors as yields fell and stocks rose was widespread. They had been lulled into a false security, believing that interest rates could not come down while the federal deficit was so large. They felt betrayed when interest rates plunged. If the truth were known, it is likely that a majority of American investors felt bitterness and betrayal, not joy, when stock and bond markets soared.

It is clear that even after both bonds and stocks had soared, confidence was tentative. Money poured into mutual funds. Investors did not have enough confidence to go it alone and pick their own stocks and bonds. They preferred the diversification and professional management offered by the funds. Stocks that moved higher attracted buyers. Stocks that languished were quickly sold as if the rush to higher stock prices was a passing phenomenon. The broad general consensus was that while it was nice that stock and bond prices were rising, the best strategy was to cash in, take profits while they lasted. Deep beneath the surface was a vague feeling that long-term optimism was justified, that things really had changed for the better. But on the surface was a widely accepted conviction that since the pessimists, the mongers of gloom and doom, had been so wrong, justice might require that the optimists suffer the same fate. Few were willing to back optimism with hard-earned cash.

Ironically, the crowd by its tentative optimism created

yet another opportunity for those with the courage to be different. If you believed that the recovery had a chance of lasting, you could buy those stocks that were either being sold or neglected. A prolonged recovery would lift the fortunes of companies that were still struggling in early 1986. Many, with the benefit of lower interest rates and lower energy costs, would be showing substantial future gains in profits. The crowd ran in one direction, with a single opportunistic strategy, leaving a broad range of opportunities in its wake. That is the point. That is what always happens. The primary engine of opportunity in the financial markets is not the government, the consumer, or the economy. It is the crowd. There is a world of opportunity. But to see it you must find the tools, techniques, and perspectives that will allow you to stand apart from the crowd. It isn't enough to be a rugged individual in your social or business life. The financial markets require their own special disciplines.

Financial success is like success in cooking, art, music, or mathematics; you must develop your skills and practice regularly. You have to take the time to concentrate on the markets, to "see" developing risks and opportunities. It is said that anyone can draw a picture. That is true. But that doesn't mean that anyone can simply pick up a pencil and instantly produce an artistic sketch. You have to learn eye and hand coordination in order to draw. Likewise in investments, anyone can be successful. But to be a survivor in the battle for financial security you also have to develop a special sense of awareness and bring out your hidden talents.

This book has several objectives. The primary one is to show you that you can acquire a new international perspective, one that will let you cut through the confusion and see the world of opportunity. In the chapters that follow you will find new tools and techniques that will lead you to greater investment profits. A second objective is to show you how to stand apart from the crowd, tap hidden personal resources, and move ahead toward your financial goals with confidence. Anyone can be wealthy. You just have to take a close look at wealthy people whom you know to see that riches are often acquired by individuals with skills and talents no greater than your own. That doesn't mean that everyone who reads this book will be rich. But by practicing the disciplines described in these pages you will come closer to fulfilling your personal, maximum financial potential.

The world of financial markets can be complex and intimidating. There are thousands of various types of investments from options to futures contracts and zero coupon bonds. It is easy to get lost amid all the variations or to shrug and run away in search of a simpler life. Hidden beneath the surface of world financial markets is always a simple truth. Once discovered, that truth will lead any investor to above-average profits. You can apply simple, straightforward strategies or indulge in the complex array of opportunities, as you wish. Conversely, miss that core of truth, make false assumptions about the state of the markets, and you will suffer, pay the price no matter what strategy you apply. The most sophisticated techniques will not insulate an investor who fails to see market conditions clearly.

The Crash of 1990

The title of this chapter is not pessimistic. It is optimistic, indicating that the earliest date that the U.S. stock and bond markets could run into serious trouble is 1990.

As the 1970s drew to a close it was popular to worry about long-waves, cycles that repeat themselves with regularity in the markets. The U.S. stock market crashed in 1929. The Dow fell from a 1929 peak of 381 to a 1932 low of 41. The stock market lost 89 percent of its value in three years. In the process, investors were devastated. Billions were lost. Some people committed suicide. Having failed to see the risks in 1929, they were unable to face the consequences of financial disaster. Others accepted fate and suffered the impoverishment of financial failure.

Based on the truism that history often repeats itself, investors began to look for a duplicate of the great crash fifty years later, in 1979. There was a popular book called *The Crash of 1979.*

The market didn't appear to be cooperative. The Dow Jones Industrial Average reached 1,000 in 1976, a level from which a devastating crash was believed to be possible. Instead of plunging to 100 or 200, however, the Dow merely drifted lower, hovering between 800 and 900 during 1979. That did not deter the doom mongers. They persisted in their forecasts of a coming crash right up to 1982, when their predictions were brushed aside by the markets. In 1982, instead of a crash, stocks entered a new bull market that carried them to a series of new highs. In 1986, six and a half years after the crash of 1979 was supposed to develop, the Dow was still strong, rising above 1,700 and showing no signs of decay.

There was no error in the original cycle theories. History did repeat itself. The error was in the perspective. The doom mongers had failed to take careful note of both the similarities and the differences between the 1970s and the 1930s. In the twenties and thirties the U.S. and world economies were on a gold standard. The value of the dollar was fixed by the government. In the 1970s and 1980s the dollar was free to float on world currency markets. In the 1920s and 1930s the economic strains that accumulated had no where to go but into the financial markets. In the 1970s financial pressure was released in the currency markets as well as in financial markets. The dollar dropped steadily between 1970 and 1979, reaching a crescendo of decline in late 1979. When the U.S. stock market and the dollar are combined, a pattern remarkably similar to that of 1929 appears. In terms of Swiss francs, for example, the Dow Industrial Stock Average fell 72 percent between 1970 and 1979. To an investor in Europe there was a U.S. stock market crash in the 1970s.

An American investor could have seen the "crash" in another way. Stocks didn't rise, even though inflation rose to double digits, significantly diminishing the value of a dollar. If stock prices were adjusted for inflation, their real value was declining in the 1970s.

From an international perspective or from an inflation-adjusted point of view, the predicted stock market crash came right on schedule.

By 1932 the U.S. economy was deep in the depression. The stock market bottomed that year and began a rebound that carried the Dow 150 percent higher to 100 in 1934. Fifty years later, in 1982, the U.S. economy slipped into "the worst recession since the Great Depression." The recession of 1982 plus the international perspective of the stock market in the 1970s were powerful suggestions that U.S. financial markets and the entire economy were following a path very similar to that of the 1930s. Consistent with that conclusion, world stock markets bottomed and began what was to become a new bull market in 1982.

By the end of 1982 the evidence was accumulating rapidly. The financial markets were not forging new ground; they were repeating fifty-year-old history.

Wall Street, investors, and the economic community are fond of finding interesting correlations. There is the Superbowl indicator, which forecasts stock prices based on which league wins the Superbowl. There are forecasts based on presidential election cycles. And in the 1970s and 1980s technical, computer-driven, statistical analysis has been the rage. In spite of all the computer and human brain power that was invested in monitoring the financial markets, few noticed the "crash of 1979," and few paid attention to the "coincidence" of the deep recession of 1982 and the depression of 1932. It even became popular completely to misinterpret the evidence. The aftereffects of the recession of 1982 were also similar to those of the postdepression period. Instead of recognizing the situation, nationally respected economists came out with warnings of doom. They argued that these signs were signs of a *coming* crash and depression. They missed the obvious, that the crash and depression of the 1970s–1980s were over.

Perhaps the problem was that too many people expected an exact duplicate of the Great Crash and Great Depression. They were not willing to admit that some of the changes that came after the depression worked. In the 1930s demand was a nagging problem. People were out of work, unemployment was inadequate, Social Security had not been enacted, and there was a monstrous shortage of cash in consumer pockets. There were too few people with enough cash to buy goods and services. The economy, lacking demand, was plagued with deflation. Prices kept falling as if in search of buyers at any price.

In contrast, by 1980, we not only had Social Security and a more adequate unemployment program, we had also a whole range of social programs that kept demand from falling as dramatically as it did in the 1930s. When the recession of 1982 struck, it did cause a massive contraction. Millions of people suffered financially. But thanks to the social programs, there was enough residual demand, enough people with cash to spend, to keep us out of deflation. Inflation came tumbling down, but we did not fall headlong into a depression. We managed to get by with "only" the worst recession since the Great Depression.

If the dollar had been connected rigidly to gold and if we had not enacted social programs, it is likely that the doom mongers would have been rewarded. The stock market would have crashed exactly as it did in the twenties and early thirties, and the nation would have plunged into a second depression. But, the differences were there, and the results, while similar to those of fifty years ago, were, in many respects, significantly different.

The Latin American Debt Theory

The doom peddlers had a favorite story, Latin American debts. In the 1930s the depression deprived Latin American economies of needed revenue. Most were not able to meet their obligations, and debt default became widespread.

In the 1970s, as in the 1920s, there was a buildup of international debts, including huge loans to countries in Latin America. High interest rates and the recession of 1982 combined to deprive Latin American countries of needed foreign exchange and, at the same time, caused a steep rise in interest costs. The result was the international debt crisis of the 1980s.

American banks had billions of dollars outstanding in loans to Latin America. Economists and investment analysts looked at the situation, remembered the 1930s, and spewed out a long stream of gloomy forecasts. The basic theme was that there would be a chain of Latin American debt defaults that would cause bank after bank to collapse, ruining the world banking system and producing another Great Depression. The idea was not frivolous. It was embraced by some of the nation's most respected economists. One went so far, in 1983, as to say that it was no longer a question of if, but a question of when, the destructive chain of debt defaults would begin.

Reports showing that many of America's biggest and most prestigious banks had loans outstanding to Latin American borrowers far in excess of shareholder equity made the frightening forecasts all the more compelling.

That situation, it was argued, meant that a widespread debt default would bankrupt the banks, wiping out shareholder equity. The doomsdayers did not stop there.

The bloodshed in El Salvador and Nicaragua was used as an example of what would happen if countries in Latin America tried to set their economies on a right path. International organizations such as the International Monetary Fund were busy trying to find solutions to the debt crisis. They offered prescriptions designed to bring down the destructive inflation plaguing most Latin American nations. In all cases, corrective economic action meant sacrifices. The U.S. economists argued that the people of Latin America would never accept sacrifice but would revolt instead. There was no solution to the debt crisis because any attempt at resolution would lead to blood in the streets. That view became so popular that money-center bank stocks sold at an all-time record low price-to-earnings ratio. No one wanted to hold the stocks for fear of losing everything when Latin America ultimately crumbled.

Generalizing about the people of Latin America turned out to be a major mistake. Argentina, for example, ousted its military government and installed a democratic civil government without revolution. The new civilian president decided to adopt the harsh economic measures needed to turn the Argentine economy around for the better. He legislated price and wage controls, caused a sharp rise in unemployment, and asked the people to make real sacrifices in the hope of a better future. The people reacted with enthusiasm. One reporter described the phenomenon by saying that a Lenten spirit of sacrifice had come early to Argentina. There was no blood in the streets. The U.S. pundits were wrong. The people of Argentina embraced economic sacrifice with courage and conviction. Within a month the inflation rate in Argentina had come down enough to justify new optimism.

In early 1986 a similar story came out of Brazil. There too a military government had been replaced with democratic civilian leadership. The new government of Brazil followed the lead of Argentina and imposed harsh economic measures to fight triple-digit inflation. Included was a one-thousand-for-one reverse split on the currency. Imagine what would happen in the United States if the government decided to give every American one new dollar for every thousand dollars. Americans take great pride in their currency and certainly would react negatively to the idea of giving up one thousand old dollars for one new dollar. In Brazil in 1986 the people accepted the harsh measures with a willingness like that seen previously in Argentina. The new Brazilian president's popularity soared shortly after the measures were imposed. The people understood what had to be done and why. They also understood that success or failure was up to them. The gloomy American analysts were wrong about Brazil too.

About the same time that Brazil was imposing harsh measures to bring inflation down, world oil prices collapsed. Mexico's oil revenue fell sharply. Fresh concerns about Mexico's ability to meet debt payments arose. Mexico, however, did not adopt a confrontation approach. It addressed the problem realistically and in a spirit of negotiation. Officials from Mexico kept the U.S. banks and the U.S. government informed and remained open to ideas on how to deal with the crisis. In the process of examining the issues it came out that what Mexico needed most was a reduction in the interest rates being paid on its debts. No sooner did that idea surface than there was a significant rally in the U.S. bond markets. Interest rates plunged, and without anything having to be negotiated, the rate of interest on Mexico's debt began to decline. The Mexican debt crisis, like those of Argentina and Brazil, began to melt down to manageable proportions.

A strange thing happened in early March 1986. The president of Mexico addressed the nation on a Friday night. The subject was plunging oil prices and the Mexican debt crisis. Considering all the headlines given over the years between 1982 and 1986 to Latin American debts, you might think that the Mexican presidential address would be front-page material. Hardly; the address was good news, not bad. The crisis in Mexico was being managed intelligently. There was no threat of revolution, no blood in the streets, and therefore no sensational headlines. There was no front-page coverage of the address to the people of Mexico. In fact, in the major eastern U.S. papers there was no mention at all until Monday and then only casual references to the event. The United States, at least the financial press, was obviously embarrassed by all the good news coming from south of the border. We had, by our arrogant conviction that the people of Latin America would revolt rather than face economic issues, insulted our neighbors, but we were too proud to apologize. So, the news was buried in hopes that no one would notice. Let the false predictions of doom die quietly seemed to be the strategy.

The basic error was not underestimating the people of Latin America; it was our failure to look closely at history and the differences in the 1980s. In the 1930s U.S. banks were also brokers. Fifty years ago the banks sold Latin American bonds to individual investors. When the depression struck, it impoverished the American investor. When the depression wrecked the economies of Latin America, there was no source of emergency capital. Latin America, in the 1930s, was suddenly cut off from financial assistance. Capital flows to Latin America stopped, leaving those countries entirely to their own inadequate resources.

Following the Great Depression, the United States passed a law called the Glass–Steagal Act, which separated banks and brokers. In the 1970s the banks were not selling Latin American bonds. They were making direct bank loans to businesses and governments south of the border. In the 1970s it was the banks that were at risk with their own capital. When the crisis struck in the 1980s, the countries of Latin America were not left stranded. They had bankers in the United States to negotiate with. The U.S. bankers did not abandon Latin America; they had too much at stake. That was perhaps the most significant difference between the 1930s and the 1980s. The fact that the recession of 1982 was not as severe as the depression of the 1930s also helped. Continued demand, an economy in the United States that at least was limping along, meant that there was opportunity to address all the problems, including the Latin American debts.

We will never know what might have happened in the 1930s had there been a similar opportunity to negotiate Latin American debts. It is clear, however, that the corrective measures taken after the Great Depression had a positive effect when the economic crises of the late 1970s and early 1980s arrived.

Investors who recognized the differences were rewarded with an opportunity to more than double their money. The money-center bank stocks rose from excessively depressed levels in 1982 to more than double by early 1986, and they were still "undervalued" relative to most other U.S. stocks.

Watching and waiting for the next stock market crash, based on Latin American debts, had another obvious fault. The disastrous string of debt defaults that marked the 1930s occurred between August 1931 and September 1932, after the great stock market crash of 1929 and about the time that the Dow was striking its all-time record low. The doomsdayers of the 1980s banked on the public having a short memory. Had there been a careful look at the past, the warnings of a coming stock market crash because of international debt problems would have been ridiculed. Anyone who *bought* stocks when Latin American debt defaults were at their peak in the 1930s would have been buying at the stock market's all-time record low. Investors who did that enjoyed substantial *profits.* The Dow climbed to 100 by 1934, a gain of 150 percent. By 1937 the Dow had risen to almost 200 for a gain of 400 percent from the 1932 low. The Latin American debt problems of the 1980s should have been viewed as a signal to buy, not a warning of coming disaster.

The stock market behaved in the 1980s much the same as in the 1930s, rising from a 1982 low of 777 to more than 1,700 on the Dow Industrial Average by early 1986. The international debt crisis of the 1980s, like that of the 1930s, was a sign that the worst was over.

The Latin American debt crisis was more evidence that history in the 1980s was following patterns established fifty years earlier. While many misinterpreted the evidence, they were basically correct to make the comparison. The 1930s hold powerful messages for the 1980s, not the least of which relates to the U.S. federal deficit.

The Federal Deficit

Americans like to think, because of the billion- and trillion-dollar numbers, that the federal deficit problem of the 1980s is unique, new, and without precedent. That is not true. The federal deficit was a problem in the 1930s. The depression devastated federal tax collections. The programs created to help lift the economy out of the depression were expensive. In 1936, President Franklin D. Roosevelt proposed tax increases to balance the federal budget.

The federal deficit of the 1980s was not new and unprecedented. Depressions and recessions are expensive for the federal government. They reduce income and increase expenses, creating deficits. In the 1980s, just like the 1930s, the federal government was faced with rising deficits and a huge national debt. Surprisingly, however, few bothered to look back at the 1930s to see how those problems were handled by the Roosevelt administration. Walter Mondale in his campaign for president in 1984 boldly argued that tax increases would eventually be necessary to balance the federal budget. He was supported in that conclusion by the economic community, which argued that the deficit had become "structural." By that they meant that it would never go away by itself. It was widely believed that the huge federal deficit, by increasing the government's borrowing requirements, was keeping U.S. interest rates high. High interest rates meant that the cost of the national debt alone would mean continued deficits. Republicans and Democrats alike feared that the deficits had become self-intensifying. The deficits cause high interest, they thought, and high interest rates make deficits worse.

The government felt the same way fifty years ago and that is why President Roosevelt and Congress enacted a tax increase. By 1937, just over a year after the tax increase, however, the economy slipped badly. The gross national product dropped, and the stock market fell from near 200 to 100. The tax increase of the 1930s, instead of reducing the deficit, caused a new recession and made the deficit worse. By 1939 the privately held national debt had risen to 37 percent of the entire economy.

The United States was saved from the full effects of the tax increase mistake of the 1930s by the buildup toward World War II. Spending on war materials gave the economy support. The gross national product recovered quickly. War spending also increased the deficit. By the end of World War II, in 1946 the privately held national debt had swollen to $231.6 billion, a modest figure by today's standards but at the time equal to more than 100 percent of the entire economy.

In the 1980s there were a few lonely voices trying to persuade people to remember that in the past a rising federal deficit went hand in hand with lower, not higher, interest rates. Between 1936, when the total, privately held national debt was 37 percent of the GNP, and 1946, when it had risen to more than 100 percent of the GNP, long-term interest rates fell from 3 percent to 2.5 percent. Our own history contradicted the most popular views of the 1980s, but few bothered to listen. The idea that rising government deficits would be accompanied by falling interest rates *seemed* ridiculous until, in 1986, just like fifty years earlier, it happened. Interest rates came down in 1986 in spite of huge federal deficits and a burgeoning national debt.

The Future

The story of the stock market, the dollar, Latin American debts, the federal deficit, and interest rates shows how, with a sense of history and some common sense, you could have penetrated the cloud of confusion that ruled the markets in the early 1980s. It was possible for an individual investor to buck the most respected and degreed economists and financial advisers and profit while they languished in error. By buying long-term bonds, money-center bank stocks, or other stocks you could have significantly increased your personal wealth.

The story of the similarities between the 1930s and the 1980s doesn't stop with a look back at what might have been; it carries us out into the future with an intriguing look at potential future profits.

Another major difference between the 1930s and the 1980s is the presidential election cycle. In the thirties a president was elected in 1932 and again in 1936. In the 1980s the years are 1984 and 1988. President Ronald Reagan and his anti-tax-increase stance will be in the White House until 1988. The pro-tax-increase forces may be able to nibble away at his position, but they will not be able to drive through a tax increase large enough to damage the economy until 1989. From the 1930s we can see that it takes time for a tax increase to show up in the economy and the markets. It took slightly more than a year in the 1930s.

If the new president and Congress decide, in 1989, to increase taxes to balance the federal budget, and the old script from the 1930s continues to be played out in the 1980s, the next major stock market correction can be expected in 1990. That is why this chapter is entitled "The Crash of 1990." This is not a discouraging theme designed to send you running for shelter. It is encouragement intended to show that there is still a world of opportunity, even in the U.S. stock market.

As the stock market rose in 1985 and 1986, many became increasingly worried about a "blow off" or a "speculative bubble" that would burst, sending stocks plunging to sharply lower prices. Rising markets are just as disconcerting as falling markets. It isn't easy to earn above-average profits, not even when the stock market is roaring ahead. In early 1986 as the Dow rose to a string of new highs, there was a widespread tendency to sell any stocks that weren't moving and shift the proceeds into stocks that were in the midst of the "action." Investors were impatient, afraid of missing an opportunity. They would rather try for the last 15 percent on a "hot stock" than invest in one of the overlooked stocks languishing at a bargain price. There was a noticeable lack of confidence. The popular fear was that the stock market was becoming ever more vulnerable as it rose to one new high after another. It was as if most were still worried that the crash of 1979 would arrive late. This left many stocks in companies with solid finances and good earnings selling at low prices. It wasn't hard to find stocks selling at book value, when the average U.S. stock had advanced to 180 percent of book value.

If you had a clear understanding of the similarities and differences between the 1930s and the 1980s, you would have had the confidence to buy the low-priced stocks and wait for the market to lift their prices later in the cycle. If you were worried about a crash in 1990, instead of looking for ghosts of past crashes, you would have the conviction and patience to hold on for above-average gains in 1986, 1987, and 1988.

The Question of a Recession in 1990

The recession of 1938 followed the tax increase of 1936. The Great Crash of 1929 followed the enactment of the Smoot–Hawley Tariff Act, a protectionist measure designed to keep out foreign farm products and save American farmers. These experiences from fifty years ago let us know that recessions, even depressions, can be caused by tax increases and protectionism. The recession of 1982 followed a deliberate and massive change in U.S. monetary policy that drove interest rates to record high levels.

Recessions are disruptions of either supply or demand on a scale large enough to affect a large portion of the economy. Tampering with consumers, world trade, or business can be dangerous to our economic health. Good intentions, such as balancing a deficit federal budget, make no difference. Economic forces are both brutal and objective. They respect no man's ideas and owe allegiance to no political party.

Until 1986 investors were protected from another round of high interest rates by the economy's lackluster performance. The Federal Reserve wouldn't risk enlarging the federal deficit by precipitating a recession with high interest rates. During 1984 and 1985 as the dollar soared, there was a rising tide of protectionism in the United States. Farmers and business were losing badly to cheap foreign imports. Congress was being pressured to take action in the form of laws reducing the flood of imports. The protectionist tide did not break out into disastrous congressional action because the dollar, in 1985, came tumbling down under the force of sharply lower U.S. interest rates.

The risk of recession is always close at hand. In the 1930s recession blossomed after the tax increase of 1936. There could be a new recession in the future. The force of deficits, presidential resolve, and the currency markets has fended off the dangers between 1982 and 1986. It is likely that those conditions will continue to fend off recession for the next year or two.

After the presidential elections of 1988, the risks will emerge again. Recession is not inevitable, but neither is there a guarantee of long-lasting prosperity.

Fifty years ago the Great Crash of 1929 and the Great Depression were followed by World War II. It takes only the slightest glance at the news today to know that tensions and violence have increased in the 1980s just as they did fifty years ago. In those days the international debt crisis left nation after nation in a state of despair. Fifty years ago the world was on a rigid gold standard, and there was no Social Security in the United States. It was every man for himself. Despair, depression, and economic isolationism led to world war. This time around there are social-spending programs, the banks are negotiating on international debts, no nation has been cut off from world credit markets, and the economic malaise is not as bad as in the thirties. This time there is hope that we can avoid the dismal consequences that followed the Great Depression. There is increased violence in the world from Lebanon to the streets of major U.S. cities. Just as we avoided a depression in 1982, there is hope that the tensions of the mid-1980s will not lead to another world war.

The absence of war will present another challenge. After World War II the United States, believing that the war had been caused by economic depravity, set out to help the vanquished nations of Germany and Japan rebuild. The objective was to preserve the peace through economic prosperity. The Marshall Plan turned out to be more than an aid package for Europe and Asia; it became the source of twenty years of American prosperity. Our generosity in helping others produced markets for American goods, created American jobs, and assured the United States of economic growth, falling national deficits, and a general increase in the standard of living.

One of the more perplexing and unanswered questions for the 1980s is, Can we produce prosperity without first going through the destruction of a world war? The answer is yes, but only if we can repeat the Marshall Plan process and create new markets for American goods.

There is an obvious opportunity to do so, and that is Latin America. The nations south of our borders need our help. They are reasonably well-developed economies, but they have a long way to go. If the United States can supply Latin America, not with short-term loans as in the 1970s but with genuine, long-term financing, there is a very good possibility that new markets for American goods can be developed. We could create new jobs in the United States and lift U.S. standards of living by helping our neighbors with long-term investment capital.

Finding prosperity, however, will require setting aside our prejudices. As long as too many Americans look at Latin America through discolored glasses there will be a problem in finding enough aid to accomplish the goal. You can't have nationally respected economists openly assuming that sound economies in Latin America produce revolution and expect to find government and private money willing seriously to consider long-term Latin American investments. We need a fresh dialogue, a new and more accurate understanding of our neighbors. We need to have confidence. Perhaps the fact that this time there wasn't a chain of Latin American debt defaults will help. The risks are great enough. On the one hand we can have prosperity through generosity, and on the other a lack of generosity can propel us back into the crash and depression we fear.

Without growth the deficits will linger as an ever-present threat. One recession and the U.S. federal deficit could run into $500 to $600 billion a year. That might be enough finally to shake people's confidence. Interest rates could soar. The dollar could plunge. The world economy could be destabilized. There could be a new depression. Only this time it would be worse. In the 1930s many people still lived on farms. The skills for basic physical survival were common. This time there are millions more people. They are concentrated in cities, and they think that hamburger comes from a fast-food restaurant. If there is a major disruption in the food-producing or food-distributing system, the result could be hunger and starvation. It is easy to say that one of the richest countries on earth, the United States, could not ever suffer like Ethiopia. But you can't eat a Social Security check from Uncle Sam.

Both the risks and the opportunities are real. On the one hand, investors can suffer when markets plunge in recessions. On the other hand, they can suffer if they miss a major opportunity to increase their capital when markets rise. Between 1976 and 1986 you had to double both your income and your capital to keep even with the effects of inflation.

It isn't easy to keep from being brutalized by the markets. It isn't impossible either. You can achieve financial security in this world of wild, volatile, and unpredictable financial markets. To do it you need the courage to take reasonable and calculated risks and a perspective, a way of looking at things, that sets you apart from the crowd. That's what the remaining chapters in this book are all about: how to develop a successful personal investment strategy by adopting an international point of view. You don't have to leave home. You don't have to study in foreign countries. All you have to do is be willing to learn some new ideas.

It all starts with the one true world money, the hinge pin for all financial markets, gold.

Chapter 2

Gold: The Hinge Pin of All Investments

THERE ARE TWO WAYS to protect yourself, your family, and your life-style from economic disaster. One is to run for cover, preserve and protect what you have. The other is to fight to increase your fortune.

Both are valid strategies. On the eve of a global economic disaster there is no choice but to preserve and protect. There is no longer, at that point, any hope of increasing wealth. In the days and years before a disaster, however, protectionist strategies can lead to disaster. Failing to embrace appropriate risks can mean more than financial stagnation; it can mean significant losses. Likewise, clinging to false optimism as disaster dawns can result in despair and financial ruin.

There is a time for taking risks and a time for staying in safe havens. Aristocrats always opt for preservation and safety. They survive by protecting their vast holdings of land, cash, bonds, stocks, and gold. Others have little or no choice. Their resources are not enough. Their only real chance for financial survival is first to increase their wealth to a level where protectionism becomes a meaningful alternative.

It is human to fancy ourselves as aristocrats. And in many ways other than financial we may be as well off as any king or queen. To indulge in financial fantasies, however, is dangerous. It is all too common to wish risk away, to make believe that we can't afford risk and to opt for safety under the false illusion that we have enough.

In the real world of ordinary people there is no choice but to take risks. The secret to financial survival is to take calculated, intelligent risks in full awareness of all the facts.

Gold is basic. To possess it is the first and essential step in developing a sensible investment strategy. Gold crosses the line between preserving a fortune and making one. Understanding gold is essential to internationalizing your investment thinking and developing a sensible strategy for financial survival in the new world of wild, unruly, and largely unregulated financial markets.

The Basic Value of Gold

Gold has emerged again as the centerpiece of world financial markets. Gold's spectacular rise in the 1970s attracted a lot of attention. People who never before thought of gold as an investment joined the crowd's mad pursuit of profits. At one point, near the 1980 peak of $835 an ounce, activity in the futures markets was so hectic that twenty-five times the world's known supply of gold was traded in the space of a few months. One thing became crystal clear. Gold, the same gold that attracted pirate's guns and adorned Egyptian kings, still holds enormous power. Other things also became clear. In the modern world, gold is more than a mere commodity. It is world money, capable of protecting wealth and providing financial security. It cannot be brushed aside or ignored. It has once again assumed its role as the hinge pin of global financial markets.

Understanding the gold market is essential for all investors. That's what this chapter is all about, understanding.

You can build a castle if you have the right tools. With three new tools you can come to grips with the complexities of the gold market.

The three tools are practical, easy-to-use devices that will deepen your understanding of the workings of the gold market. They can be used to accumulate long-term gold positions at the lowest possible cost. They can be used to make trading gold profitable. They are equally valuable to investors whose primary focus is on stocks, bonds, silver, currencies, real estate, or other investments. The tools provide a realistic view of past, present, and likely future trends. This may sound too good to be true. It isn't. The magic lies not in the tools but in the nature of gold itself.

Man's fascination with gold stretches back as far as history and archaeology can see. Imagine the excitement, the rush of uncontrollable emotion, the breathlessness of being the first to open a pharaoh's tomb. After long, arduous hours in libraries, more hours of meticulous planning, days plodding in the dust, endless months of not knowing, not daring to be optimistic, suddenly there it is—gold. Not just rough, natural gold but gold that captured the hearts and minds of people who lived thousands of years ago. Gold that was worked into objects of beauty by men worshiping god-kings. Gold that would make you rich today.

Yes! There are undiscovered tombs of Egyptian kings, tombs so well hidden in desolate valleys that not even the indomitable, lucky Howard Carter (who discovered Tutankhamen's tomb in 1922) was able to find them.

The Origins of Gold's Value

The economy of ancient Egypt was based on barter and regulated by deep religious convictions. The gold of Egypt, until the great famine in the year of the hyena, was used for adorning pharaohs, who were believed to be gods, and not for base human purposes.

Famine, when the yearly flood waters of the Nile receded in the year of the hyena, irrevocably changed the orderly, religious ways of ancient Egyptian society. Hunger and fear produced intense competition for status, power, and enough to eat. Gold, formerly revered as a symbol of godly power and respect, was suddenly desired by all. After the famine, it became necessary to hide the tombs of the kings because plundering tombs for their gold had become too popular. Some of those postfamine tombs have never been found. Archaeologists know they exist, but no one has yet discovered their location.

In the days of Egyptian prosperity, gold was truly priceless. It had a value far above the coarse, commercial affairs of mere mortals. In a very real way, gold has never completely lost its timeless, priceless character. The gold of the Egyptians still holds fascination and value. It can still make a person rich and provide protection and security. It will still buy food, even in times of famine. And it is still an object of beauty and a symbol of immortality.

Gold is one of the few assets that an investor can accumulate with confidence that it will be of real value for ten, fifty, or even the next hundred years.

The Split Personality of Gold

Gold serves investors in two very different ways. First, it is a storehouse for accumulated wealth. Second, it is a route to making money. It doesn't pay to mix or confuse the two. Many investors have paid dearly for not having their objectives clearly in mind at the outset. They bought gold for short-term profit. But when the market went against them, they rationalized holding on with tales of gold's lasting value. There is no doubt of gold's lasting value, but in the short run the price of gold can and often does fluctuate widely. If you buy gold to make a profit, stick to your strategy. Don't fall victim to gold's allure. Treat gold as you would any other investment. Likewise, if you are accumulating gold as insurance against a possible future economic catastrophe, hold on through thick and thin. Don't become a short-term trader with your basic financial insurance.

When you buy gold, or any other investment for that matter, ask yourself these questions:

1. Am I trying to make money?
2. Am I trying to protect accumulated wealth?
3. Am I looking for security, financial peace of mind, insurance against a possible economic catastrophe?

Gold can be used for all three purposes. It pays to keep your gold holdings clearly separated into these three categories. Always have your investment objectives clearly in mind. Write them down. Keep records. Don't switch strategies as the market rises and falls.

Gold's Long-term Rate of Return

In 1984 Barry Clifford found a shipwreck off the beach in Wellfleet, Massachusetts. It was identified as a pirate ship named the *Widdah,* which went down two centuries earlier in a North Atlantic storm. Most hunters of pirate treasure had assumed that the *Widdah* must have been picked clean by local Cape Cod residents. Barry Clifford thought otherwise. One day in 1984 he managed to excavate a trench in the sand. To his delight he found it overflowing with gold and silver coins. The treasure had not been plundered. It had lain just beneath the sand a short distance off one of the most popular summer beaches on the Eastern seacoast, untouched for 267 years.

Experts determined that the original value of the *Widdah*'s cargo was the equivalent of $4 million. The value in

1984 was estimated at $400 million, proof positive that gold not only holds its value but appreciates over the years.

The problem for investors is that the annual compounded rate of return on the *Widdah*'s precious cargo works out to a slim 1.75 percent each year. That is another way of saying that over those 267 years the value of the dollar declined at an average rate of less than 2 percent a year. The gold didn't change. It held its value. It was the dollar that declined and caused the price of gold to rise.

The story of the *Widdah* is more than a fascinating tale of pirate treasure; it is an important lesson about the true nature of money and gold. Gold is the constant. Paper money fluctuates in value.

In 1984 and 1985 it was, at times, popular to be tantalized by forecasts of gold costing $2,000 an ounce within a year or two. Those forecasts and their popular acceptance point to the treacherous nature of misconceptions about gold. When there is a political catastrophe or a massive economic disaster, it doesn't matter what the price of gold is in terms of paper money. During the hyper-inflation in Germany in the 1920s no one cared that the price of gold went from hundreds to thousands of marks per ounce. No one cared because no one wanted marks. The German currency became worthless, of no value at all.

In 1985 if you carefully thought about what it would take to produce a rise in the price of gold to $2,000 an ounce, you would have realized that the underlying assumption must be for an apocalyptic event. In that case it wouldn't matter if the price was $2,000 or $200,000 an ounce. The true story of the *Widdah* tells us that governments ordinarily destroy the value of paper money at a far slower pace than most people realize. From time to time there are interludes when the destruction moves at a faster clip. That was the situation in the 1970s, although even then it could be argued that the dollar's decline was at least partially a reflection of several decades of erosion. That erosion had been covered up by an artificially high exchange rate for the dollar. Once the cover-up ended, the markets moved quickly to bring the dollar down. When analysts forecast the rapid destruction of a currency as a route to profit, they are seductive but unrealistic. If inflation moves so fast as to justify a rise in the price of gold from $300 to $2,000 in a short time, then the economy, like that of Germany during hyper-inflation, stands on the edge of financial disaster.

The point is simply that it is essential to distinguish between gold as insurance against disaster and gold as a route to increasing your wealth. You don't need tantalizing forecasts of skyrocketing gold prices to make a killing in the gold market. Millions of dollars have been made (and lost) trading gold and currencies. In most situations the strategy has included borrowed money. By using leverage (borrowing to buy gold), the profits from relatively modest changes in the gold price can be enormous.

The first rule when dealing with gold is to separate gold as long-term insurance from gold as a path to near-term profits.

Investment Characteristics of Gold

Gold has three investment characteristics: It may be a storehouse for accumulated wealth, a parking place for wealth between investments, or a money-making asset.

Gold as a Storehouse of Value

Every investor with a reasonable amount of accumulated wealth should own gold. A gold position of 5 percent to 15 percent of total liquid assets is about right. As your portfolio grows, you must begin to adopt a strategy of diversification. You can't be right all the time. There are few things worse than struggling for years to accumulate a sizable portfolio only to see it wither away because of a strategic mistake. Continually adding to a basic gold position is one way to assure that your portfolio will hold its value.

In 1985 a financial planner was asked how much it took to provide for a comfortable retirement. The answer was $700,000. An investor with $200,000 might have been tempted to look at U.S. government bond yields of 12 percent and jump to the conclusion that a portfolio of high-yielding bonds was perfectly safe. After eleven years a $200,000 portfolio would grow to $700,000 compounding at 12 percent. The problem with that once-popular point of view is inflation.

Between 1966 and 1984 inflation devalued the dollar substantially. It took 300 percent more assets in 1984 to provide the same purchasing power as in 1966. Over a period of ten to fifteen years the amount needed to provide a comfortable retirement will change by the amount of inflation. The $700,000 target would become $2,100,000 if inflation were to run at the same levels as it did in the 1970s. Investing in government bonds at 12 percent wouldn't provide enough protection. Gold appreciates in a direct relationship with inflation. The gold portion of a portfolio offers protection against the possibility of future inflation. That may well be the single most important reason for including 5 percent to 15 percent gold in every portfolio.

Gold as a Cash Reserve

Gold offers another characteristic. Too often we think of cash, meaning a money market account or treasury bills, as the best parking place for investment reserves. That isn't always true. There are times when gold is a better parking place. When the gold price is low, an investor can take profits in other assets, such as stocks or bonds, put the cash in gold, and sleep well, knowing that the funds will be available for the next bull market.

In 1976, when gold sold at $100 an ounce, for example, it was one of the best parking places for investment reserves.

Trading Gold for Profit

Gold's third characteristic is as an asset for making money. Buying gold at the right time and selling after a bull market run can produce substantial profits.

Using gold effectively demands a clear-headed, no-nonsense, hard-hearted attitude on both a subjective and objective level. Gold's unique characteristics challenge investors. It is easy to become lost in the glitter of gold, to switch strategies in midstream and to end up with losses.

In considering gold, keep these four points in mind.

1. Always be clear about your personal reasons for buying gold. If you buy for the long term, hold on and don't change attitudes as the price of gold rises and falls.
2. Include gold as a basic portfolio building block.
3. Think of gold along with cash as a logical parking place between investments.
4. Use gold as an asset that can increase your wealth.

Evaluating Gold

In every situation you must have a model for determining gold's value. If you are buying for long-term insurance, you want to keep the cost of that insurance as low as possible. If you are buying as a reserve, you need to be able to compare gold to paper currency, money market accounts, and treasury bills. It is relative values that count. There are times when gold is best and times when paper currency is best. It is obvious that making money in gold means being on the right side of the market at the right time.

Over the years all sorts of methods have been offered for evaluating gold. There have been seasonal approaches where gold's rises and falls have been linked to the seasons of the year. There are supply-and-demand models. Analysts look at mining output and match those figures with demand from industry and investors. There are technical models based purely on charts.

All methods have their merits, and all have their limitations. Charts have become the most popular for a simple reason. It is hard to obtain accurate figures for supply and demand. It is much easier to keep track of the published figures for the price of gold. Charts are within the reach of every investor. The problem is that neither charts nor supply-and-demand models have proven to be a sure-fire route to accurate forecasting. In 1985 when all the charts were bearish, investors in all major gold-trading centers sold short. They expected the downtrend to continue. Then, unexpectedly the downtrend reversed. Gold shot up by $30 an ounce, and the short-sellers suffered huge losses.

It is basic that when a particular technique becomes too popular it loses its value. When everyone is watching the same charts, they are of little or no predictive value. Following the crowd is never a route to profits. More often than not it is a route to losses. Success in investing means staying at least one step ahead of the crowd.

Success in dealing with gold means being able to determine when gold is overvalued and when it is undervalued. When the gold price is too high, it becomes vulnerable. When it is too low, mysterious buying can develop and produce a substantial and profitable advance.

Placing a value on gold, the world's basic money, may seem an insurmountable task. It isn't. Any investor who is willing to grasp the basics and work at keeping well informed can be a successful gold trader. You don't have to be an international economist. You don't have to watch the gold market hour by hour. You don't have to have inside information. You do have to have a set of comprehensive tools. You do have to understand them and use them.

Relative Value: An Essential Investment Concept

All investment values are relative. When we say that the price of gold or a stock or any other asset is high, we mean high relative to other values. If you were stuck on an island far from world news and a bottle washed up on shore with a message saying that gold was trading at $1,000 an ounce, you wouldn't know if that was high, low, or just right.

There might have been years of inflation while you were on that island. The gold price might have risen to $1,500 and fallen back to $1,000. Or there might have been a mad speculative rush into gold that drove it up to $1,000 while inflation and most other values were down. Without a point of reference a single price is meaningless. The secret to successful investing is adopting a correct frame of reference. A disciplined approach to comparing values is all that any investor needs.

In the 1960s U.S. investors became enamored of the idea of growth. Relative value was cast aside. What counted was future growth, not relative value. If IBM's earnings grew at a good rate, the future price for the stock would be higher. That fascination with growth was understandable. After World War II the United States enjoyed twenty years of growth. Those were remarkable days. Growth was a route to successful investing.

But, as with most popular investment ideas, things went too far. Investors bid up the prices of stocks to unsustainable levels. The idea that growth would come to an end simply never came into their thinking. They assumed that there would always be growth and that all an investor had to do was be in the right place to enjoy growth's benefits. When the growth stocks plunged, losses multiplied geometrically. Investors became disillusioned, frightened, and pessimistic. They had forgotten another principle of traditional investing, relative value. If the growth stocks at forty and fifty times earnings in the early 1970s had been compared to gold, real estate, stocks in other countries, or commodity prices, someone might have realized that growth or not, the growth stocks were too high.

Even during those rare times when growth is common, relative value is important. Looking at growth alone can result in a total loss of perspective. Keeping a firm hold on relative value and comparing prices will keep your investment thinking centered. Investors who can relate one group of asset prices to others aren't swept away with the crowd. They don't suffer the monstrous losses when markets suddenly turn. The crowd, with its unbalanced investment ideas, is often left with a stream of losses.

The loss of perspective that comes from failing to consider relative values explains why gold was not popular in the United States until long after it became a legal investment. Gold is at the opposite end of the spectrum from investing for growth. Gold doesn't fit into growth thinking. Gold is a never-changing metal. It doesn't grow and it does not shrink. It is basic value. Investors in the 1960s and early 1970s became so caught up in growth ideas that they never had a chance. Had they balanced their growth-stock ideas with relative-value concepts, they might have bought gold when it was low in the early 1970s.

Many people who look back and ask, "Why didn't I see gold at $100 in 1976 as an attractive investment?" simply don't know about relative values. If they did, they would quickly and easily understand that when you are all caught up in growth, gold seems dull and uninteresting. Of course, looking at gold as "simply another commodity" or as dull and uninteresting is a tip-off. That attitude, in and of itself, is a clear signal of an unbalanced approach to investing. An unbalanced approach will always end in disaster. Keeping a balanced attitude, staying focused on relative values, is one way to assure success in your entire investment program.

In this sense you don't ever have to buy an ounce of gold to benefit from a clear understanding of the gold market. Another of gold's benefits is that it is a standard of value. The gold market works two ways. You can compare prices and assets to gold, or you can use other prices to determine whether gold is high or low. Knowing gold's relative value can be of great assistance in determining when stocks, bonds, or real estate are undervalued and overvalued.

Gold truly is an investment hinge pin. Every investor should have a thorough understanding of gold.

Basic investing begins with gold and relative value. Trading gold for profit, using gold effectively as a cash reserve, or buying gold for long-term insurance starts with a clear idea of relative value. Gold isn't always cheap. You can't buy gold willy-nilly and expect to build a successful portfolio. Gold is world money. Gold holds its value through political and economic disaster. Gold can make you rich. Nevertheless, gold's benefits flow only to those disciplined investors with a trained approach to establishing gold's relative value.

Establishing Relative Value: The Three Tools

In real estate the experts say that there are three considerations: location, location, and location. In investing there are also three considerations: discipline, discipline, and discipline.

No human being can carry in his head all of the complex international financial factors that push and pull the gold market around. We are selective in choosing those factors that receive our attention. We dismiss some and embrace others. The most common mistake is continually to shift the direction of our focus. We have a natural tendency to run with the crowd. If the most popular concern is inflation, then we judge the gold price and its likely future based on inflation. When interest rates dominate the investment community, we look to interest rates for the answers to our gold questions.

It takes but a few minutes reading past articles on gold to see that this human failing affects amateur and professional alike. When the United States was selling gold in the 1970s in an effort to stem the antidollar tide, most experts focused on those sales in making their assessments. By 1979 all eyes were on inflation. In 1980 and 1981 the gold experts were riveted to interest rates.

This kind of haphazard following the crowd does not provide a consistent basis for formulating a profitable gold strategy. It leads instead to a stream of misjudgments. Once the crowd has focused its attention on a specific set of conditions, it is too late. All that information is already in the market price for gold. When the newspaper headlines speak about gold and interest rates, you can be sure that all aspects of that relationship have been discounted. An individual investor can add nothing more. You could know with a certainty what the next move in interest rates was going to be and still not be assured of a profit in gold. The only way you can deal in gold successfully is by anticipating what the crowd will be likely to do next. Profits come from being one step ahead of the crowd, not from following in the crowd's footsteps.

Getting Your Bearings

Sailors have an investment advantage. They must think in terms of "bearings" to keep track of where they are and where they are going. Those of us who travel exclusively on land easily fall prey to one-dimensional thinking. We follow the road signs and expect to arrive at our chosen destination. Investing is more like being at sea. There are no roads and no road signs. Without proper bearings it is easy to become lost and founder on the rocks.

From a position at sea, but within sight of a coastline, a sailor can keep track of the ship's position and calculate the course to a safe harbor by a method called triangulation. The idea is simply that you need at least two bearings to find your position. If you sight on only one shore-based landmark, you end up with a line, such as line A on the navigation chart on the next page. Your ship could be anywhere on that line. You could be on the right course or headed for disaster. By taking another bearing and determining a second line (line B), you can find your exact position. The ship is located where the two lines cross. If you take three or four bearings, the reliability of your conclusion goes up. The more bearings the better.

The same is true for gold. The more bearings the better. And you need at least two to have any chance at all of knowing whether gold is high or low. If all you watch is the gold price in terms of dollars, you are like a sailor at sea taking only one bearing. You have some idea of your position, but you still might be headed for trouble.

The three tools that follow are ways of taking additional bearings. Using them will increase the accuracy of your analysis and decisions. They aren't magic formulas. They are essential tools that will help every investor.

Practical Landmarks

Experience has taught us that the gold price rises and falls in some relation to inflation, oil prices, and the exchange rate for the U.S. dollar. These three, inflation, oil and the dollar are like landmarks to a sailor. They enable us to get additional bearings on the current state of the gold market.

Sailors had to create the compass and work out a scheme of navigation in order to convert landmarks to a practical

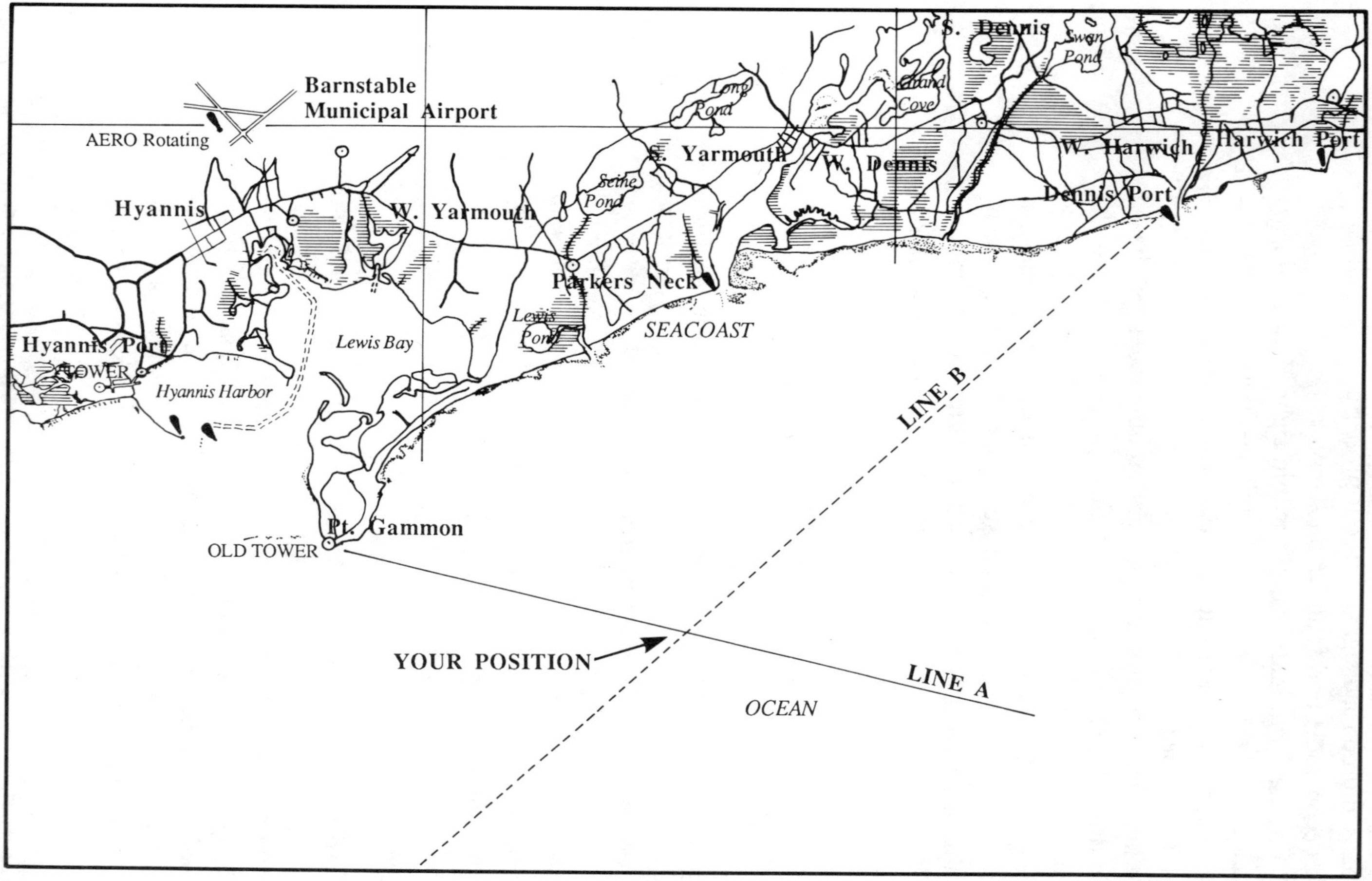

Barnstable
Municipal Airport
AERO Rotating
Hyannis
W. Yarmouth
S. Yarmouth
Long Pond
Seine Pond
Grand Cove
S. Dennis
Swan Pond
W. Dennis
W. Harwich
Harwich Port
Dennis Port
Parkers Neck
Lewis Pond
SEACOAST
Lewis Bay
Hyannis Port
TOWER
Hyannis Harbor
Pt. Gammon
OLD TOWER
LINE B
YOUR POSITION
LINE A
OCEAN

use. Investors, likewise need to take the financial landmarks and find a method of converting them to useful information.

Don't worry. You won't have to invent the financial equivalent of the compass. The three landmarks have already been converted into three tools. Using these tools will give you an accurate way of determining where the gold market is, where it has been, and where it is likely to go.

The three tools are called: (1) the long-term, inflation-adjusted gold price; (2) the gold-oil pendulum; and (3) the value of gold in Swiss francs.

The long-term, inflation-adjusted gold price allows you to determine gold's basic current value. From that determination you can discover if gold is too high or too low relative to inflation.

The gold-oil pendulum relates the gold price to the world's most significant commodity, oil. From this tool you will know how the gold price stands compared to oil. It is a second and valuable "bearing".

By watching the gold market in terms of Swiss francs you will be able to sort out gold's value relative to the dollar.

The three tools, used in combination with the conventional U.S. dollar price, provide a deadly accurate method for getting a fix on the gold market. Once you know whether the gold price is high or low, you will be able to make investment decisions with the odds on your side. You will know more about the risks you are taking. You will know when gold is a "screaming buy," as it was in 1976. And you will know when things have gone too far. You will know when to stay out of the gold market. You won't be shocked to see gold collapse from peaks such as the $835 price set in early 1980.

No matter what your investment skills or preferences, you will find genuine value when you use these tools. Traders can use them to improve their results. Long-term investors can use them to make better-timed decisions. Investors looking for financial insurance can use them to keep the cost of that insurance to a minimum.

The tools are based on complex financial and economic factors. They go to the root of international economic forces. They are not difficult to understand or use. In fact, they simplify the task of keeping track of far-reaching, complex events. Anyone can use them. You don't have to understand the basis for the tools. They work for everyone.

Some of the techniques are new. They may seem strange at first. But, with a little practice you will soon become an "expert" at using these tools. By using them you will often know more about the true state of affairs in the gold market than many experts. Too often "experts" get mired down in details. They forget where they are. They become like sailors arguing over the merits of the ship and lose their way only to be sunk by the unforgiving sea.

Use these tools. Take your sightings. Get your bearings. You will then be able to sail from one investment objective to the next safely and in comfort.

Tool Number 1: The Long-term, Inflation-Adjusted Gold Price

There is no doubt that inflation and the price of gold are related. When inflation rises, there is money to be made in gold. Conversely, during times of low inflation or deflation, gold is an uninteresting investment choice. (See the chart on the next page.)

The connection is twofold. First, inflation is the great destroyer of paper money. Inflation eats away at the buying power of even the mighty U.S. dollar. As the value of a dollar falls, it takes more and more dollars to buy one ounce of gold. Or, putting it the other way around, one ounce of gold buys more and more devalued paper money.

GOLD PRICE AND INFLATION

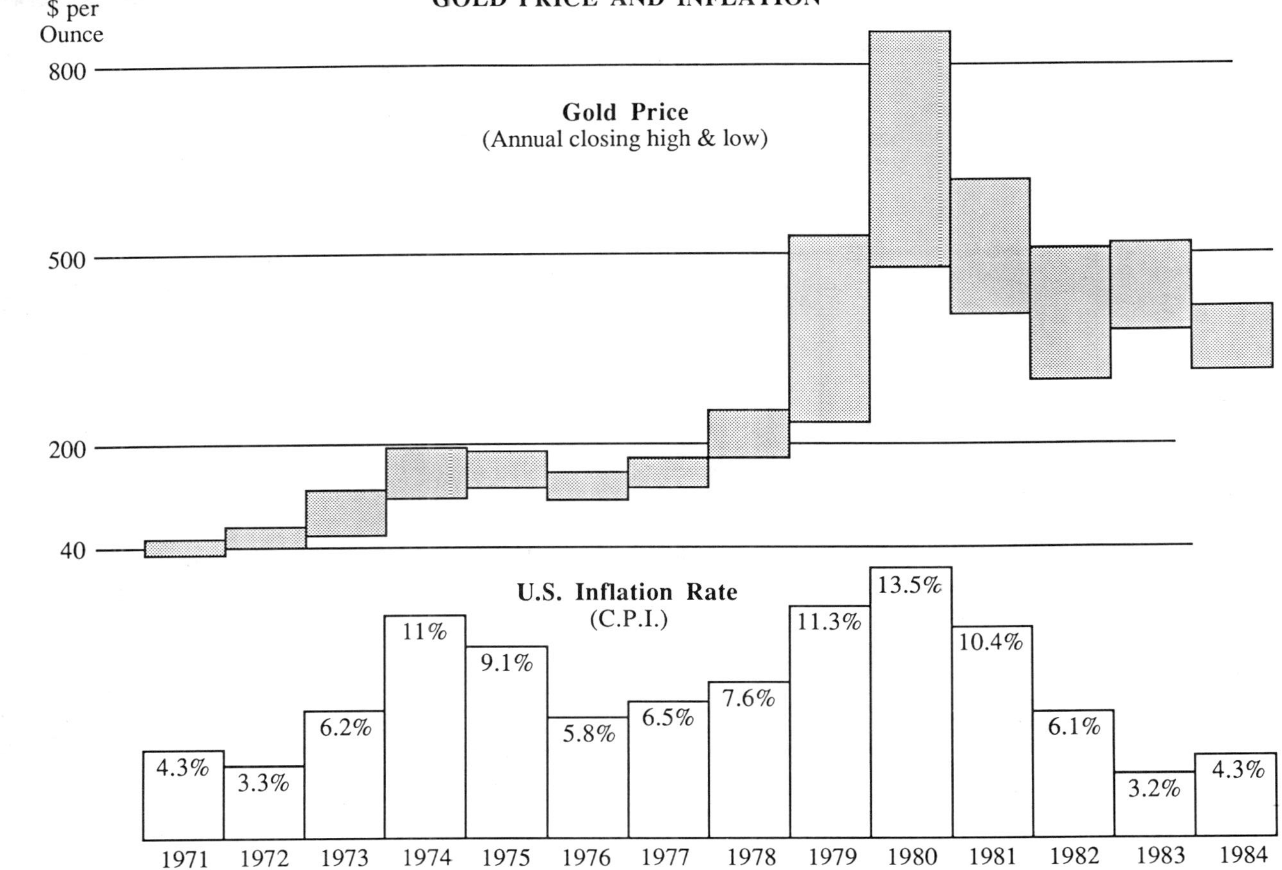

Gold	1971	1972	1973	1974	1975	1976	1977	1978	1979	1980	1981	1982	1983	1984
High	$44	$70	$127	$195	$185	$140	$168	$243	$524	$850	$601	$481	$508	$405
Low	$37	$44	$64	$116	$129	$103	$120	$166	$232	$477	$390	$297	$375	$308

Source: Compiled by the author. U.S. inflation rate figures from *Economic Indicators*, President's Council of Economic Advisors.

Second, investors anticipate the future. Gold's price is not only determined by actual past and present inflation, it is affected by investors' opinions about the future for inflation. The crowd will buy aggressively in anticipation of higher future inflation. Likewise, gold can come under intense selling pressure when inflation expectations cool.

Between 1976 and 1980, inflation in the United States rose steadily. It peaked at an annual rate for the Consumer Price Index of 13.5 percent in 1980. That long period of ever higher inflation rates caused a modern American gold rush. At first it was investors looking for long-term financial protection that lifted the gold price from below $200 an ounce to above $300. At the end, however, there was a mad speculative rush that culminated in a gold price of over $800. Inflation produced not just a solid long-term gain in the price of gold; in 1980 it also produced a wild and unruly rush into the yellow metal.

The crowd expected inflation to keep rising until it destroyed the world's paper currencies. The crowd was wrong. In 1981 and the following few years, inflation fell precipitously. By 1985 the U.S. consumer rate of inflation was down to 3.3 percent. Lower actual inflation brought lower and lower gold prices as the crowd revised its expectations.

The same connection between gold and inflation was evident in the early 1970s. As U.S. inflation rose to a 1974 peak of 11 percent, the price of gold rose from less than $50 to near $200 an ounce. When the recession of the mid-1970s trimmed the inflation rate, the price of gold declined, falling back to near $100 an ounce in 1976.

There have been times when the gold-inflation connection was in doubt. In 1983 the rate of inflation declined, but the price of gold rose. Gold in that year was able to buck the inflation trend, throwing doubt on the gold-inflation connection. The year 1983 was ruled not by actual inflation but by investors' opinions about the future for inflation. Seeing a rapid expansion of the U.S. economy and money supply, investors thought that higher inflation would follow. They were behaving just as expected. The problem was that the fundamentals did not cooperate. Inflation did not rise. Investors turned out to be wrong. Neither rapid money growth nor an expanding U.S. economy brought a quick return of inflation. The gold market responded to lower than expected inflation by falling throughout most of 1984.

Markets in the seventies and again in the eighties have demonstrated the age-old investment principle that gold is, in fact, directly related to inflation. At times human expectations can rule the market. But in the long run, inflation will determine the price of gold.

What an Ounce of Gold Is Worth

Governments keep records. We can find out about past rates of inflation. Using past inflation, it is possible to calculate what an ounce of gold is really worth today.

Once we know that value we can distinguish between the underlying market forces and human expectations. We will be on the way to a deeper and very practical understanding of the gold market.

Taking this theory and applying it effectively means using some common sense and some mathematics. To reduce the error we will need first to look at a long period of past inflation. Second, we will have to select a valid starting point.

Fortunately history helps at both steps. Prior to the Great Depression it was difficult to determine if the official price for gold was correct or not. Governments have a habit of overvaluing their paper currencies, meaning that they set official gold prices too low. The depression is solid evidence for the conclusion that prior to 1929 the official gold price of $20.67 was indeed too low.

The final proof came when the gold price was raised to $35 an ounce. Following that move, the U.S. economy began to recover from the devastation of the depression. Raising the gold price, devaluing the dollar, and thereby allowing the U.S. money supply to expand was the needed medicine. The response of the economy and the markets tells us that the price of $35 in 1934 was a lot closer to "correct" than the earlier official price of $20.69. No doubt it is possible to go back even farther and find another point when the official gold price was "right." Fortunately, that isn't necessary. The 1934 starting point is good enough. That date is far enough back in history to provide a fifty-year string of calculations.

The next step is to adjust the 1934 price for all intervening inflation and deflation. We will then find out what an ounce of gold should be worth today to be exactly equal to $35 an ounce in 1934.

There are various ways of measuring inflation. It can be done through comprehensive, commodity-price studies, through the producer price index, or through the consumer price index. The last is the best choice for several reasons.

Investors must concentrate on the real, or practical, world. That is the world of final consumption. The producer price index, for example, is valid for businesses. But there would be no businesses without consumers.

The consumer price index is also a good choice because it is fairly easy to track, follow, and use for keeping information up-to-date.

The bottom line, is, as you will see in the chart on page 45, that we are not searching for an academic figure. We are not trying to calculate the most scientifically precise price for gold. We are in search of a useful tool in a world of relative values. The most important thing is to be clear, crisp, and consistent. We would err by switching from one index to another. It would be wrong to start with the consumer price index and then use the producer price index half way through the calculations. By choosing the consumer price index, however, with all its faults and foibles, and sticking with it over a truly long period of time, we will reduce error and end up with a usable result.

Adjusting the 1934 gold price of $35 an ounce for all inflation results in some truly startling observations. For example, taking account of inflation showed that an ounce of gold by 1970 was worth more than $100. It had been worth as much as $78.84 in 1959. All the while, between 1959 and 1970, the U.S. government was willing to settle international claims at far less than gold's real value. The U.S. government had clung to the $35-an-ounce price for far too long.

No wonder there was an outflow of U.S. gold in the late

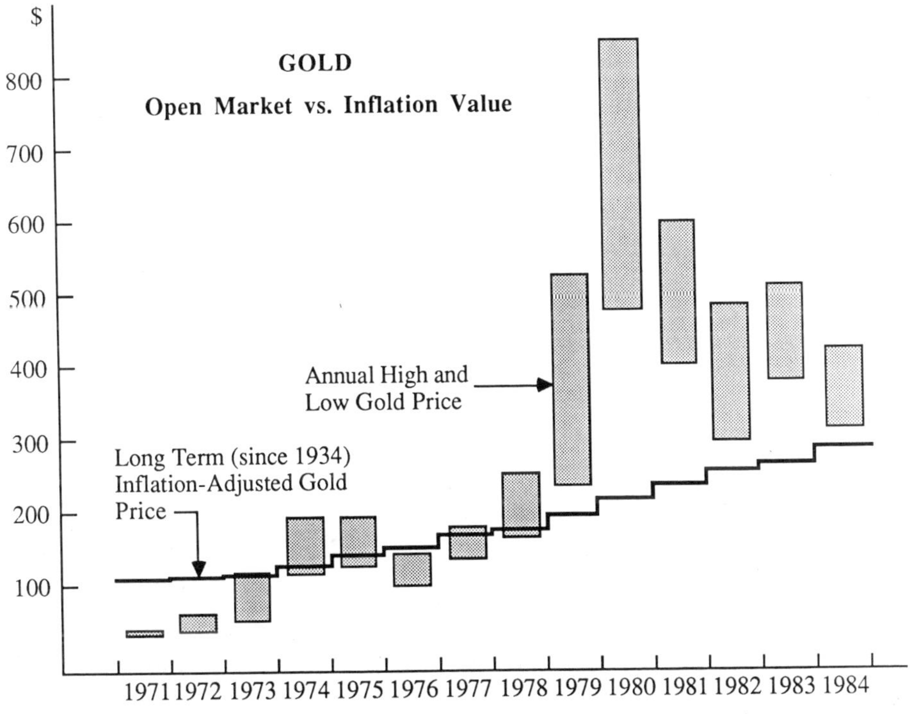

Source: Compiled by the author.

1960s. The United States was willing to sell at bargain-basement prices. Anyone with a calculator and the gold-inflation calculations could recognize quickly the benefits of exchanging dollars for gold at official prices. Many did. As the 1960s came to a close, a crisis was brewing. The dollar was overvalued, the official gold price was too low, and something had to be done. In the early 1970s President Richard Nixon was forced by the harsh facts of international economics to cut the connection between dollars and gold. After his action the dollar could not be exchanged for U.S. gold. The U.S. gold hemorrhage was stopped.

The calculation of the long-term, inflation-adjusted gold price was right on the mark by the end of the 1960s. It provided a full and complete explanation for the outflow of U.S. gold, which eventually ended with the severing of the connection between the dollar and gold.

By 1973 the free gold market caught up with the long-term, inflation-adjusted gold price. The high that year was $127 and the calculated value was $120.16. An investor who had used the long-term, inflation-adjusted value as the basis for buying gold in the early 1970s enjoyed handsome profits. Gold was up some 300 percent by 1973.

In 1974 and 1975, bouyed by rising inflation, the gold market exceeded the target, or base line. The market price for gold rose to near $200, while the long-term, inflation-adjusted price was at $145. Investors bid up the price of gold in anticipation of future inflation. In the long run those expectations would prove correct, but in the short run recession intervened. Inflation first fell and gold followed.

After being "above the line," gold fell back below its long-term, inflation-adjusted value. By 1976 the calculated value had risen to nearly $154, while the market value, overreacting on the down side, fell to near $100. Investors with calculators and common sense were once again presented with an outstanding opportunity to buy gold at bargain levels. From those unsustainable low levels of 1976, gold shot back to and above the line in a bull market that did not end until early 1980 at $835 an ounce.

Buying based on the long-term, inflation-adjusted gold price worked again in 1976. In fact it provided an unbelievable profit opportunity. The great bull market finally went too far. It went so far that wild and unthinking speculation took hold of the market. On January 18, 1980, when the real, underlying, long-term, inflation-adjusted value for an ounce of gold was roughly $200 an ounce, the market reached $835 an ounce on the London afternoon fixing. The market had boiled up to a level 400 percent higher than real value.

The gold price, with rallies along the way, tumbled from its lofty 1980 peak to a January 1985 low of $285. At that level, while many "experts" were confidently forecasting a continued slide, the market reversed and moved back above $300. Professionals who had sold short were caught by surprise. Instead of easy gains, they were faced with huge losses. At least one major international gold-trading firm was broken by the reversal.

Inflation had continued, albeit at a rate well below the blistering pace of the late 1970s. By the end of 1984 the long-term, inflation-adjusted value for an ounce of gold had become $280.48.

The market had returned to the line and from that level had rebounded. The market's performance through the 1970s and the first half of the 1980s validates the use of the long-term, inflation-adjusted gold price. Reality and actual market performance confirm that by starting in 1934 and using the consumer price index we can arrive at a useful conclusion.

The market has not only validated the calculations, it has demonstrated the value of the long-term, inflation-adjusted gold price as a tool for increasing investment profits.

Practical Applications

From the chart on page 45, you can see that the calculations of the long-term, inflation-adjusted gold price produce a very useful base line. When the actual market price for gold falls below the line, there is an outstanding opportunity to buy gold for extraordinary profits.

When the market price is above the line, investors should use caution. There is the ever-present risk of a fall back down to the line. That doesn't mean that gold priced above the line must always be avoided. It means that when the market is above the line there are real risks that must be taken into account.

The line is the calculated, long-term, inflation-adjusted gold price. You don't have to keep charts to use this tool. All you need to know is the current long-term, inflation-adjusted gold price and then compare that price to the market.

Long-term Insurance against Financial Disaster

Gold is the best financial insurance available. It belongs in every portfolio because, when it comes to the future, there are no guarantees. Gold coins or bullion bought today will provide bread, butter, and housing tomorrow. They will even provide for your grandchildren and great-grandchildren if you are fortunate enough to escape financial and political disaster. Gold acquired as financial insurance should be held through thick and thin. That portion of a portfolio does not represent a profit maker, it represents insurance. Just as you don't ever cancel insurance on your house, you should never liquidate the insurance portion of a portfolio.

The long-term, inflation-adjusted gold price is a tool for minimizing your financial insurance premium. By buying gold only when the market price is near or below the line you will be sure of accumulating gold at attractive, long-term prices. Your insurance premium will be at the minimum because you will have bought gold low.

The long-term, inflation-adjusted gold price is your guide to accumulating gold as protection against a possible future economic catastrophe. Using that gold price will not assure you of being in with the crowd; it will assure that you, unlike the crowd, pay the minimum for your gold-based financial insurance. The crowd tends to rush into gold when there is an obvious threat. The crowd's stampede drives the gold price up. Gold will be low only when the crowd is busy in other markets. Dull, uninteresting times are those when gold is attractively priced. When most people feel secure that inflation is down and out, when you really don't need gold's protection, that is the best time to be a buyer. The long-term, inflation-adjusted gold price will give you the discipline needed to buy your golden insurance at the right price.

Trading Gold for Profit

Gold can also be a source of capital gains. It can add to your wealth. That means buying low and selling high. The selling is the difference. Gold bought as insurance should never be sold unless there is an economic catastrophe. The opposite is true for gold bought to enhance and increase wealth. The key is to sell at a higher price, hold cash, and be ready for the next buying opportunity.

The long-term, inflation-adjusted gold price is one of the most valuable tools for determining when gold is low and when it is high. From 1978 through the first half of 1985 the market price for gold stayed above the line (above the long-term, inflation-adjusted gold price). It never dipped below the line. Over the course of eight years gold did not give a clear buy signal as it did in 1976. As a practical matter this means that investors trying to make profits in gold must have a strategy for dealing with gold when the price is relatively high.

The reason for gold's above-the-line performance is continuing inflation. As inflation rolls along, even at relatively low annual rates, it continually increases the underlying value for an ounce of gold. Investors, believing that inflation will continue indefinitely, buy gold with confidence that its value will keep rising. They are willing to pay a price that is above the line today because the line is a moving target. Inflation keeps the line moving higher and higher. Therefore, there has been a tendency for gold to trade above the line in anticipation of future inflation.

When gold is above the line, you must be cautious but also sensitive to trends. From a low of $300 in 1982, when the long-term, inflation-adjusted price was $260.58, gold rose to $500, far above the line, before succumbing to a new decline. There was a profit opportunity for a courageous investor willing to follow that trend. The point is only that you should be very nervous when you are trading gold above the line. It is better to sell too soon than to hold too long when gold is above the line.

The Calculations

Every investor should be aware of the true, underlying, long-term, inflation-adjusted gold price. It is an important piece of information for all investors, even those with no special interest in gold.

The calculations are not difficult and can be done by anyone with a calculator. First, you need some background information.

In 1918 an ounce of gold could be purchased for $20.67. That official price endured the Great Crash of 1929 and the Great Depression that followed. The Great Depression proved beyond any reasonable doubt that the official price had been too low for too long. A low gold price translated into too little money growth and a high value for the U.S. dollar.

Economic events always tell the truth. Looking back through history, it is much easier to see whether government policies were right or wrong.

In 1934 the official gold price was raised to $35 an ounce. That allowed a massive expansion of the U.S. money supply and devalued the dollar. The increase in the official gold price worked an economic miracle. The U.S. economy began to respond. The dark days of the depression gave way to growth and hopes for renewed prosperity.

The economy's reaction to a $35 gold price is solid evidence of the conclusion that at $35 an ounce in 1934 gold was "priced right." At least we know that the $35 price was a lot closer to "right" than the previous, predepression $20.67 price.

Once a starting point is determined, it is a tedious but simple matter to adjust that "right" price for all intervening inflation and deflation. The following is a summary of that string of calculations:

Starting point = 1934 at $35 an ounce; at year end:

1939 = $37.54
1949 = $64.45
1959 = $78.84
1969 = $99.17
1970 = $105.02
1971 = $109.53
1972 = $113.15
1973 = $120.16
1974 = $133.38
1975 = $145.52
1976 = $153.96
1977 = $163.97
1978 = $176.43
1979 = $196.18

1980 = $222.67
1981 = $245.60
1982 = $260.58
1983 = $268.92
1984 = $280.48

To keep this table up-to-date all you have to do is take the year-end 1984 price of $280.48 and adjust it for any and all future inflation or deflation.

For example, suppose that the final rate of inflation for 1985 were 5 percent. Here is the math:

$$1.05 \times 280.48 = \$294.50$$

Remember that when we deal with inflation rates we are dealing with percentages. Mathematically there is a second way to determine the effect of inflation on gold's basic value. We can compute the increase alone and add it back in to arrive at the final result. That calculation would look like this: 5 percent of $280.48 is:

$$0.05 \times \$280.48 = \$14.024$$

That is the amount of the *increase.* The result must then be added to the base:

$$\$280.48 + \$14.024 = \$294.524, \text{ rounded to } \$294.50$$

If there had been deflation at the rate of 5 percent, you would have subtracted the $14.024 from $280.48, and the answer would have been $266.456, rounded to $266.46.

The short-hand math would be:

$$0.95\ (100 - \text{the } 5\% \text{ deflation rate}) \times 280.48 = \$266.46$$

Once you have the long-term, inflation-adjusted value for 1985 you use that as the base and calculate the effect of inflation or deflation for the following year, 1986, and so on.

For those with calculators here is a simple, step-by-step formula. In case of inflation:

1. Divide the inflation rate by 100.
2. Add 1 to your answer.
3. Multiply the result times the base, in this case the 1984 inflation-adjusted value, and you have your answer.

In case of deflation:

1. Subtract the deflation rate from 100.
2. Divide the answer by 100.
3. Multiply the result times the base or result for the previous year.

Testing Popular Forecasts

Understanding the concept of the long-term, inflation-adjusted value and knowing the calculations add reality to your gold forecasting.

In 1983 and 1984 forecasts of gold at $2,000 captured the imaginations of many investors. They rushed out to buy gold with confidence that they would make a killing as people had in 1980. They were disappointed. Gold declined as inflation remained moderate. Had they known about the long-term, inflation-adjusted value, they could have avoided that loss.

Starting with gold's basic year-end 1984 value of $280.48 and adding in the effects of inflation running at 25 percent a year, it would take nine years before the underlying basic value rose to $2,000. In other words, to believe the forecasts of gold at $2,000 you had to believe that the U.S. economy would be wracked by record-high inflation at 25 percent until 1993. That was obviously a radical assumption, given the fact that inflation, at the time, was running closer to 5 percent than 25 percent. When you took into consideration the likely reaction at the U.S. Federal Reserve, the forecast became unbelievable. If inflation rose to 10 percent, the Fed would act to tighten money, drive interest rates up, and cool the rate of inflation.

Likewise, the long-term, inflation-adjusted value can be used to "test" the forecasts of deflation. In 1985 there were many who warned of a coming collapse in the gold price. They talked about gold at $25 an ounce. If instead of inflation we were to have deflation, the underlying value for gold would decline. But it would take deflation at the rate of −10 percent a year for eight years to result in an underlying value for gold of $125 an ounce. That would mean a depression worse than the 1930s. While possible, it was highly unlikely in early 1985, given the fact that the Fed was allowing the U.S. money supply to expand rapidly.

Radical forecasts are always tantalizing. They can become obsessive. If you don't have your personal forecasts firmly planted in reality, they can lead to substantial losses. The long-term, inflation-adjusted gold price is a tool that will keep you in touch with reality.

Certainly the gold market can be whipped again to a speculative frenzy like that in 1980. If you keep track of the long-term, inflation-adjusted value for gold, however, you will understand what is really happening.

Making Your Own Forecasts

Forecasting is the art of rational expectations. It isn't a guessing game where you try intuitively to predict each new wiggle in the speculative market. You can make sensible, common sense forecasts of your own before buying or selling gold. The long-term, inflation-adjusted gold price can be projected, based on various inflation or deflation rates. Here is a table based on gold's long-term, inflation-adjusted value using three different inflation rates out to the year 1990:

Gold's Value

Year	Inflation rate 5%	 8%	 10%
1984	$280.48	$280.48	$280.48
1985	294.50	302.92	308.53
1986	309.23	327.15	339.38
1987	324.69	353.32	373.32
1988	340.93	381.59	410.65
1989	387.97	412.12	451.72
1990	375.87	445.09	496.89

Source: Compiled by the author.

This table might be called "Rational Expectations for Gold Through the End of the Decade." It tells what an ounce of gold really will be worth in terms of dollars at the various inflation rates. It demonstrates that an ounce of gold bought at $300 in 1985 will show a reasonable profit by 1990, even if the United States manages to hold the line on inflation. It also shows what will happen if inflation gains momentum.

The next step, of course, is to add in the effects of the market. There is no doubt that if inflation increases up to 10 percent the market will anticipate the 1990 price of nearly $500. It might not take five years to earn a substantial profit on a gold position acquired in 1985. Investors could drive gold to $500 long before that price is fully justified by inflation fundamentals.

This table is an example. You can make similar tables for years out to 1995 and beyond using whatever inflation rates seem sensible at the time. You can change the table when the inflation outlook changes. You can make sensible forecasts even in changing times by using this approach based on gold's long-term, inflation-adjusted value.

The Effects of Deflation

In the 1980s deflation is synonymous with economic disaster. If prices were to fall, farming, mining, and manufacturing would be in serious trouble. The Catch-22 with a deflation scenario is that governments always fight deflation. Even in the depression of the 1930s the U.S. government *increased* the price of gold in order to start the economy growing again. A prolonged period of deflation would actually increase the value of gold.

Gold, after all, is basic financial insurance. In a recession or depression the value of a dollar would be threatened, and the price of gold would rise as investors flocked to gold instead of paper money. That is the penalty for running huge domestic and trade deficits. In a recession, government spending on unemployment and welfare increases as tax collections fall. A recession increases government deficits. If the federal deficit were to double again, with the national debt at more than $2 trillion, there would be a financial crisis. Confidence would be shattered. Interest rates would skyrocket, and the dollar would plunge. Paper money would become extremely risky, and investors would prefer gold.

Nevertheless, it is theoretically possible for there to be a period of mild deflation that lasts for several years. Keep in mind that it would take sixteen years at a deflation rate of 5 percent before gold's underlying value declined to $125 an ounce. More rational is a down-side risk to $250, and even that seems highly unlikely. In any event, you can forecast the effects of temporary deflation using gold's long-term, inflation-adjusted value.

The real risk of a falling gold price comes *after* gold has shot to levels far above the long-term, inflation-adjusted value. It isn't deflation that brings gold down. It is that investors, after being carried away on the up side, overshoot on the down side in their dash to return to a more realistic assessment of gold's value.

Don't be carried away with scare stories about deflation. In the long run, gold tends to rise, not fall. The real problem is that gold's value tends to increase at rates far slower than many people seem to realize.

If you could use but one tool to enhance your personal fortune, it should be gold's long-term, inflation-adjusted value. With that single concept you can determine the current state of the gold market and correctly assess both risks and opportunities.

Tool Number 2: The Gold-Oil Pendulum

Remember the earlier discussion about navigation and bearings? When you are at sea it pays to have as many bearings as possible. By taking two or three bearings you can more accurately determine your position. The same is true for investors.

Gathering substantial profits means knowing where you have been, where you are, and the best route to your financial harbor. The long-term, inflation-adjusted gold price is a valuable tool. By itself it will improve your understanding of the market. By adding a second tool, the gold-oil pendulum, you can arrive at an even more accurate assessment of the market and its most likely future course.

Gold tends to rise and fall as inflation increases and decreases. That is what the long-term, inflation-adjusted gold price is all about. Gold also tends to rise and fall as the price for the world's most important commodity, oil, advances and declines. The connection between gold and oil can be seen from a comparison of the price of oil and the price of gold over the long term. (See the chart on the next page.)

Some investors have looked at charts of gold and oil and

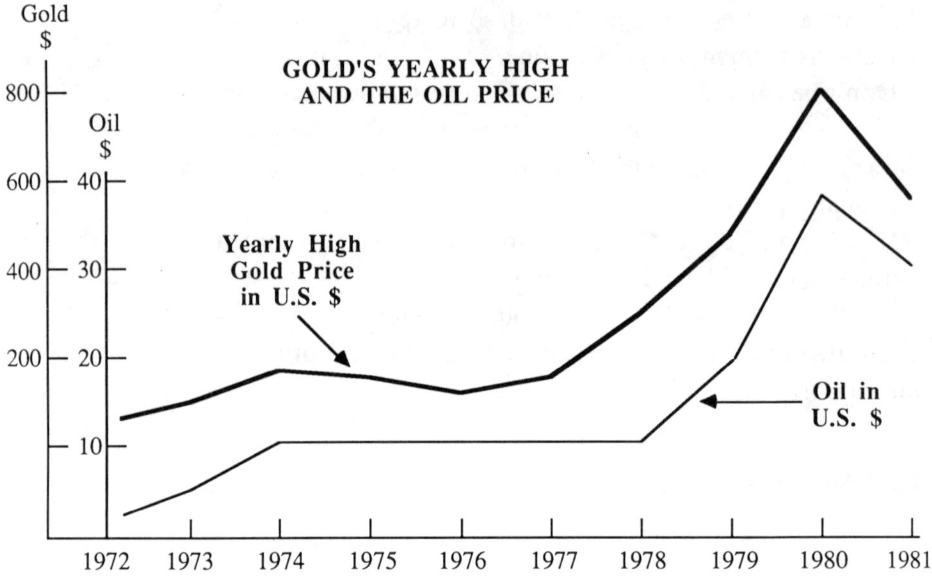

Source: Compiled by the author.

jumped to the simplistic conclusion that gold and oil are locked together in a rigid relationship. That is not true. The relationship is more complicated. The problem with the chart is that both gold and oil are expressed in terms of a single currency, the U.S. dollar. The chart tells nothing about the price of gold and oil in other currencies. Since both are international in character, we need to look at the relationship in some other way.

The solution is to remember the basic nature of gold as world money. Since gold is money, what we should ask is, What is the price of a barrel of oil in terms of gold? How much gold does it take to buy one barrel of oil?

Surprising Facts from the Market

The law of supply and demand holds that when demand increases and supply shrinks, the price will rise. Conversely, when supplies increase and demand shrinks, prices will fall. While this law is generally true, the opposite has been true for oil in terms of real money—gold. When demand rose in the late 1970s, the price of oil in terms of gold fell. Conversely, as demand eroded and supplies increased in the early 1980s, the gold price for a barrel of oil increased. This upside-down phenomenon is not a puzzle. It is an important clue to the underlying nature of free markets and their interaction.

In 1934 the world was caught in a depression. Demand for oil was depressed by sluggish economies. Not surprisingly the price for a barrel of oil declined during the depression days. It cost 1.79 grams of gold to buy one barrel of oil in 1929 and 0.94 grams in 1934.

By 1959, when the world was in the midst of an economic expansion, the cost for a barrel of oil rose to 2.59 grams of gold. Until the dollar was severed from gold in the 1970s, the markets behaved as expected. When demand for oil rose, so did its price in terms of gold. When demand was low, the gold price for oil declined.

After the separation of the dollar from gold, things began to change. The relationship between gold and oil reversed. When there was an oil shortage, the gold price for a barrel of oil declined. That is the opposite of what conventional supply-and-demand analysis would indicate.

At one point, during the height of the oil crisis in the late 1970s, the gold price for a barrel of oil declined to 0.94 grams. That was as low as it had been during the days of the depression. Likewise, during the early 1980s and until the summer of 1986, when oil supplies had grown and demand had slumped, the gold price for a barrel of oil rose to more than 2.59 grams per barrel, as high as it had been in 1959. It wasn't until the summer of 1986, when oil prices plunged to $10 a barrel that the real or gold price for oil began to behave in accord with traditional understanding of the law of supply and demand.

There is no doubt that the interaction of gold and oil surprised economists, oil analysts, and gold owners alike. The market swung through some strange territory. The gold price for a barrel of oil acted as a limit on the markets. After all, it makes no sense for the gold price of oil to rise when demand is falling. Likewise, it made no sense for the gold price of oil to fall during an oil crisis. Once the gold price for oil reached a ridiculous point, both gold and oil "corrected."

The two markets, gold and oil, while free to go their own ways, have in fact stayed within defined limits. The limits appear when the two markets are combined by looking at the gold price, rather than the dollar price, for a barrel of oil.

In January 1980 the gold price suddenly peaked and began to decline. Oil demonstrated the same pattern. When the gold price for a barrel of oil fell to depression levels at 0.94 grams per barrel, the markets reversed. A natural limit had been reached.

Many investors were caught by surprise when gold peaked and fell in 1980. Investors who had been watching the gold price for a barrel of oil, however, were not caught off guard. They understood that the markets had gone too far, that a correction had to come.

One lesson from the market's behavior in late 1979 and early 1980 is that it pays to watch the real cost of a barrel of oil. It is worth the effort to calculate how much gold it takes to buy it. The gold-oil pendulum is based on this concept. The gold price for a barrel of oil is a tool for determining the current state of the gold market and its likely future course.

Before digging into the details of the gold-oil pendulum, however, it will help to understand something about why the markets behave as they do.

The Self-limiting Nature of Free Markets

The laws of supply and demand still work. They work for gold and they work for oil. But in the new era of free-floating currencies, gold and oil formed a new, self-limiting relationship.

In the old days, when the price of gold in dollars and other currencies was fixed, there was no self-limiting relationship. Gold and oil moved in lockstep because governments controlled the price of gold. Once gold was free to respond to the market, its character as a market limiter began to emerge. The gold market has become a behind-the-scenes, natural, free-market regulator.

For example, in the worst of the oil crisis, in the 1970s, investors, economists, and politicians were terrified that the industrial nations would run out of oil. The price of oil rose, and so did the price of gold.

But the industrial nations had an unrecognized option. They all held huge gold reserves. They could have decided to pay for the oil they needed in gold. When the gold price for a barrel of oil fell to 0.94 grams, the gold reserves of the United States and the other industrialized nations would have bought as many barrels of oil as in the depression days. The gold reserves could have been used to assure enough oil to see the industrialized countries through the worst of the oil crisis. That option was not exercised. Instead the industrialized countries decided to fight inflation with tight money and high interest rates. But the gold-for-oil option did exist. It was there lurking in the background.

At one point in the late 1970s, the United States came close to exercising that option. The Treasury sold gold to raise cash. The stated objective was to keep the gold price down. The hidden objective was to convert gold to dollars that could be used to buy oil. While indirect, that method accomplished the same purpose as a direct exchange of gold for oil.

On the other side, in the Organization of Petroleum Exporting Countries (OPEC), the connection was clearer and more direct. Gold is still a basic form of money in much of the Arab world. For example, after the fall of the Shah of Iran, in 1979, the new government immediately reorganized the country's banking system in favor of a gold-based system.

The OPEC oil producers were, during the 1970s, selling oil, taking the proceeds, and buying gold. When the price of both oil and gold rose, they found that it was taking more and more oil to buy the same amount of gold. They knew that they were losing the oil price battle. They were far more sensitive to the relationship between gold and oil than the paper-based economies of the oil-consuming world. Dollars cannot be used in Iran or Saudi Arabia, but gold can. The Arab world's preference for gold over dollars meant that all along they fully understood the concept behind the gold-oil pendulum.

Charting the Gold Price for Oil

The first step in reducing the gold-oil relationship to a practical, usable tool is to look at the gold price for a barrel of oil over a long period of time. Between 1971 and 1986 the gold price for a barrel of oil fluctuated but remained within fairly well-defined limits. The gold price for a barrel of oil fell to less than one gram per barrel in 1973. From that low the price moved higher, exceeding three grams per barrel in 1976. From that peak the price retreated until it breached the one-gram-per-barrel price again in 1980. Once again that proved to be a limit. From the 1980 low, the price began to rise again and continued rising until it passed three grams a barrel in 1982.

This graphic look at the gold price for a barrel of oil confirms that the relationship is self-limiting and fairly well defined. The chart on the next page shows that the gold

THE GOLD OIL RELATIONSHIP
Grams of Gold per Barrel

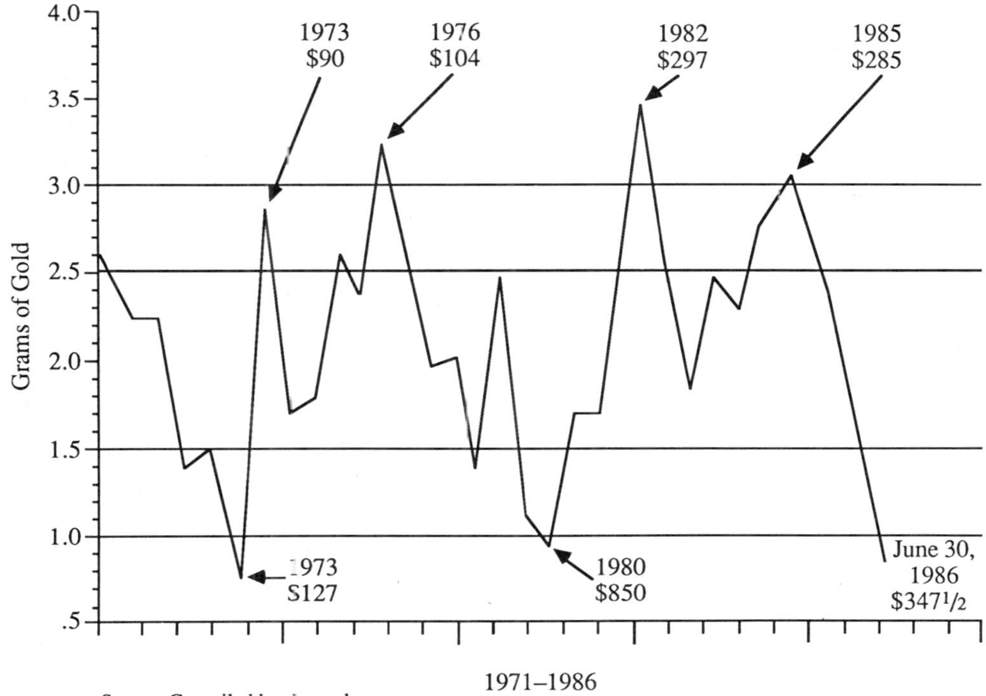

Source: Compiled by the author.

price for a barrel of oil stayed within limits through fifteen years of economic turbulence. The chart covers times of inflation, disinflation, skyrocketing oil prices, plunging oil prices, soaring gold, declining gold prices, and both a weak and strong U.S. dollar. Through it all the gold price for oil swung, like a pendulum, first toward one extreme of the range and then back toward the other.

You can keep track of the gold price for oil with a simple calculator. The math is not overly complicated. Here is what you do:

Example using oil at \$29 a barrel and gold at \$500 an ounce:

1. Divide \$500 by 31.103 (the number of grams in one troy ounce).

$$\$500 \div 31.103 = \$16.07$$

This gives you the gold price in dollars per gram.

2. Divide the oil price by the per gram gold price. $\$29 \div \$16.07 = 1.80$ grams per barrel

Example using oil at \$28 a barrel and gold at \$300 an ounce:

1. $\$300 \div 31.103 = \$9.64$
2. $\$28 \div \$9.64 = 2.90$ grams per barrel

Both the gold price and the oil price can be found in the popular financial newspapers. You have to know that there are 31.103 grams in a troy ounce. With this information you can calculate the gold price for a barrel of oil at any point in time.

You can keep track of the gold price for oil daily, weekly, or less often. How frequently you do the calculations depends on whether you are trading gold, holding for the long term, or trying to determine the best long-term buy-and-sell points.

As a practical matter, a monthly calculation is enough for most investors. Keeping track monthly will alert you when the market becomes especially hectic. During times when gold is moving rapidly it will be beneficial to calculate more frequently. Even then, weekly is usually enough.

Think of the relationship as a pendulum. Sometimes understanding complex financial relationships can be made easier by visualizing the relationship, for example, the gold-oil relationship. Any inverse relationship is difficult to grasp. (See the illustration on the next page.)

Having a mental picture of a pendulum makes the relationship easy to grasp. Pendulums swing from one side to the other.

Don't look for instant results. The gold market, like any other, cannot be predicted with scientific precision. In investments you are always dealing with ranges, calculations, and probabilities. Sometimes the market will move all the way to an extreme. At other times it will enter the range at one end or the other, reverse, and swing back toward the opposite extreme.

The extremes define major moves. The ranges define the intermediate moves. You have to use judgment to know if you are investing based on a major or an intermediate move.

The gold-oil pendulum defines one set of investment parameters. It clearly tells you when a major move has reached the limit. Buying and selling only at the extreme limits may not make your broker happy, but it will assure above-average profits over the long term.

THE GOLD-OIL PENDULUM

A Tool for Buying and Selling Gold

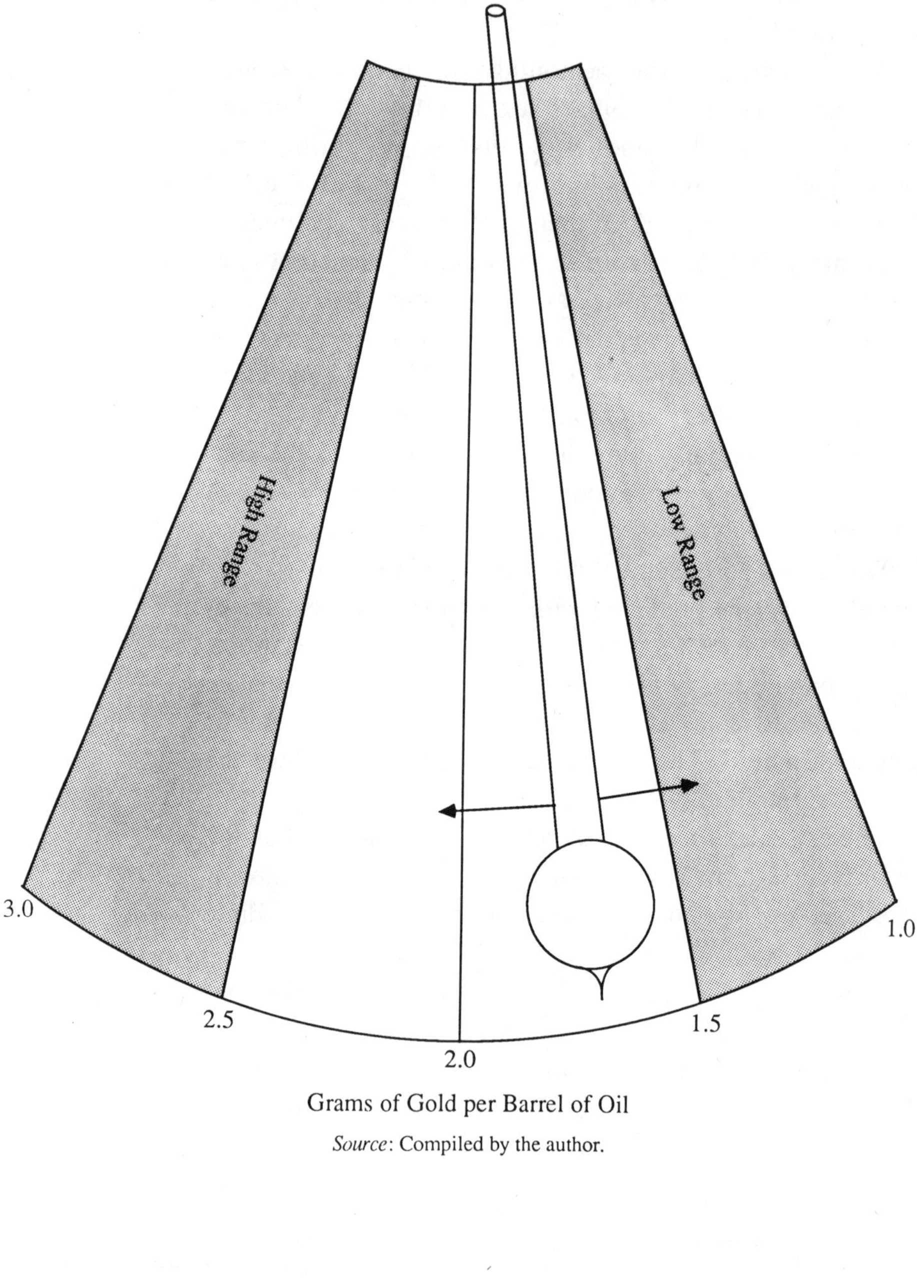

Grams of Gold per Barrel of Oil

Source: Compiled by the author.

The Gold-Oil Pendulum as a Tool for Forecasting the Gold Price

There are two variables at work in the gold-oil relationship, the price of gold and the price of oil. The pendulum's movements are determined by the action of both. At either extreme you can be sure that the pendulum will swing back toward the opposite limit but you must always ask will that happen because of a change in the oil price or the gold price or both.

In the 1970s things were fairly simple. As oil prices rose, money was concentrated in OPEC hands. People in the Middle East had a natural inclination to buy gold. As they became more prosperous they bought more gold. The pendulum's swings were then determined more by the changes in gold than by the changes in oil. Through the 1970s and into the early 1980s you simply bought gold when the pendulum was at the high gold price for oil and then sold when the pendulum had swung back to the low gold price for oil.

As oil prices fell in the 1980s, the fundamental background for gold changed. Money no longer accumulated in the hands of people ready to buy gold rather than assets. Instead the oil-consuming countries won the money tug-of-war. Cash began to accumulate in the hands of people who had a broader appetite for investments. Gold became one of rather than the primary receptacle for excess cash.

At an extreme an investor now has to look at the fundamentals and determine which is the most logical, a change in oil prices or a change in gold prices. The pendulum is still operating. But, the simple days of the 1970s have given way to the more complex days of the 1980s. That may make your task in applying the gold-oil pendulum a bit more difficult but it will also mean more opportunity. In a more complex environment many will become confused and do the opposite of what is sensible. There will be aberrations in the gold market that can work to your advantage.

The Basic Data

To help you in your work, here are the major high and low points for the gold price of oil between 1971 and 1984. They are the points used to develop the graph of the gold price for oil.

The Gold Price for Oil
(In grams of gold)

Year	*High point*	*Low point*
1971	2.58	2.18
1972	2.18	1.37
1973	1.50	0.75
1974	2.80	1.67
1975	1.76	2.54
1976	2.33	3.15
1977	2.50	1.94
1978	1.97	1.34
1979	2.41	1.07
1980	0.94	1.66
1981	1.65	2.55
1982	3.35	2.45
1983	1.78	2.40
1984	2.23	2.77
1985	3.02	2.27

Source: Compiled by the author.

The Oil Price Plunge of 1986

In the 1970s, especially the latter half, oil and gold went hand in hand. When oil prices skyrocketed in 1979 gold was never far behind. In the 1980s as oil prices came down, so too did the price of gold. When oil prices collapsed in 1986 there was a temptation to expect gold and silver prices to follow oil's lead and plunge to extreme lows. Gold did not cooperate, raising questions about the value of the gold-oil concept.

The problem by July 1986 was that the gold price for a barrel of oil, because of oil's plunge, had fallen back into a "sell" range.

Things changed in 1986.

There is an old and valued investment adage: "The only valid investment rule is one that works in reverse."

This may seem puzzling. Ordinarily we think of rules as being rigid. How can investors cope if rules say sell today and buy tomorrow? The answer is that markets do not respect investor's needs or wishes. Market's behave as they will regardless of what anyone thinks. Many analysts tantalize investors with rigid applications of otherwise valid rules. For example with the gold price for oil back below one gram a barrel it would be easy to make a strong case for selling gold. After all that was the right thing to do in 1973 and 1980. Why isn't it the right thing to do now?

In the 1970s rising oil prices acted as a mechanism for collecting cash from millions of consumers and delivering to a relatively few selected beneficiaries in the OPEC countries. Hundreds of billions of dollars were transferred to individuals who were inclined to buy gold.

The gold market is like any other. It takes investors with cash, willing to buy to push the gold price to higher ground. Rising oil prices and rising gold prices went hand in hand because so much cash was accumulating in the hands of people who wanted gold.

The fall in oil prices was accompanied by a deep worldwide recession. Lower oil prices meant less money in OPEC hands for gold purchases. The recession, by impoverishing millions of potential gold buyers, left the gold market without support. The "sell" signal given by the gold price for oil was a warning that the world was headed into a recession and that OPEC was not going to have unlimited funds to buy gold. Likewise the "sell" signal given in 1973 was a warning of recession.

In 1986 the gold price for oil fell at the same time that interest rates plunged and central banks around the world were madly pumping up money supplies in an effort to stimulate continued growth. The low gold price for oil, in July of 1986, was indicative of an entirely different situation. It was still a harbinger of change but in 1986, the most logical conclusion was that the oil price would rise rather than that the gold price would fall.

The question in mid-1986 was: How low will oil prices go before the turn is made. The answer was: Low enough so that supply and demand and market psychology could accomplish a reversal. Falling oil prices do act as a drag on the gold price. The gold-oil pendulum indicates that as long as oil prices remain weak it is unlikely that gold will manage a sustained upward move.

On the other hand, falling oil prices produce additional pressure on governments and central banks to do more to prevent recession and stimulate growth. Falling oil prices are therefore the seeds of their own reversal. Just as gold shot to unsustainable highs in 1980, oil was plunging to unsustainable lows in 1986.

Continued economic growth in the oil-consuming industrialized nations will mean more people with cash to invest in gold. The most logical conclusion from the gold-oil pendulum in 1986 was not that gold should be sold but that when oil prices stabilize and begin to rise, gold will slowly but surely advance to $400 an ounce.

Tool Number 3: Gold in Swiss Francs

Many sailors are satisfied with taking only two bearings. Mathematically that is all you need to determine a point on the sea. Many a ship, however, has gone aground or been lost in fair weather and broad daylight because the captain didn't have an accurate fix on the ship's position.

The same is true when it comes to finance. It may seem like too much work to use three tools. After all, the first two do provide an accurate view of the market. But like a sailor at sea, an investor can avoid surprises or find the best course to reach his objective by taking the time to calculate that "extra" bearing.

The first two tools go a long way toward informing you of the true condition of the gold market. When gold is selling far above its long-term, inflation-adjusted value, you should know that the market is vulnerable.

When the price of gold is low, based on its relationship to oil, you should step in, take risks, and be prepared for profits when the upward surge develops.

The third tool, the price of gold in Swiss francs, is more short-term oriented. It refines the information from the first two tools and it will increase your level of confidence.

Confidence, when it comes to making money, is the single most important factor. It is one thing to make a huge percentage gain. It is quite another to translate percentages into meaningful sums of money.

An investor who doubles a $10,000 investment is sure to be proud of that accomplishment. And $10,000 is not a small profit. But how much nicer it would be to have a profit of ten times that amount. A gain of $100,000, no matter what the percentage might be, would make a much greater difference in everyday life. In the end, the real difference, the one that determines the amount of your profit, is confidence. If you are confident of your analysis and conclusions, you will invest more, even use borrowed money, and enjoy much larger profits. Investors with less confidence will nibble, earn small gains, and then brag about the percentages. Adding the price of gold in Swiss francs to the long-term, inflation-adjusted value and the gold-oil pendulum can fine-tune your thinking and lift your confidence high enough to make a real dollars-and-cents difference.

Gold as a Dollar Asset

The gold market is a market quoted in dollars. Even in London or Zurich, gold is first quoted in terms of U.S. dollars and then converted into pounds or Swiss francs. Gold's primary relationship is to the dollar. That wasn't always true.

Years ago, in the days when the British Empire was the leading world economic force, gold was priced in terms of British pounds and then converted to other currencies. The morning and afternoon London gold fixings, which are still market benchmarks, date back to the days when the primary gold market was in terms of pounds. World War II and the gradual decline of the British Empire changed the character of the gold market. After World War II the United States emerged not only as the victor but also as the dominant world economic force. The gold market was transformed into a dollar-based market. After decades as a sterling asset, gold became a dollar asset.

The fact that gold is a dollar asset leads some investors to think that the only price that counts is the gold price in dollars. They watch the dollar price alone and think they know the market. They are completely insensitive to the fact that gold is world money, not another form of U.S. currency. To obtain a true picture of the gold market you must take into account the dollar as well. Traders the world over understand that gold and the dollar are inversely related. When the dollar is falling, gold generally is rising. When the dollar is strong, gold prices tend to be weak.

During the 1970s the dollar declined steadily for ten long years. As it fell, gold rose. The bear market in the dollar and the bull market in gold did not end until the great climax of early 1980.

From 1981 until early 1985 the dollar gained strength. Its steady climb resulted in a bear market in gold. Gold fell from the 1980 high of $850 to a 1982 low of $297 and a lower low of $285 in 1985. The strong dollar was bad news for the gold price.

Given that long experience you might think that it would be common to focus on the currency aspect of gold. You might even assume that most investors watch gold in several currencies just to be sure that they have the basic underlying trends in clear focus. That, however, is not true. Many investors do realize that the dollar and gold are inversely related, and they do watch the dollar as well as gold. But their attention is just that. They watch the dollar and then they watch gold independently. Few go the next step and watch gold in several currencies.

When you go the extra step and become sensitive to gold in terms of several currencies, you often see a picture of the gold market quite different from the picture seen by those who watch only in terms of dollars. Between March and December 1984, for example, the gold price in dollars was down 13.4 percent. That led to the conclusion that the gold market was extremely weak. It was even popular in those days to forecast a steep fall in gold, down to $250 or lower.

If the bears had been watching the gold market in Switzerland, they would have noticed that in terms of Swiss francs, gold declined over the same period by only 1 percent. In terms of Swiss francs the gold market in 1984 was relatively flat. In terms of British pounds the gold price climbed by 16.7 percent. A London gold watcher would have dismissed the gloomy bearish forecasts with a laugh.

You must watch gold in terms of dollars. That is the primary market. You must also watch the dollar, however, versus other currencies. You cannot expect to have an accurate picture of the gold trend unless you watch gold in terms of at least one other currency.

Gold Prices in 1984

	Gold price		
	1/3/84	*12/6/84*	*Change*
U.S. dollars	381	330	−13.4%
British pounds	234	273	+16.7%
French francs	3,215	3,090	−3.9%
German marks	1,051	1,008	−4.1%
Japanese yen	88,659	81,246	−8.4%
Swiss francs	843	832	−1.0%

Source: Compiled by the author.

Gold in Swiss francs makes relative value simple. We know that all things are relative. That includes gold and the dollar. What you need to know is how gold is behaving *relative to the dollar.* That can be done in several ways. Most are quite complicated. By watching the price of gold in Swiss francs, however, you will be able to tell at a glance how the gold market is behaving relative to the dollar.

The study of the gold price in several currencies in 1984 shows that gold was not moving in lockstep with the dollar. Back in the great bull market of 1979, gold rose at about the same rate in dollars, pounds, Swiss francs, and other currencies. The bull market cut across all currencies. In 1984 gold was rising in pounds, relatively stable in Swiss francs, and sinking in dollars. In other words, gold was not falling as fast as the dollar was rising. The bear market that appeared in terms of dollars was only half the story. If gold had been down sharply in Swiss francs and dollars, then there would have been good reason to worry about a bear market. It wasn't. Instead the mixed results indicated that the worst of the decline from the $850 peak in 1980 was over. The view of gold in other currencies contradicted the gloomy bearish forecasts that were so popular at the time. And gold in Swiss francs was the messenger of truth. In early 1985 gold bottomed at $285 and recovered to a level above $300.

Why the Swiss Franc?

The dollar and the Swiss franc are opposites in terms of trade and economic significance. When it comes to trade, official reserves, financial markets, and international fundamentals, the dollar is dominant. The Swiss franc doesn't account for enough international trade to be noticed in the statistics. When it comes to safety, personal security, and private investment, however, the situation is reversed. In those terms the Swiss franc is number one.

The dollar is number one in trade and economics. The Swiss franc is number one when it comes to investor sentiment. Combining the two, watching the dollar-Swiss franc exchange rate, provides a perfectly balanced perspective.

By watching the price of gold in Swiss francs you combine both in a single tool. Gold in Swiss francs includes the might of the dollar, because gold is a dollar asset, and the influence of the Swiss franc.

Switzerland is a tiny country with roughly 6.2 million people. Switzerland and its currency are dwarfed by Germany, Japan, and the United States. Nevertheless, individual investors from every corner of the globe turn to tiny Switzerland for bank accounts, investments, privacy, and financial safety. They respect both the discipline of the Swiss banking system and the gold reserves standing behind the franc.

The Swiss deserve the respect. They have steadfastly guarded the privacy of their clients against the U.S. Internal Revenue Service, the Nazis during World War II, and the pressures and threats of various governments in Africa and the Middle East.

The famous numbered account system grew out of the Swiss passion for bank secrecy. During World War II the Nazis sent agents to Switzerland. Their mission was to penetrate the Swiss banks and discover the names of German Jews with money in Switzerland. The Swiss responded with the numbered account. All the German agents could find were numbers, not names. The code that linked names and numbers was locked in a secret vault open only to the top two or three bank officers.

Americans often sneer at Swiss banking secrecy. Officials of the U.S. government, believing that the secrecy is only to protect criminals, take periodic legal shots at the Swiss banks. In the United States it is easy to forget that innocent people need the kind of protection offered by the Swiss banks.

When the Shah's government in Iran was replaced by the extremist, anti-Western regime of the Ayatollah Ruhollah Khomeini, Iranians withdrew hundreds of millions of dollars from U.S. banks and deposited the cash in Swiss banks. The outflow from the United States was not a flight from the dollar. Most of the money, after being deposited in Switzerland, was reinvested in U.S. bank certificates and U.S. assets. The investors were terrified that the new, "holy" government would discover their bank accounts and arrest them or worse. It is too easy, in an open country like the United States, to find out all about a person's financial affairs.

In the case of Nigeria, a few years earlier, the United States made an innocent but terrible mistake. In an effort to help that less-developed country, we offered to train Nigerians in the art of U.S. banking. While on the job some Nigerians took home copies of computer printouts with the names and balances of Nigerians. Later when there was a coup and the government changed, those printouts became lists for arrest and persecution. The government forced depositors to withdraw the cash from the U.S. banks and turn over the funds to the new government. Trusting the U.S. banking system proved fatal in some instances.

Switzerland is one of the very few places where people can find real, tested protection against such risks. Privacy, even secrecy, is a way of life in Switzerland. The Swiss regard bank secrecy as essential to the development of a free financial market. Without secrecy, investors would not dare to risk investment in the less-stable and less-developed countries.

The Swiss franc itself is another part of the story. The Swiss have a healthy regard for the value of their currency and despise the ravages of inflation. The Swiss franc is unofficially backed by gold. The Swiss operate their monetary system "as if" they were still on a gold standard.

You should pay attention not to what people say but to what they do with their personal funds. Investors express their sentiments about the international economy and the international payments system through the language of financial transactions. Transactions cause fluctuations in the value of the Swiss franc.

When there is real doubt about the future for global inflation and the international economy, not even the Swiss franc can hold against the tide. Under those circumstances investors will prefer gold itself to any paper currency. The price of gold in Swiss francs will rise. During times when investors fear deflation and a long decline in the gold price, they will prefer paper currencies, especially the Swiss franc. In those periods the price of gold in Swiss francs will decline.

Gold in Swiss francs will tell you about the true, underlying gold-market trends. This is not to say that watching gold in Swiss francs is "better" than watching it in dollars alone. It is to say that the price of gold in Swiss francs presents a far more complete picture of conditions in the gold market. Gold in Swiss francs includes the dollar, the Swiss franc, and gold itself.

The Way to Calculate the Price of Gold in Swiss Francs

Calculating the price of gold in Swiss francs is simple and can be done by anyone with a newspaper and a calculator.

The first step is to find the section called "Foreign Exchange" in your favorite financial newspaper. Read down the list until you come to Switzerland. What you find should look something like this:

FOREIGN EXCHANGE

Friday, June 6, 1986

The New York foreign exchange selling rates below apply to trading among banks in amounts of $1 million and more, as quoted at 3 p.m. Eastern time by Bankers Trust Co. Retail transactions provide fewer units of foreign currency per dollar.

	U.S. $ equiv.		Currency per U.S. $	
Country	Fri.	Thurs.	Fri.	Thurs.
Argentina (Austral)	1.1614	1.1614	.861	.861
Australia (Dollar)	.6990	.6928	1.4306	1.4434
Austria (Schilling)	.06397	.06352	15.63	15.74
Belgium (Franc)				
Commercial rate	.02153	.02191	46.45	45.65
Financial rate	.02139	.02176	46.75	45.95
Brazil (Cruzado)	.07262	.07262	13.77	13.77
Britain (Pound)	1.5050	1.4950	.6645	.6689
30-Day Forward	1.5014	1.4914	.6660	.6705
90-Day Forward	1.4954	1.4856	.6687	.6731
180-Day Forward	1.4883	1.4783	.6719	.6765
Canada (Dollar)	.7158	.7184	1.3970	1.3920
30-Day Forward	.7167	.7175	1.3952	1.3937
90-Day Forward	.7191	.7153	1.3907	1.3981
180-Day Forward	.7225	.7123	1.3840	1.4040
Chile (Official rate)	.005274	.005274	189.90	189.90
China (Yuan)	.3131	.3109	3.1935	3.2159
Colombia (Peso)	.005291	.005291	189.00	189.00
Denmark (Krone)	.1214	.1207	8.2350	8.2850
Ecuador (Sucre)				
Official rate	.009153	.009153	109.25	109.25
Floating rate	.006329	.006329	158.00	158.00
Finland (Markka)	.1929	.1917	5.1825	5.2175
France (Franc)	.1411	.1404	7.0870	7.1250
30-Day Forward	.1411	.1403	7.0885	7.1260
90-Day Forward	.1412	.1403	7.0910	7.1290
180-Day Forward	.1409	.1402	7.0950	7.1340
Greece (Drachma)	.007143	.007105	140.00	140.75

Country	U.S. $ equiv. Fri.	U.S. $ equiv. Thurs.	Currency per U.S. $ Fri.	Currency per U.S. $ Thurs.
Hong Kong (Dollar)	.1280	.1280	7.8110	7.8115
India (Rupee)	.0796	.07876	12.56	12.69
Indonesia (Rupiah)	.0008857	.0008857	1129.00	1129.00
Ireland (Punt)	1.3555	1.3525	.7377	.7394
Israel (Shekel)	.6720	.6720	1.488	1.488
Italy (Lira)	.0006549	.0006523	1527.00	1533.00
Japan (Yen)	.005968	.005940	167.55	168.35
30-Day Forward	.00598	.005953	167.18	167.99
90-Day Forward	.006006	.005978	166.48	167.27
180-Day Forward	.006043	.006015	165.48	166.25
Jordan (Dinar)	2.9727	2.9727	.3364	.3364
Kuwait (Dinar)	3.3829	3.3829	.2956	.2956
Lebanon (Pound)	.03174	.03174	31.50	31.50
Malaysia (Ringgit)	.3826	.3811	2.6140	2.6240
Malta (Lira)	2.5125	2.5125	.3980	.3980
Netherland (Guilder)	.3994	.3971	2.5035	2.5180
New Zealand (Dollar)	.5620	.5560	1.7794	1.7986
Norway (Krone)	.1317	.1309	7.5925	7.6400
Pakistan (Rupee)	.05993	.05896	16.85	16.96
Peru (Inti)	.07168	.07168	13.95	13.95
Philippines (Peso)	.04876	.04876	20.51	20.51
Portugal (Escudo)	.006678	.006596	149.75	151.60
Saudi Arabia (Riyal)	.2667	.2666	3.7500	3.7505
Singapore (Dollar)	.4498	4492	2.2230	2.2260
South Africa (Rand)				
Commercial rate	.3970	.3980	2.5188	2.5123
Financial rate	.2340	.2413	4.2735	4.1442
South Korea (Won)	.001129	.001129	889.20	889.20
Spain (Peseta)	.007029	.006988	142.25	143.10
Sweden (Krona)	.1393	.1385	7.1775	7.2200
Switzerland (Franc)	.5455	.5427	1.8330	1.8425
30-Day Forward	.5465	.5438	1.8297	1.8388
90-Day Forward	.5488	.5462	1.8220	1.8308
180-Day Forward	.5525	.5499	1.8100	1.8185
Taiwan (Dollar)	.02614	.02614	38.25	38.25
Thailand (Baht)	.03789	.03789	26.39	26.39
Turkey (Lira)	.001451	.001451	689.00	689.00
United Arab (Dirham)	.2723	.2723	3.673	3.673
Uruguay (New Peso)				
Financial	.006885	.006885	145.25	145.25
Venezuela (Bolivar)				
Official rate	.1333	.1333	7.50	7.50
Floating rate	.04924	.04885	20.31	20.47
W. Germany (Mark)	.4494	.4458	2.2250	2.2430
30-Day Forward	.4504	.4468	2.2200	2.2881
90-Day Forward	.4523	.4380	2.2108	2.2831
180-Day Forward	.4552	.4517	2.1970	2.2140
SDR	1.16424	1.15635	0.858932	0.864789
ECU	0.962358	0.952504	...	...

Special Drawing Rights are based on exchange rates for the U.S., West German, British, French and Japanese currencies. *Source:* International Monetary Fund.

ECU is based on a basket of community currencies. *Source:* European Community Commission.

z-Not quoted.

The figure you want is the spot quotation under "currency per U.S. $." In the example shown for September 5, 1985, the figure is 2.3720.

That quotation is the number of Swiss francs per dollar. If you were traveling in Europe with traveler's checks in dollars, you would receive 2.37 Swiss francs for every dollar when you cashed your traveler's checks at the bank in Switzerland.

The other quotation (.4216) is the value of one Swiss franc in terms of dollars. That figure is popular in the United States where everyone thinks and operates in terms of dollars. It is not, however, the figure used by currency traders around the world and it is not the figure you want to calculate gold in Swiss francs. You want to know how many Swiss francs per dollar. On September 5, 1985, that was 2.37.

The next figure you need is the dollar price for an ounce of gold. The only caution is to obtain the cash, or spot, figure and not the option, or forward, figures that are frequently reported by some news services. On September 5, 1985, the spot price for gold at the close was $325.75.

The final step is to multiply the Swiss franc price by the spot gold price to determine the Swiss franc price for an ounce of gold. On September 5, 1985, that price was

2.37 × $325.75 = 772.0275, rounded to the nearest Swiss franc = 772 sfr

Watching the price of gold in Swiss francs is no more demanding than watching gold in U.S. dollars. The difference is familiarity. It takes time, patience, and effort to develop sensitivity to the price of gold in Swiss francs. You won't find the figure headlined in popular gold reports. You must do the calculating yourself. That is one of the attractions. When everyone is doing something, you can be sure that when it comes to investments, much of the effectiveness has been lost. Staying one step ahead of the market means having unique tools. It means having a perspective that is more complete than, and different from, the popular view.

The price of gold in Swiss francs, the third unique tool in this chapter, rounds out your perspective. It fills in the gaps and adds dimension to your market analysis. It helps to internationalize your investment thinking. Once you are accustomed to thinking about gold in Swiss francs and not just in dollars you will have an international view of the gold market. You will "feel" about gold much the same way that wealthy, successful international investors do.

You will have to calculate the price of gold in Swiss francs regularly for some time before it becomes familiar and easy. Make the calculations daily for a week or two. That should provide an initiation period. Then you can calculate the price as often as suits your investment style and strategy. The results will be worth the effort.

Remarkable Forecasts from Gold in Swiss Francs

After gold's spectacular rise to $835 in January 1980, a new crowd of gold enthusiasts developed. There is nothing like a rising market to attract attention. Many investors seem to feel that history will immediately repeat itself so they can apply yesterday's news to make tomorrow's fortunes.

In 1981 forecasts of new heights in the gold price were common. (See the chart on the next page.) Some people confidently predicted gold at $2,000. They were not watching the price of gold in Swiss francs. In 1981 and the first half of 1982 gold in Swiss francs told a clear, unambiguous story. Anyone following gold in Swiss francs in that period had no doubt that the popular forecasts were going to be wrong. During 1981 and early 1982 the price of gold in Swiss francs steadily declined from over 1,000 Swiss francs per ounce to less than 700.

GOLD IN SWISS FRANCS
(Monthly-Opening)

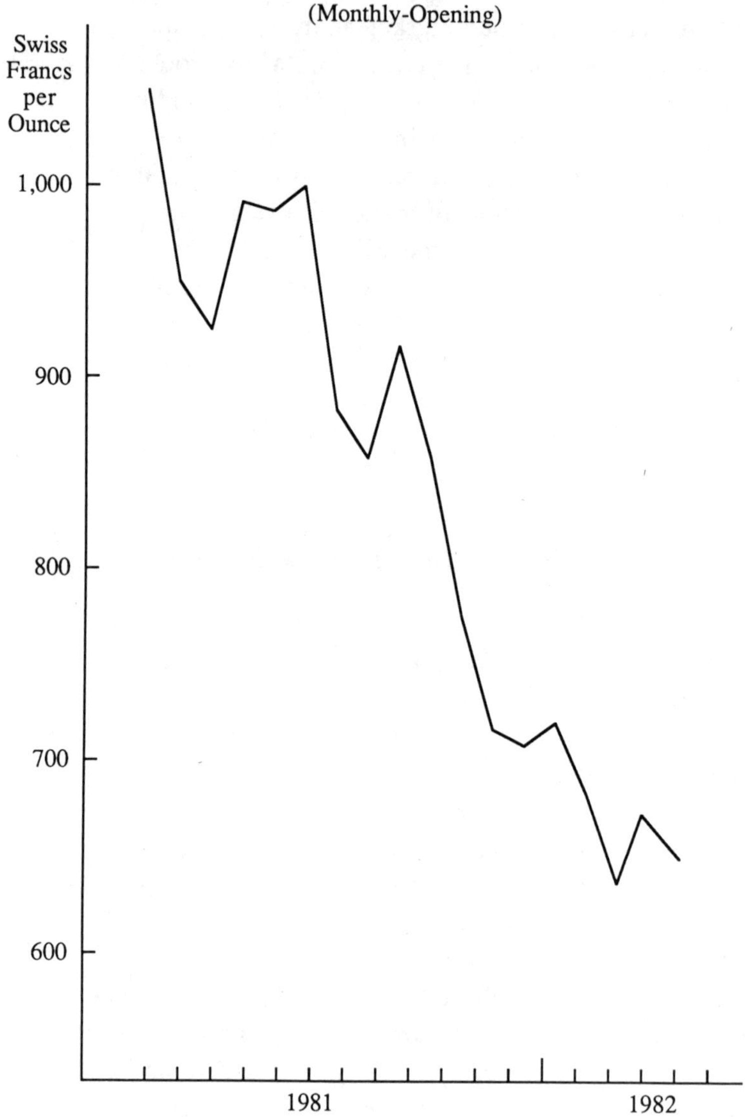

Source: Compiled by the author.

Many investors lost considerable amounts as they bought gold during that period. Gold's tantalizing undulations in dollars combined with the popular forecasts of a coming new bull market were alluring. You needed a unique and distinct perspective to stay out of the treacherous gold market of 1981. The bottom did not come until the price had dipped below $300 in 1982. Gold in Swiss francs was an effective and useful tool in 1981 and 1982.

From the 1982 the low price of gold began to climb. It reached almost $475 in September, fell back, and then climbed again to $500 in early 1983.

For those watching only the dollar price of gold (see the chart below), this fluctuation was again very seductive. Gold was reaching higher highs. That kind of action whets

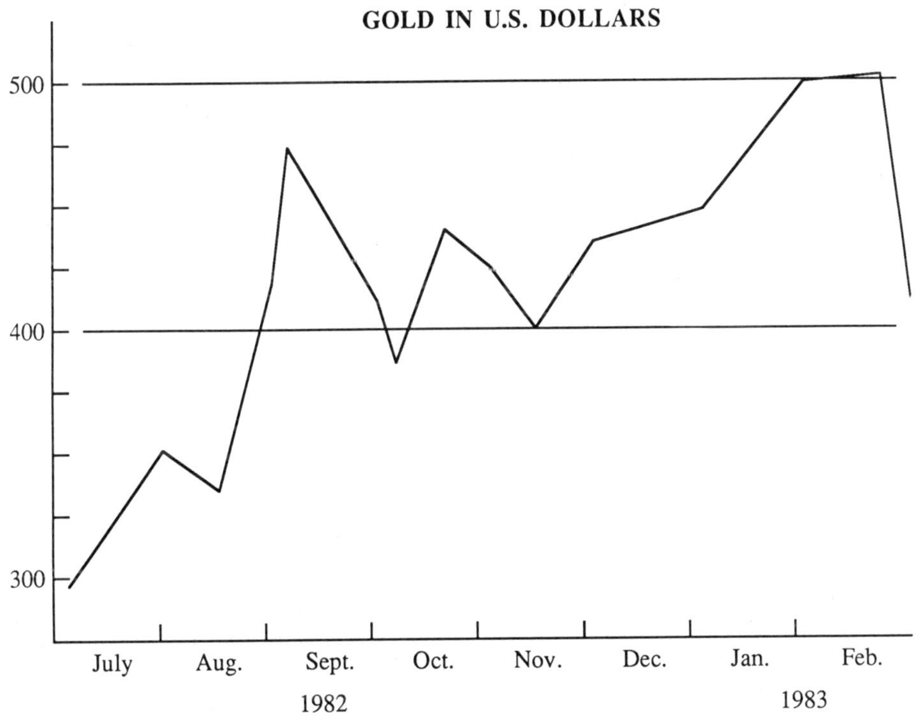

Source: Compiled by the author.

an investor's appetite. It is commonly believed that a market making higher highs is gaining strength.

Once again, in 1983 the forecasts of gold at $2,000 emerged and were believed. And once again they were wrong. Gold did not fulfill those dreams of a new bull market. Instead, after reaching $500 in 1983, the gold market began a dull, dreary retreat that did not end until a lower low was established in early 1985.

While the price of gold in dollars was seducing so many investors, the price of gold in Swiss francs was issuing warnings. In August 1982 the price of gold in Swiss francs crept above the 1,000 level. That was an early warning. That level had held the U.S. stock market captive for over a decade, and it has acted as a ceiling in many markets the world over. Gold's failure in 1982 to maintain its position above the 1,000 level was an early signal of coming market weakness.

From 1,000 in August, the price of gold in Swiss francs, like its price in dollars, retreated. Then in late 1983 gold in Swiss francs staged a second assault on the 1,000 level. The second assault carried only marginally above the earlier attempt. It too failed. The market quickly slipped back below 1,000 Swiss francs per ounce of gold. Instead of higher highs, the chart of gold in Swiss francs showed a pattern that looked ominous even to investors with little knowledge of technical analysis. In technical jargon the market had made a double top, a clear warning.

The Swiss franc chart proved correct. Gold fell to $285 before the slide was arrested.

Over long periods of time, financial markets can be efficient. The dollar price of gold will adjust to the underlying trend. If a long-term chart is drawn of the price of gold in Swiss francs and in dollars, the lines will generally follow each other.

You can rely exclusively on the price of gold in Swiss francs with confidence that you will have a better perspec-

GOLD IN SWISS FRANCS
Stopped at 1,000 Again

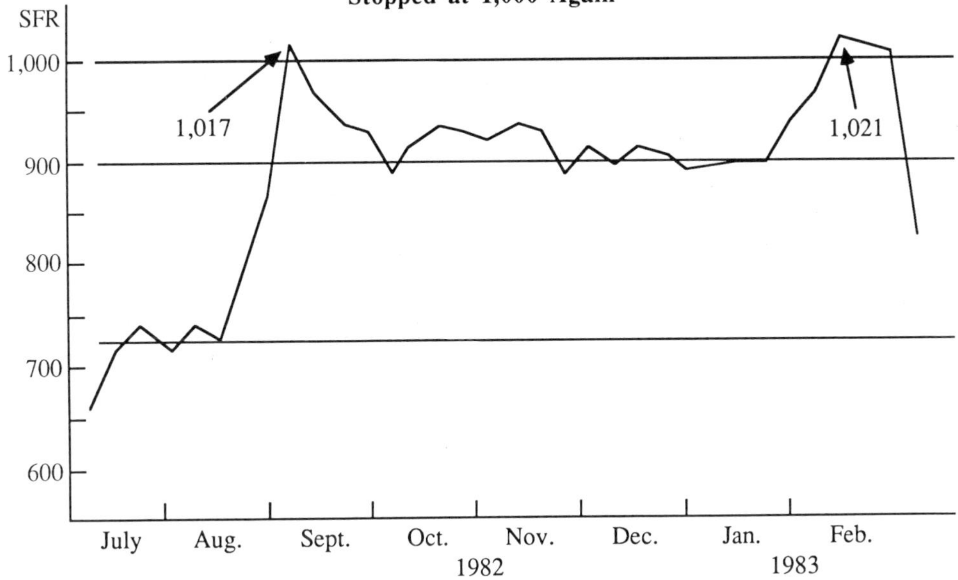

Source: Compiled by the author.

tive on short-term trends and not be misled when it comes to long-term trends. (See the chart above.)

Short-term Comparisons

Because the price of gold in Swiss francs tends to portray more accurately the underlying trend, it can be used to detect trading opportunities. The dollar price is not locked to the Swiss franc price. Over short periods of a year or less, the dollar price can and often does move away from the basic trend. These "errant" moves in the gold market present a trading opportunity.

For trading purposes you want to be sensitive to the prices of gold both in dollars and in Swiss francs (see the chart on the next page). Look for those times when they go in different directions. If you are sure that you have a correct analysis of the Swiss franc chart, you can make investment decisions with confidence. The odds are that the

GOLD IN DOLLARS VS. GOLD IN SWISS FRANCS

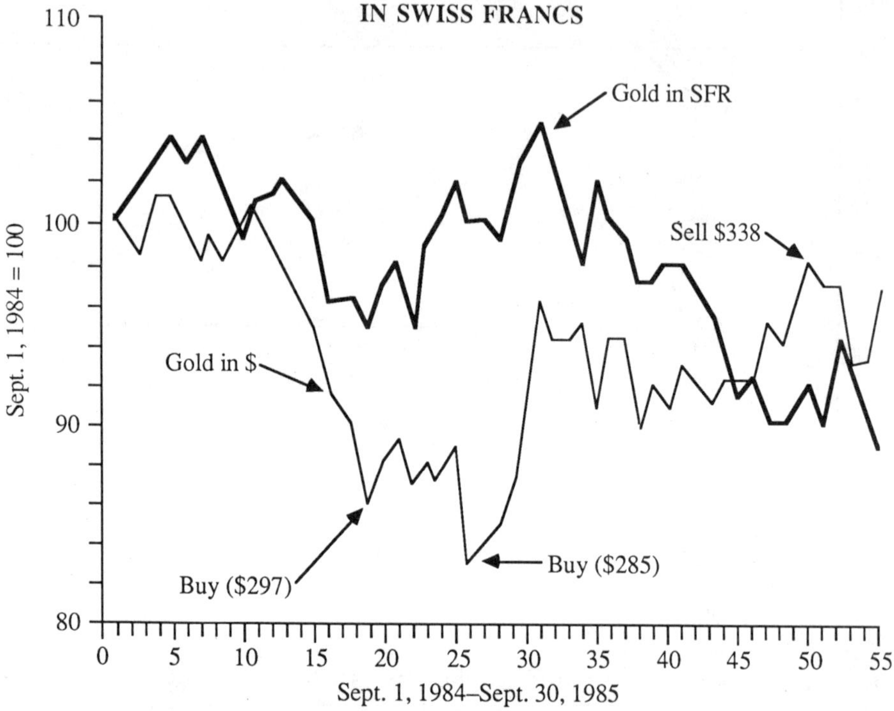

Source: Compiled by the author.

dollar gold price will "correct" and later follow the trend being described by gold in Swiss francs.

Using the Three Tools Together: A Case Study

Used together, these three tools make a potent combination. In January 1984, gold traded at $380. There were sharp differences of opinion. Some argued that a new bull market was coming. Others warned of a plunge in the gold price. A huge bulge in the U.S. money supply supported the optimists, while persistently low-current inflation pointed towards the pessimists. It was easy to become confused, lost among the conflicting fundamentals.

Charts of the price of gold in dollars were not much

help. Gold had spent much of 1983 hovering around $400. The graphs were more or less trendless. The three tools described in this chapter cut through the conflicts and confusion with surgical skill.

The price of gold in Swiss francs was down from 1,000 to 820. Gold's long-term, inflation-adjusted value was $269, while the market was considerably higher. The gold price for a barrel of oil was 2.37 grams, well along towards one extreme of the gold-oil pendulum.

The three tools portrayed a picture of vulnerability. There was no uptrend in the Swiss franc gold chart. Gold was high relative to its basic long-term value, and the gold-oil relationship indicated that a further downward move in gold was probable. Caution flags were flying. You bought gold at your peril.

The tools were correct. Oil prices fell, the dollar soared, and gold's next move was down to $285.

The three tools worked at the market low in 1976. They worked again at the top in 1980. And they worked during 1984, a year of confusion in the gold market. The tools were not the product of special foresight. They were born in the confusion of the 1970s.

Many investors fall prey either to tantalizing forecasts or to gold's "religious" character. They count their losses too often. Successful investing is the result of practiced discipline. You can increase your understanding of the markets and your profits by using these three tools. Use them to question forecasts and opinions of others. Use them to make your own forecasts. Use them to make buy-and-sell decisions.

Silver

Silver, like gold, is a precious metal and a form of money. In some countries, India, for example, silver is the precious metal of choice. Silver tends to be popular when governments make it illegal to own gold. When gold was illegal in the United States, many Americans turned to silver.

While there are differences, silver generally follows gold because it too reacts to inflation, the devaluation of paper currencies, and international crises.

One way to trade silver is simply to follow the gold market. When gold signals it is time to buy, you purchase silver instead. When gold peaks, you sell your silver holdings. Because silver trades at a lower dollar price, the percentage moves in silver can be greater than in gold. Trading silver using the gold trends can, therefore, result in greater profits (and losses) than dealing in gold.

Specializing in Silver

Two of the three tools for market analysis can be adapted for silver. The long-term, inflation-adjusted silver price can be determined in much the same way as it is for gold. Likewise, you can calculate the Swiss franc price for silver. The third tool, the gold-oil pendulum, is specifically for gold.

Calculating the long-term, inflation-adjusted price for silver is somewhat more difficult than finding that price for gold. Because in the late 1920s silver was more volatile than gold, it is harder to find a firm base from which to start a string of inflation calculations for silver. From 1919 to 1932, the price for silver dropped sharply. It had reached a peak of $1.375 an ounce in 1919. By late 1932, the price for an ounce of silver had fallen to $0.24.

Two things account for silver's volatility, and both apply to today's market. As 1920 approached, inflation was rising (similar to 1979). In 1920 U.S. consumer prices rose at an annual rate of 15.8 percent. Rising inflation produced a spike in silver not unlike the gold-market spike of early 1980. In 1921 inflation gave way to deflation. Consumer prices fell by 10 percent that year. Deflation produced a sharp fall in silver prices. The experience of both the 1920s and the late 1970s indicates that silver follows inflation rates in an exaggerated fashion. The market tends to overreact in both directions. The same is true today. The prices of both silver and gold will follow inflation or deflation, exaggerating on the down side when inflation falls or deflation threatens.

The question is, What was the right price for silver back in the 1920s or early 1930s? After the 1919 spike and before the Great Depression down turn, silver settled at $0.70 per ounce. At that level silver was, arguably, at a true equilibrium price.

Using $0.70 an ounce and adjusting for inflation produces a theoretical price of $0.48 in 1932. The actual market price that year was $0.24, well below the target line. In 1940, the calculated price was $0.49, in 1950, $0.84, and in 1960, $1.06. At each of these points the market was very close to the calculated long-term, inflation-adjusted silver price. These market facts confirm that $0.70 is the right starting price.

Taking the calculations out to the 1980s produces a long-term, inflation-adjusted silver price of $3.60 in late 1982, $3.71 in late 1983, and $3.86 in late 1984.

The figures may seem shocking. Silver climbed to $48.40 in 1979, and many investors still relate to that peak. It is hard to realize that silver was fourteen times too high in late 1979 and early 1980. We tend to believe that the markets are always right. Somehow, we imply, a group of investors banding together to form a market can forecast the future when no individual investor can. This faith in the crowd is wrong. Crowds, brought together by ideas, often move irrationally. The markets are fallible. The spikes in gold and silver in early 1980 are proof of that conclusion. The shocking aspect of silver is to understand just how much the market can exaggerate a trend.

Bullion vs. Coins

Gold can be purchased in the form of bullion or coins. The gold bars that you see in ads for gold and silver are bullion. Coins are either monetary or numismatic.

The three tools in this chapter apply to bullion and the monetary coins. Numismatic, or collector's, coins follow another path. They tend to advance or decline in line with personal income more than inflation or prices for gold bullion. Collectors will buy rare coins when they can afford the price. Rising personal income makes rare coins more affordable for more collectors.

Monetary coins are coins issued by governments as a medium of exchange. Examples are the Canadian Maple Leaf and the South African Krugerrand.

In Switzerland, over lunch, it is common to hear a debate. The question is: In a depression, which would be better, coins or bullion? The debate rages on and has never been completely resolved. Both have their merits and their shortcomings. One way to answer the question is in the context of personal need.

An advantage of coins is that they can be acquired for relatively small amounts of money. Whenever you have the extra cash you can buy a coin or two and put it away in a safe deposit box. If you do this regularly over many years, you will accumulate a substantial gold position without having to invest a large sum at any one time. Coins are also very attractive. It can be a pleasure just to look at fine gold in the form of coins.

Never take delivery of bullion. If you do, you will have a problem when it comes time for sale. The dealer won't know if the gold bar has been tampered with and will insist on an expensive assay.

The bottom line is that it really doesn't matter which you choose, coins or bullion. What matters is that you make a choice and begin your gold-investing program.

There is one exception. In the event of a depression Americans probably would be well served to hold some silver coins such as silver dollars. The long period when gold was illegal for Americans has taken a toll. Merchants and grocers are not as familiar with gold coins as they are with U.S. silver dollars. Put a few silver dollars away in your safe deposit box, just in case.

Mining Shares

During the days when it was illegal for Americans to own gold, it was legal to own gold-mining shares. Many U.S. investors, not wanting to flout the law, chose gold-mining shares as an alternative to gold bullion or monetary coins. Of all mining shares, those in South African companies became the most popular. By the 1970s Americans owned fully 25 percent of all the outstanding shares in South African mining companies.

Mining Shares and Dividends

Mining companies pay dividends. Gold pays no income at all. Dividends proved to be a powerful attraction even after gold had begun its 1970 bull market. Not many investors switched out of gold-mining shares into gold. They did not have to. The results on the mining shares were spectacular.

If you bought gold in 1976 at $101, you would have enjoyed a capital gain of 750 percent by early 1980. A $10,000 investment grew to $85,000.

Mining shares provided an even greater profit. A $10,000 investment in Driefontein at the 1976 low would have become $95,083 in early 1980, including dividends. Driefontein, a fairly conservative South African gold mine, outperformed gold in those volatile four years.

After the 1980 peak the argument in favor of mining

shares grew more impressive. An investor who held on to gold after 1980 saw his $85,000 dwindle to $31,000 by the end of 1984. An Investor holding shares in Kloof had first enjoyed a gain from $10,000 in 1976 to $179,666 by early 1980. The still more impressive result came after gold peaked and fell. The holding of Kloof shares dropped only to $172,424 at the end of 1984. The dividends not only had increased the total return, they had protected the value of mining shares when bullion prices fell.

It is tempting to look back at past results and form hard-and-fast conclusions. The spectacular results from mining shares, especially South African mining shares, lured many investors into a trap. They thought that mining shares were better than gold itself.

That was an illusion. Looks, from past performance, can be deceiving. Mining is a tough business. The dividends come from sales of gold at a profit. Once the gold is depleted, the mine will be a worthless hole in the ground. Dividends are, in the case of mining, a gradual return of the capital invested.

Of course mining companies do not pay out all the profits in dividends. They retain some profits and invest in new mines and new mining properties. Some mining companies have been in business, paying dividends, for decades. That doesn't change the basics, however.

Mining shares are not a substitute for gold. Mining, like any other business, can and does suffer setbacks, bad years, and even periods of depression. If a mining company closes because of poor management, labor strife, or other reasons, the shares will be worthless, and there will be no dividends.

Gold-mining shares are "shares" first and a gold play second. Once that concept is accepted, mining shares can be explored as an interesting and, at times, exciting opportunity.

Mining Shares and the Cross Currency Phenomenon

South Africa's controversial government has sensitized the investment community to the political risks in gold-mining shares. The news tends to exaggerate everything, including South African apartheid-related violence. The headlines obscure the financial landscape and make it easy to forget the basics. Gold mining outside the United States is a business with a substantial cross-currency exposure.

Gold is a dollar asset. This means that the price, no matter where you are in the world, is first set in dollars and then converted to local currency. South Africa may sell gold for Swiss francs in Zurich, but the basic price level is still linked to the dollar. Consequently, the income for a South African or other non-U.S. mining company is directly or indirectly in U.S. dollars.

This is an important concept. It isn't easy to grasp. Once you understand it, it seems easy enough. But for those who don't regularly deal in foreign currencies, it can be a tough idea to capture. Spend some time. Use a pencil and paper. But don't quit until you have firmly grasped the idea that gold sales, anywhere in the world, are connected to the U.S. dollar.

South African mining companies sell a U.S. dollar-denominated product, gold. But their expenses are denominated in South African rands. This situation is called a cross-currency exposure. Income is in one currency, expenses are in another. A cross-currency exposure can work in favor of or against a mining company.

In the early 1980s it worked in favor of mining companies. The dollar was strong and other currencies, including the rand, were weak. Gold was also weak but not so weak as the rand. The strong dollar made up for much of the revenue lost owing to the fall in gold. When income and expenses were stated in rands, mining profits and therefore mining dividends held up very well. It was the weak rand that accounted for the phenomenon and not a general increase in the mining business.

The weak rand also had negative effects. It caused inflation in South Africa. Mine wages were not able to keep up with inflation. Real, after-inflation wages fell, and recession took hold. Violence erupted, and South Africa was again in world headlines.

The weak rand, while protecting mining profits for a while, led to severe problems later. At the 1983 high, an ounce of gold sold for $508, and the dollar-rand exchange rate was 1.2285. For each ounce of gold, South Africa received 624.07 rands (1.2285 × 508) to meet payroll and other expenses. In December 1984, an ounce of gold sold for $325, down 36 percent. The dollar-rand exchange rate was 1.852. South Africa received 601.90 rands (1.852 × 325) for every ounce of gold. Proceeds in terms of rands fell only 6 percent, a fraction of the decline in gold.

With income based on dollars and expenses on rands, South African mining companies benefit from a strong dollar. During the period 1980–1984 South African mining shares outperformed gold, and the cross-currency exposure was the reason.

In a different financial climate the results can be reversed. For example, when the dollar is weak, coming down from a peak, and gold is relatively stable, the cross-currency exposure works the other way. Income falls while expenses do not.

There are mining companies in Canada, Australia, and other countries. Remember, when considering investing in any mining company outside the United States, that you must take into account the cross-currency exposure. When analyzing a mining company, look first at the cross-currency exposure, second at the business fundamentals, and third at the gold price. That is the right order of priority. Mining shares can be a source of substantial profits. But don't take shortcuts. Keep your priorities in order.

Investing in mining shares is more complicated than investing in gold or silver. Don't be seduced by dividends. Before buying or selling mining shares, go through the exercise of evaluating the mining business. Look at local politics, local inflation, and the outlook for the local currency before making a decision. And as with any investment, if you can't buy low, don't buy at all.

Chapter 3

A World of Opportunity: How to Profit from an International Stock Market Strategy

RISKS AND OPPORTUNITIES in investments have changed significantly since the beginning of the 1970s. The world's markets will never be the same again. Nevertheless, many investors go on applying old techniques and then wonder why their results are disappointing.

Money flows freely from one market to another. Satellites and computers provide instant, worldwide quotations. The days when investors could focus on familiar home markets and feel secure are gone. No investor can afford anything less than an international perspective.

There is only one reason for bothering to follow stock markets around the world, and that is performance. When it comes to stock market profits, we do what must be done to keep one step ahead of the crowd. As of the mid-1970s that includes following at least the major world stock markets. If you don't know anything about markets in Europe and Japan, you are at a disadvantage. Investors who make judgments about U.S. stocks without first comparing them to other markets will make costly and unnecessary mistakes.

Sometimes the motive for watching stocks on foreign markets is direct profit. We hope to earn an above-average profit by a direct investment in a foreign stock. Other times the reason for watching foreign stocks is to improve the odds on profits at home in the U.S. stock market. No matter what your motive, even if you never intend buying a foreign stock, knowing about foreign stock markets is essential in this new era of wild, unregulated markets.

Foreign investors know all about the U.S. markets. They buy and sell U.S. stocks easily and comfortably. They are your new competition in the battle for financial survival. If you hide your head in the sand, pretending that the U.S. stock market is the only stock market, then you will be giving the competition the game. They will end up with the profits, and you will end up with only what dumb luck allows.

Following foreign stock markets does require some additional work. But it is not difficult. There are techniques that you can master that will bring the world of international investing within your daily grasp. Following stocks in Germany or Japan is really no different from following stocks in the United States. The basic rules are the same. The economic fundamentals that move stocks in Europe are the same as those that move markets in the United States.

The secret to successful investing is a combination of selectivity and discipline. That is true whether you are investing in U.S. stocks or following world stock markets. No one can do it all. Following all markets and all stocks is just too much for any individual, even with the aid of a computer. By limiting yourself to the five major world markets and a small group of representative stocks, you can become familiar with world stock market trends and patterns without having to strain your natural human resources. You can do it. You can become your own expert on world stock trends.

The Basics: What Every Investor Needs to Know

There are three things that every investor needs to know:

1. The basic condition of modern markets
2. How things are different from the past
3. The right questions to ask your broker or investment adviser

The Basic Condition of Modern Markets

Thanks to OPEC and the rising oil prices of the 1970s, there has been a worldwide rush towards deregulation of financial markets. Americans think of deregulation as a U.S. phenomenon. We deregulated our banking and airline industries. That pattern has not been confined to the United States. Governments in Europe and Asia have also rushed to deregulate. It is the international dash to deregulate financial markets that is of most concern to investors.

When capital flowed out of the industrialized nations to pay for high-priced OPEC oil, a crisis developed. The capital outflow was so massive that it threatened governments and financial markets. The industrialized countries wanted the money back, and they decided to get it back in the form of OPEC investments and bank accounts.

In the beginning the process was called recycling. As it developed it became a rush to deregulate in an effort to make financial markets as attractive as possible for the investment of the OPEC billions. By the early 1980s the rush to deregulate had gone far enough to make most financial markets free and open to both inflows and outflows of capital.

Modern financial markets have become wild and largely unregulated. Oil prices began to decline in the early 1980s, stripping away the OPEC surplusses. The original motive for opening up financial markets diminished. Nevertheless, deregulation marched on, freeing pension-fund managers to look around the world for opportunity.

Pension-fund managers in London can now move millions by a telephone call. They can buy or sell stocks in the United States or any other market. Japanese corporations, flush with cash, can buy and sell like their British counterparts.

Foreign investors look at the United States from an international perspective. They automatically compare the country with their home market and usually go further and compare all major world markets before deciding which stocks to buy or sell. If a U.S. company's stock looks cheaper than a stock in a competing German company, they will buy the U.S. stock. When a U.S. stock looks high by comparison, it is vulnerable to sale.

Just as American-made cars must compete in a world car market, so must U.S. stocks compete in a global capital market. As an investor you are in a position similar to that of a U.S. car dealer. You can't afford to ignore the competition. If you do, you are likely to come up with substantial losses.

How Things Are Different from the Past

The principal legacy of the great stock market crash that began in 1929 was a resolve to do something to prevent it ever happening again. The United States government was a leader in creating rules, regulations, and whole agencies to monitor activity in the financial markets. At one point, when the trend towards regulation was at its peak, the United States enacted the "interest equalization tax." That was a tax paid by any U.S. investor who invested in a foreign market. The intent of the tax was to keep American money at home. And it worked. Perhaps too well. Thanks to the interest equalization tax, Americans had a good excuse for not bothering to learn about investing in foreign markets.

Other countries also had rules, regulations, and taxes that acted as barriers to the free flow of capital. This type of regulation is usually known as "exchange controls." The first difference between markets in the 1980s and markets in earlier decades is that many exchange-control barriers have been eliminated.

For decades after World War II, the United States was the world's dominant economy. There was no reason to venture far from home. Attractive U.S. investments, especially in stocks, were plentiful. Investors made millions investing exclusively in U.S. stocks. As other world economies grew and prospered, the situation began to change. At first there was no threat to the dominance of the U.S. markets. While there were attractive investments in foreign lands, there was no necessity to leave U.S. shores. As the idea of international investment opportunity blossomed, professional U.S. money managers advanced the notion that you could participate in worldwide opportunity by investing in U.S. companies doing business in foreign countries. The idea was that the U.S. company would do the foreign investing on behalf of shareholders. The conclusion, at the time, was that investing directly in foreign stocks was ill-advised. This conclusion proved to be too self-serving. Like the interest equalization tax, it was an excuse for not bothering to look around the world for opportunity. The idea was valid only so long as an overvalued dollar made it cheap for U.S. corporations to buy assets in foreign markets. As long as a U.S. business could use overvalued dollars to buy land and build a plant overseas, U.S. business was assured of its dominance.

In the 1970s the dollar began a long decline. The situation reversed, and finally it became cheap for foreign businesses to acquire U.S. assets. The world of international competition changed. The United States lost its dominance and a new era began.

A second difference today is that the basic business environment has changed. U.S. businesses are no longer insulated from foreign competition. When you buy stock in a U.S. company, you are now buying into fierce global competition. The company and therefore the stock must be evaluated in light of foreign as well as domestic competition.

The third difference deals with one of the most cherished national U.S. ideas. The United States has long been called the land of opportunity. The implication is that there is no other land of opportunity that can match the United States. No doubt that was true after World War II and probably in earlier days of the nation's history as well. As much as many people wish it were still true, the fact is that today there are other lands of equal opportunity. That is especially true when it comes to stock markets.

Between 1970 and the end of 1984 the Mexican stock market advanced 1,102 percent, Hong Kong stocks rose 762 percent, and Japanese stocks 501 percent. The U.S. stock market rose during the same period but by a far more modest 154 percent. (These figures are based on Capital International's stock market indices.) In the 1970s the best stock market opportunity was outside the United States.

In 1985 that pattern was repeated; there was more opportunity in foreign markets than in the United States. (See the chart on the next page.) German stocks, for example, rose 131.5 percent in terms of U.S. dollars in 1985. An investment of $10,000 in German stocks at the beginning of the year grew to a startling $23,150 by year end. An investor who stayed at home in the U.S. market enjoyed a far smaller 27 percent, or $2,700 gain. This 1985 comparison is all the more revealing when you know that the German stock market is known as a stodgy market composed largely of big international companies. There was more opportunity in lumbering German stocks in 1985 than in presumably more vital and exciting U.S. issues.

In 1985, in fact, a U.S. investor was better off in any of the other major stock markets than at home. That year the U.S. stock market lagged behind. The land of opportunity was a disappointment. The most significant difference between decades past and today is that there is now a world of opportunity.

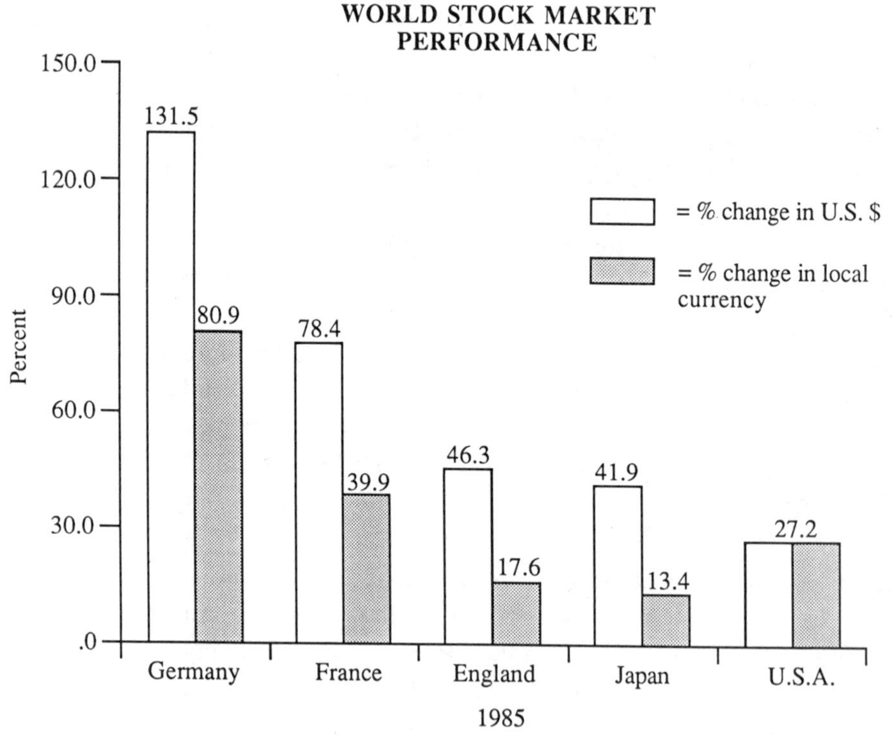

Source: Morgan Stanley Capital International Perspective, Geneva, Switzerland.

The year 1985 proved beyond any doubt the value of watching foreign markets. By year end the U.S. Dow Jones Industrial Average had soared to more than 1,500, almost double the low of 1982, the year the bull market began. In December Henry Kaufman, the widely followed economist from Salomon Brothers, came out with another of his gloomy forecasts that U.S. interest rates would rise. Joe Granville published a book explaining in great detail why the U.S. stock market was vulnerable and ready for a collapse that would rival the Great Crash of 1929. Many investors were confused. Opinions were split. Some believed the Granville analysis and thought that Kaufman's higher interest rates would be the tug that pulled the rug out from under an overvalued U.S. stock market.

Investors with an international perspective not only were not confused, they saw the U.S. stock market in an entirely different light. They had seen the spectacular rise in German stock prices. They knew that U.S. stocks had been lagging behind a powerful worldwide bull market. U.S. stocks selling on average at 1.6 times book value were hardly overvalued compared to German stocks at nearly 3 times book value and Japanese stocks at 2.8 times book value. Investors with an international perspective were not surprised when the U.S. stock market roared into 1986, climbing 100 points on the Dow to 1,600 in just over a month.

The year 1985 demonstrated in a spectacular way that watching world stock trends really does open up a world of opportunity. Better yet, watching world trends gives a new level of understanding and confidence that allows bigger commitments. It is one thing to double a small investment. It is another to have the confidence to take meaningful positions and intelligent risks and change your entire standard of living for the better.

The modern world is different in significant ways that demand a new approach to investing. The business world is international and fiercely competitive. Consumers in the United States can choose from products made in Germany, Japan, Hong Kong, Korea, and a host of other countries. Investors from Britain or Japan can drive U.S. stock prices up when they buy and crush them unexpectedly when they sell.

The financial world has changed. Either you change with it or you proceed at your peril.

The Right Questions to Ask

The very least you should do is learn the right questions to ask. When a banker or broker approaches with an investment idea, you should be able to poke into the right issues in order to assess correctly the underlying risk and opportunity.

For example, suppose you are interested in buying shares in a U.S. company. The first challenge is to find out about the company's competition, including foreign competition. The last thing you want to do is buy in just before the company's sales are battered by cheap products from a foreign company. Be sure to ask, Who are the competitors? And, Is the company gaining or losing its share of market to foreign products? If you don't get satisfactory answers, don't buy the stock. There are always lots of investment opportunities. There is never a shortage of ideas. The challenge is to keep your losers to a minimum. It is better to miss an opportunity than to buy when you don't have enough facts.

The second line of interrogation relates to the stock itself. Not only do you want to know about competing products, you want to know about the competitor's stock price. You may discover that the shares of a competitor are cheaper and therefore more attractive. Ask if the competition's stock is publicly traded and on which market. If the competition is a foreign company, ask if the shares are traded in the United States. Find out what the dividend yield is on the competition's shares. Look into the usual tests of a stock's value—price-earnings ratio, ratio of stock price to book value, and the ratio of the stock price to cash flow per share.

Don't be put off if your broker or adviser belittles the question. That often means that he or she has been caught unprepared and can't answer your questions. The answers do exist and you need to know before investing. Insist on getting complete answers. If your broker or adviser can't supply the information, try the library or another investment advisory service. You don't have to fire your broker. The whole idea of an international perspective is relatively new in the United States. That means that many brokers and advisers don't have the information you need at their fingertips. In time they will. Meanwhile, the fact that a minority of investors know the right questions to ask gives you a distinct advantage.

When it comes to stocks, be sure to ask about the market. An individual stock may be attractive on its own merits and still fall if the entire market comes under pressure. You need to know if the market itself is high or low compared to other markets.

Here is an example of what can happen when you look around the world and comparison shop before investing. Between 1979 and 1984 Eastman Kodak stock rose a respectable 15 percent, from $65 a share to $75. Many analysts and investors were encouraged by Kodak's rising stock price. At the same time, however, one of Kodak's principal competitors, Fuji Photo Film stock, rose from 650 yen to 1,700 yen for a gain in yen of 161 percent. The dollar recovered during the period, but even after taking currency losses into account the gain on Fuji shares was 111 percent. An American investor interested in the photography industry would have been far better off buying Fuji shares than Kodak. The tip-off was that Fuji's share of the U.S. film market was rising while Fuji was holding its market share in Japan. The question about market share was the one that would have pointed in the direction of Fuji. Remember that both Kodak and Fuji were well-financed, sound companies at the time. There was nothing wrong with Kodak. Nevertheless, there was a far greater stock market opportunity in Fuji.

Don't be shy when it comes to investments. Be tough and demanding. Insist on an international point of view before buying anything.

A Simple, International Wealth-Building Strategy

Not everyone needs to jump into a full-blown international investment strategy. You may have assets tied up in a business or real estate and not have enough liquid funds available to justify buying individually selected foreign stocks. No matter, that is no excuse. With as little as $1,000 you can and should become an international investor. Decades ago they didn't exist in the United States. Even five years ago there weren't many. Today there is a growing selection of U.S.-based mutual funds that invest exclusively in foreign stocks, bonds, and currencies. Some are no-load mutual funds that you must find and contact yourself. Others are load funds that charge a sales fee. Those are available through your broker or investment adviser. The choice of a fund is not the critical part of this strategy. Any fund that invests in markets around the world but not in the United States qualifies for use in this basic international strategy. Balanced funds that invest both in the United States and in foreign markets are sound investment choices but are not suitable for this approach to increasing wealth. Likewise, funds that concentrate on stocks in a single country, such as Korea or Japan, are not for use with this basic international strategy.

In the early 1970s President Richard Nixon severed the connection between the dollar and gold, as previously noted. That released the dollar so that it could fluctuate on world currency markets. Initially the dollar was very high, overvalued. During the 1970s that was corrected by the markets. At the end, in late 1979, the markets overshot on the down side and the dollar became undervalued. In the early 1980s the dollar rose again. By early 1985 the U.S. currency was back to a high, overvalued level. From that lofty perch the dollar once again began to decline. The dollar's wild fluctuations present an opportunity for you to profit.

When the dollar is high, that means that you can buy foreign assets such as stocks and bonds cheaply. When the dollar falls, those assets will appreciate in terms of U.S. dollars and you will profit. The basic idea is to use overvalued dollars to buy cheap foreign stocks and then sell after the dollar has corrected or overshot on the down side. By doing this you will add a new dimension to your financial plans. You will, like the mighty international traders, be able to enjoy profits from the dollar's wild swings.

Don't be skeptical. It really can be done, by anyone willing to read between the headlines. You can tell when the dollar is overvalued or undervalued without having to know anything about the currency markets. Basic common sense is all that is required. Financial analysts and currency traders dig deeply into the details of the currency markets and the underlying economic fundamentals. That is their business. They are trying to make decisions that will show profits week to week and month to month. They have boards of directors and corporate treasurers to impress. You can judge the state of the dollar not by looking into the dull statistics of the currency markets but by watching people and what they do with their money.

One of the easiest ways to judge the value of the dollar is through the "tourist test." In 1984, a flood of U.S. tourists visited Europe. Stories about shopping at Harrod's in London made the evening news on television. There was an abundance of ads for inexpensive vacations in Europe. Americans were told plainly by the travel and tourist industry that Europe in particular hadn't been so reasonable in over a decade. When there is a flood of American tourists visiting Europe and Asia, you know that the dollar is at least close to being overvalued. The basic characteristic of an overvalued currency is that it makes meals, hotels, services, investments, and real estate in another country look like a bargain. When a good dinner for two costs $125 in New York and $30 in London, you know that something is wrong, and that something is the currency. When everything outside the United States, from hotel rooms in Zurich to cab fares in Hong Kong, looks cheap, you can be sure that the dollar is overvalued.

This tourist test is not a cute gimmick. It is sound, basic financial analysis. The best way to judge the state of any market is to watch transactions, not listen to opinions. It is what people do with their money that counts. They often say one thing and do another. Watch people and transactions and you will always be a step ahead of those who rely on opinion. When millions of Americans flood Europe and Japan, you know that the dollar is high. And that is all you need to know.

Investing is as simple as "buy low and sell high." But when it comes to a currency, people become confused. How do you "sell" the dollar when it is high? We live in a dollar-based economy. You can use dollars to buy cars or television sets. But for the ordinary, individual U.S. investor, selling dollars to make a profit was a challenge until the introduction of U.S.-based international mutual funds. When you sell one currency, you buy another. Overvalued dollars can be "sold" by investing them in foreign assets. What do you do with an overvalued dollar? You use it to buy cheap foreign stocks.

Investing in an international mutual fund makes life easy. You only have to decide when to buy and when to sell the fund's shares. The professional investment managers at the fund will figure out what to do with the fund's assets. They will pick out the individual stocks, bonds, and other investments. For example, in 1984 or early 1985, when Americans were flocking to Europe and the tourist test indicated that the dollar was overvalued, all an investor had to do was pick out an international mutual fund and buy the shares. The fund took care of everything else.

The tourist test will also tell you when to sell. When the dollar falls and foreign currencies rise, there will first come a point where the flood of U.S. tourists going abroad slows and later a point when the flood works in reverse. When you find mobs of foreign tourists at your favorite vacation spots in the U.S., when you can't help but hear French, German, and Japanese on the beach, that is a signal that the dollar has fallen to an undervalued condition. That is the time to sell.

Don't think that you have to start watching the papers more closely. In fact don't change your habits at all. I'm sure that you can look back and say, "Yes I remember when the headlines were full of tourist stories."

Those were the decision points. They are so obvious that you can't help but notice. The last thing you want to do is start looking for stories that aren't there. Let your normal instincts guide you. Only buy or sell when it is really obvious that the dollar is undervalued or overvalued.

Don't expect to be making lots of decisions. Applying this strategy will leave you with plenty of free time to travel or enjoy America's beaches. This strategy calls for decisions only every few years. In fact, it took an entire decade for the dollar to go from overvalued to undervalued in the 1970s. And it took four years for the dollar to complete the swing to the opposite condition in the early 1980s.

You can be more sophisticated in the analysis of the dollar's value. You can look at trade figures, relative interest rates, relative inflation rates, and track several currencies relative to the dollar. That isn't necessary, however. The sophisticated techniques are valuable for those who are applying a more comprehensive international strategy. For example, the managers of the mutual fund will be looking at all those factors and more in their work on international markets and individual stocks. When you are applying this basic, mutual fund approach to international investing, all you need is an understanding of the concept and the tourist test. Your objective is simply to profit from the dollar's gyrations. You want to buy into an international mutual fund when the dollar is clearly overvalued. Hang on for years and sell at an embarrassingly high profit when the dollar becomes clearly undervalued.

It is possible to construct a more complicated mutual fund strategy. I'm sure that the managers of an international mutual fund can make an excellent case for holding on to the shares of the fund they manage indefinitely. Investors have a penchant for making things more complicated than necessary. Don't fall prey to that attitude. Keep your strategy simple, clear, and effective. Follow the tourist test and let your fortune grow.

The results can be spectacular. For example, in 1985 the T. Rowe Price International Fund grew by 45.3 percent. The Scudder International Fund grew by 46.4 percent. If you had invested $10,000 in the T. Rowe Price International Fund in late 1984, when the tourist test was screaming that the dollar was grossly overvalued, you would have enjoyed a profit of $4,530 by the end of 1985, and that does not count dividends. If you had picked the Scudder Fund instead, your profit would have been $4,640.

You don't have to worry about being right on the money in applying the tourist test. In fact, you could have been way off the mark in the early 1980s and done well. Here is the record of the T. Rowe Price International Fund from its inception in 1980 through the end of 1985:

1980 (6 months)	+11.87%
1981	−01.8
1982	+06.27
1983	+28.62
1984	−05.9
1985	+45.3

An investment of $10,000 in 1980 grew to $20,530 by the end of 1985, and that does not include dividends. Following a dividend reinvestment program would have produced an even greater gain.

Here are the names and addresses of three international funds to get you started:

T. Rowe Price International Fund
100 East Pratt Street
Baltimore, MD 21202
Tel: 1-800-638-1527

Scudder International Fund, Inc.
175 Federal Street
Boston, MA 02110
Tel: 1-800-225-2470

Templeton Foreign Fund
c/o Securities Fund Investors, Inc. Underwriters
405 Central Ave.
P.O. Box 3942
St. Petersburg, FL 33731
Tel: 1-800-237-0738

This is far from a complete listing of all the available international funds. Their number was growing rapidly by 1985. This is just a start. The first two are called no-load funds. That means there is no sales charge when you buy or redemption charge when you sell. The Templeton Fund is sold through brokers and does involve a sales charge.

The type of fund you choose should be determined by your personal preferences and life-style. Some people like to be independent, do their own digging, and take care of all the details themselves. A no-load fund is right for that person. If, however, you customarily do business with a broker and enjoy the benefits of that relationship, then you might prefer a load fund such as the Templeton Fund. The choice is yours. Relax. This is not a stressful decision. You can't make a mistake. The differences in performance over the time you will own the shares in the fund will not be significant no matter which fund you choose.

An International Strategy for Outstanding Profits

The simple tourist test, mutual fund strategy is surprisingly sophisticated. It can be used even by investors with large sums. For example, you could invest $1 million to $2 million in the T. Rowe Price International Fund and still not represent too large a piece of the total fund.

Just as with anything else in this life, however, there are limitations and greater opportunities. With the mutual fund approach you are limited to the performance of the fund you choose. Mutual funds are fairly large pools of money that are reasonably well diversified. A fund's performance is, by definition, a composite of all the investments in the fund. Some of the fund's investments will do much better than others. There is no doubt that an individual investor, willing to take on the extra responsibility, can earn greater profits through individual selection.

For example, an investor who decided to concentrate on German stocks in 1985 enjoyed a capital gain of 131.5 percent in dollars compared to 45 percent for the international mutual funds. A $10,000 investment in German stocks at the beginning of 1985 was worth $23,150 at year end. That is substantially greater than the $14,500 for a similar investment in an international mutual fund.

There is a world of opportunity, and it comes in varying degrees of risk and reward. You can choose the level at which you wish to participate. There is nothing wrong with the 45 percent gain on the international mutual funds in 1985. Likewise, there is nothing wrong with going to the next level of sophistication in pursuit of even greater gains.

The next level, picking individual markets and individual stocks, intimidates many U.S. investors. They think about strange languages, companies they have never heard of, and currency fluctuations. They assume that the risks are great and give up on the idea of foreign investing after a cursory examination of the challenge. Don't be intimidated by the prospect of choosing markets and individual stocks around the world. The task, through the application of common sense, can be reduced to something manageable by the average U.S. investor. You don't have to open a foreign bank account. You don't have to study international economics. You don't have to learn foreign languages, and you don't have to spend a fortune on sophisticated publications.

Armed with your present sources of information, and by understanding a few new rules, you can move money from country to country without leaving the United States and without changing brokers.

Levels of Involvement

The age of computer games has made the idea of levels understandable. When you first begin playing a new game, you start at the first level of difficulty. As you become more skilled, you move up to new levels of challenge. The same concept can be applied to investing. Of course, there is one difference. You can choose not to play a computer game, but there is no escape from the rigors of financial management. You need money to survive. You are involved in the financial markets every day of your life, like it or not. You can trust to luck, let things go their own way, and hope for the best. Or you can become an active participant and take command of your own future. But you cannot avoid the consequences of the twists and turns of the markets as they push your income and net worth first up and then down. The best course always has been to become a willing participant.

There are eighteen significant world stock markets, including the United States. It is possible to watch all eighteen, become expert at their individual peculiarities, and move money confidently from one to the other. It is also possible to pare down the universe, concentrate on a few markets, and still substantially increase your performance over the simpler tourist test strategy. You don't have to jump, all at once, into a full-blown program of international investing. You can choose your level of participation.

The Five Major Stock Markets and Representative Selections

Out of the eighteen markets five can be described as "major." The major stock markets are in the United States, Japan, Germany, Britain, and France. The first step at this second level of participation is to concentrate on those markets exclusively. That means ignoring markets in places such as Austria, Italy, and Mexico no matter how attractive they may, at times, seem. You can master the five major markets in a reasonable time. If you don't exclude the others, you risk becoming confused, diluting your efforts, feeling frustrated, and being tempted to give up on the whole idea. Following the crowd to whatever market seems exciting at the moment is a route to poor performance. Be selective. Concentrate on the five major markets and leave the others until later.

The next step is to identify "representative investments." There are thousands of stocks listed on all five major markets. It is not practical to follow too large a universe. You must be selective not only in choosing markets but in choosing individual stocks. The idea behind choosing representative stocks is that a rising market tends to push all stocks in that market to higher prices. The thrust of this strategy is to concentrate on markets, not individual stocks. When you decide that a market is attractive, you want stocks that will follow, not beat, that particular market. The idea is to improve your profits by being in the right market at the right time. All that is asked of the individual stocks is that they do as well as the market.

A very successful professional money manager in Switzerland once commented that investing in stocks is easy. He argued that you only needed to pick a bank, an insurance company, a major manufacturing company, and a major retail firm each market. Then, he went on, "The trick is to be in the right market at the right time."

In recent years countries such as France have nationalized the banks, so his prescription needs some modification. But he was and is essentially correct. Simply pick a few representative stocks and you will enjoy profits equal to the market of your choice.

Here are representative stocks for each of the five major markets:

United States:	IBM
	General Motors
	Citicorp
	Sears Roebuck
Japan:	Bank of Tokyo
	Honda Motor
	Fuji Photo Film
	Tokyo Marine and Fire Insurance
Germany:	Dresdner Bank
	Siemens
	Hoechst
	Mannesmann
France:	Moët-Hennesy
	L'Oréal
	Source Perrier
	Club Mediterranée
Britain	Reed International
	Marks and Spencer
	Chadbury Schweppes
	Plessy

This list does not fit the specifications of choosing a bank, an insurance company, a major manufacturer, and a major retailer; it is more of a mixed bag. Nevertheless, these are stocks that can be expected to follow their respective markets both up and down. This list has one overriding attraction. In every instance there are American Depository Receipts (ADRs) traded in the United States. You can buy or sell these stocks through your present U.S. broker without undue complication. When you buy and sell, the transactions will be settled in dollars. You don't have to worry about collecting dividends in a foreign currency or switching from currency to currency. And the ADR traded in the United States is the equivalent of the foreign shares. Owning an ADR is just like owning the shares through a foreign brokerage account but much simpler. You have all the advantages of holding foreign stock without the hassle of managing a foreign brokerage account. This may sound too good to be true. It isn't. The answer lies in understanding what an ADR is all about.

The Importance of ADRs

There are technical differences between markets in Europe, Asia, and the United States. For example, on the one hand, Americans feel more comfortable having a stock certificate registered in their name. They can take delivery of the certificate, put it in a safe deposit box, and not worry too much about loss or theft. Europeans, on the other hand, prefer bearer stock certificates. They don't want anyone to be able to trace the stock to them. They worry about unfriendly governments and tax collectors tracking them down through registered stock certificates. Over the years the markets have learned to adjust for these differences. The ADR is one example of how the peculiarities of one market can be accommodated for investors in other lands.

Understanding ADRs

An ADR is a receipt issued by an American bank certifying that the bank holds an equivalent number of foreign shares. ADRs have been available for most of this century. The concept originated in Europe. European investors wanted to buy U.S. stocks but did not like the idea of having the stocks registered in their names. Dutch trust companies came to the rescue with an ingenious technique. In the 1920s they bought the U.S. stocks, had them registered in the trust company's name, and then sold certificates in bearer form. The certificates were freely traded in Europe. Through the bearer certificates of the trust company Europeans were able to own U.S. stocks without exposing themselves to the long arm of an unfriendly government or tax collector.

The concept crossed the Atlantic and was transformed in the process. Americans like the security of registration. They feel more comfortable with their own familiar system. European and other foreign stocks in bearer form did not appeal to U.S. investors. Banks came to the rescue for American investors just as the Dutch trust companies had for European investors. American banks bought European bearer stocks and tucked them safely away in bank vaults. The U.S. banks then issued receipts indicating that the bank held the underlying foreign shares on deposit. The idea met with investor approval and the U.S. ADR market was born.

The system is secure. The banks are audited regularly and must always have the requisite number of foreign shares to support the ADRs. Only a few U.S. banks are involved. They are Morgan Guaranty Trust Company, Citicorp, and Bank of New York. All three are giant U.S. banking organizations of great reputation. The banks are simply custodians. They earn a small fee for holding the foreign shares and issuing the ADRs. The banks are not involved in the market-making process for ADRs. That is done by U.S. brokers.

The market price of an ADR is the price of the underlying foreign stock plus the exchange rate. There is no practical difference for an American investor between owning the foreign shares directly or owning ADRs.

The relationship between the foreign stock and the ADR is not always one to one. Sometimes, there will be two or more ADR's for each foreign share or the other way around, with one ADR equaling more than one foreign share. That is done to bring the price for each ADR more in line with the U.S. markets. Some foreign stocks trade at very low prices. Others trade at very high prices. Each market around the world tends to have a price per share that investors accept. The ADRs not only adjust for registration preferences, they adjust the price to local conditions.

The Safety of ADRs

Safety is a prime concern of investors in these days of failing banks and brokerage firms. A logical question is, How safe is it to hold a receipt from a bank? The answer is, Very safe. The alternative would be to buy the European shares directly and take delivery. The problem is that you would be dealing in bearer certificates. Those certificates are like cash, which is also bearer in form. Whoever holds the certificates can collect the dividends and has the right to the proceeds of sale. Just imagine the practical problems you would encounter trying to take delivery of European stocks in bearer form. These problems mean that, as a practical matter, you would open a bank account in the foreign country and have the bank hold your certificates in your account. The bank would send you statements showing your securities' positions. You would then be relying on the foreign bank to be honest and trustworthy. You just can't escape the clutches of the banks when it comes to foreign stocks any more than you can escape their clutches when it comes to handling cash. The advantage with an ADR is that it is under the protection of U.S. laws, rules, and regulations. That doesn't mean that the FDIC will guarantee the value of your stock holdings, but it does mean that the federal and state authorities in this country are watching the bank to make sure that there is a foreign share for every ADR. In the event of a loss you would be able to make a claim against the U.S. bank and its insurance or bonding company. An ADR is safe and secure, safer and more secure than leaving foreign shares on deposit with a foreign bank.

Another question is, Can you take an ADR to the foreign country and sell it there? The answer is generally no. The ADR says that the bank is holding the foreign shares. That certification theoretically should be acceptable to a European bank or broker. But as a practical matter, Europeans don't want registered ADRs; they want the underlying bearer shares. The task of switching ADRs and the underlying foreign shares is best left to the professionals—the banks, and the market makers. ADRs are meant for the U.S. market. They are bought and sold between U.S. investors. The bank custodians and the market makers adjust the ADR market to meet demand in the United States. When U.S. investors lose interest, the market makers end up with large holdings of ADRs, which they are able to arbitrage on the foreign market, and the ADR market shrinks. When U.S. demand grows, the opposite happens and the number of available ADRs increases.

Over the last couple of decades the largest ADR market has been in South African mining stocks. American investors have become so accustomed to buying South African mining ADRs that they often don't remember the connection. South African mining ADRs are bought and sold as if they were the underlying foreign shares. Frequently, investors buying South African mining stocks for the first time are puzzled when they receive a different-looking stock certificate. Millions of South African mining shares have been bought and sold in the United States for years in the form of ADRs. Thanks to the active trading in South African mining shares, the ADR process has been proven in the thick of action. The fact that so many U.S. investors don't know that they are buying and selling ADRs is proof positive of the soundness and efficiency of the ADR system. Between 1970 and 1985 the U.S. appetite for South African mining shares both grew and diminished. At times U.S. investors increased their holdings of such shares. At other times interest waned and U.S. holdings of South African gold stocks declined. The U.S. ADR system was able to accommodate both phases of the market without strain. The experience with South African mining shares is solid evidence that Americans can buy and sell foreign securities in the form of ADRs with confidence and security.

The same ADR system that has so well supported American interest in gold mining shares also supports all other ADRs. If you have ever owned a South African mining stock or thought about doing so, you can move on to other ADRs in other markets with confidence and understanding.

There are limits to ADRs. Not all foreign stocks are traded in the U.S. in the form of ADRs. By confining your universe to ADRs you impose restrictions on your ability to pick and choose stocks in foreign markets. The ADR market has grown large enough, however, to support the strategy of buying representative stocks in the five major world stock markets. Sticking with ADRs may not satisfy a professional pension-fund manager with tens of millions to invest overseas. But ADRs are more than adequate for the effective and profitable implementation of this market-oriented strategy.

Country Funds

Investing in foreign markets became increasingly popular in 1986. More and more U.S. pension and retirement funds wanted the benefits of international diversification. Individual investors were lured to foreign stocks by their outstanding performance in 1984 and 1985. Money managers and brokers teamed up to introduce a host of new closed-end funds listed on U.S. exchanges. Typically each fund would specialize in the securities of a particular country.

The Scandinavia Fund, for example, trades only in the securities of the Scandinavian countries. By mid-1986 there were funds for Australian, Korean, Scandinavian, Japanese, Mexican, French, and German securities either launched or well along in the planning stage.

The concept is sound. A closed-end fund is different from the ordinary mutual fund. An ordinary, or open-ended mutual fund continually sells and redeems shares. A mutual fund can grow from $100 million to several billion dollars, as did the Magellan Fund, when investors flock to participate in the fund's concept. Many foreign markets are relatively small. If American investors decide that a particular market is a good investment and billions of dollars suddenly descend on that market, the market could quickly become saturated and stock prices, being chased by too much money, could soar beyond rational limits. Foreign markets could be swamped by an open-ended U.S. mutual fund that specialized in one single market. The closed-end funds sell a specific number of shares and then those shares are traded from one investor to another. These funds will initially bring $50 or $60 million to any given market but will not be continually flooding that market with new cash.

If the trend toward closed-end country funds continues, it won't be long before American investors have another avenue for investment overseas. You will be able to "buy" an attractive foreign market by investing in a closed-end country fund whose shares are traded in the United States.

The technique for picking the right fund at the right time is exactly the same as buying ADRs. First, you must carefully select the markets that are attractive using the same methods. There is one additional layer of complication. At times a particular country's stock market can be very popular among U.S. investors. The shares of a closed-end fund can be bid up to a premium. The shares may sell for a price that is greater than their underlying net asset value. Never pay a premium for a closed-end country fund. When a fund is selling at a premium the wiser course will be to go direct and buy ADRs in representative stocks in that market. More often than not, however, the most attractive markets will be those that are out of favor. In that case closed-end country fund shares may sell at a discount to their net asset value. In that event the closed-end fund shares will be more attractive than the underlying shares themselves. An investor would be better off buying shares in the closed-end fund than buying ADRs in representative securities.

There is no doubt that shares in closed-end country funds should be added to your list of possible investment choices. When you find a fund in an attractive market consider buying those shares. If the fund happens to sell at a discount to net asset value at the time, then choose the fund over ADRs in representative shares. If, on the other hand, the fund shares sell at a premium to their net asset value then you should stop and reconsider your strategy. The fact that the fund's shares are popular enough to demand a premium may be a warning that the underlying market itself is so popular that prices are too high and the risk too great.

The basic investment rule is to buy into low-priced, out-of-favor markets with promise. Following trends, buying into popular markets can produce gains but also will carry greater risk when you are wrong.

Choosing the Right Market at the Right Time

The moment you say choose a market, visions of past U.S. stock market disasters come to mind. Throwing in four more markets may seem like adding to the problem. However, just as the tourist test is a practical, easily applied solution to a complex challenge, the goal of choosing the right stock market can be reduced to manageable proportions.

There never has been any mystery about what makes a

stock market rise or fall. When an economy is flush with money, the price of stocks and many other items rises. In an economy starved for cash, stocks will suffer. The common denominator when it comes to choosing the right stock market is the money supply. In modern economies the issue is the rate at which the particular country's money supply is expanding. When the rate of money growth increases, there is more liquidity in the economy and interest rates decline. Investors have more money to invest and are reluctant to hold bank accounts and other short-term investments in a falling-interest-rate environment. Stocks rise because, under those circumstances, they are more attractive than other forms of investment. Choosing the right stock market means looking for countries whose money supply is expanding. While that is not difficult, since money-supply statistics are widely published and readily available, that sort of data lies more in the realm of economics than practical, day-to-day investing. Don't despair. You don't have to subscribe to dull reports on world economics and money growth. In fact, they would not be of that much help. The task of an investor is not to buy into a market *after* the money supply has begun to expand. It is to buy into the market *before* the money supply increases. You have to be one step ahead of the crowd to make money in stocks.

It is well known that lower interest rates and an expanding money supply are bullish for stock prices. Once it is clear that the money supply is growing, stock prices will already be well up from their lows. You can't wait for the money-supply data to be published; you have to construct a set of characteristics that will anticipate an expanding money supply and higher stock prices. Believe it or not, that is actually easier than studying esoteric money-supply figures.

Look for a market where the conditions are right for the money supply to begin expanding and you will have found opportunity. The easiest way to understand the signs of opportunity is by first looking at the opposite, the conditions that call for a tightening of the money supply. When a currency is weak or when inflation is rising too fast, the government is forced to take steps to protect the value of the country's currency. That is one of the first responsibilities of any government, to defend the value of the currency. It ranks right up with protecting the citizens from crime at home and invasions from abroad. Defending the currency has been a top priority since the first society. Governments don't always succeed. Sometimes they fail and the currency collapses. That doesn't matter. As investors we expect to be out of a market long before there is a collapse of the currency.

Three Characteristics of the Right Market

What we look for are the early signs of change. A falling currency on world exchange markets or rising domestic inflation rates are the warning signs that growth in the money supply will be slowed. Those are the danger signs. The positive indicators are the opposite. Attractive markets are found in nations with the other problem, the three characteristics of low inflation, high unemployment, and a strong currency. The most significant of these is high unemployment. Governments abhor unemployment because it means disgruntled voters and rising expenses. If they have the latitude to act, governments will always try to increase employment. One of the principal tools they use is the money supply. By allowing the money supply to expand at a faster rate, they make more cash available for investment in new plants and new jobs.

Look for news reports of high unemployment. Then look further, at the country's inflation rate. When you see a low inflation rate and a high unemployment rate, your task is nearly finished. That is a perfect combination. Then you only have to check the currency. If you find that it is firm or strong, don't hesitate, take the plunge. If the currency is weak, you probably should wait before buying. A weak currency often means a temporary bout of high interest rates to stop the currency's slide. The high-interest-rate medicine, when applied, might drive stock prices down, creating a later buying opportunity.

The information you need about unemployment and inflation in the five major countries can be found in the national U.S. press. Most of the major U.S. newspapers have an international section and regularly report on economic conditions in the other four major-market countries. All you have to do is read those sections regularly with a very specific purpose, to find out about inflation and unemployment in the five major countries.

Finding all three characteristics present at the same time, while not unusual, is not common either. More often you will find one or two of the desired characteristics but not all three. For example, you might find high unemployment combined with a relatively high inflation rate or a weak currency or both. In these common situations you will have to weigh the evidence and decide if it is better to wait for a buying opportunity to develop or plunge in and take the risk of being wrong. Once you find high unemployment, you should take the time to dig further. You can be sure that the government will try to bring unemployment down. Almost no matter what tactics are used, they will eventually be positive for the stock market. A relatively high inflation rate acts as a limitation on what the government can do. It makes no sense to increase the money supply if the only result is higher prices for everything. Governments are usually faced with difficult choices, to fight inflation or fight high unemployment. The government might decide that inflation was the first priority and tighten the money supply inspite of high unemployment. But you can be sure that whatever they do, the long-term objective will be to bring down the high unemployment rate. Knowing this, you can watch and wait, looking for an opportunity.

A low inflation rate is a somewhat different matter. Unlike high unemployment, a low inflation rate does not pressure a government into action. People generally like stable prices, and that is what a low inflation rate means—prices of goods and services are not rising very much. But a low inflation rate does give the government the latitude to expand the money supply if it wishes. When you see just a low inflation rate, the logical conclusion is that the government can increase the money supply but is not under any pressure to do so. Your task then is to ask yourself if there is any reason to expect that the money supply will grow faster. If your conclusion is yes, there are pressures to increase the money supply, then you have found an attractive market.

The third characteristic for the right market is a strong currency. Like unemployment, the currency markets can and often do pressure governments into action. A weak currency is negative for stock prices because it demands that the government tighten the money supply or raise interest rates. Conversely, a strong currency is positive because it puts pressure on the government to increase the money supply and bring interest rates down. A strong currency alone, like high unemployment, is a signal that there is potential in that market.

Analysis of the Right Market

Confining yourself to this kind of analysis, looking at only three economic factors—unemployment, inflation, and the currency—is a disciplined way of forcing yourself to ask all the right questions. The bottom line is always, Do you think that the money supply is going to expand at a faster rate or not? By sticking with this disciplined approach you will stay focused on the central investment question of risk versus potential reward.

There is another advantage in watching the five markets in this way. As you compare one to the other you will also see their common characteristics. You will be alert when unemployment is low worldwide or when inflation is creeping to higher levels. When you see this kind of uniform situation, you will know that it is time to cut back on all stock holdings and wait for the coming storm to clear. Conversely, you will also know when conditions are right for a new, worldwide bull stock market. It truly is a small world. While there are usually significant differences from one major country to the other, there are also times when all are more or less in line, for better or for worse. More significantly each of the five major markets is drawn along the collective path. A booming stock market in one country is often followed by a booming stock market in another. By following the five major markets you will have an international perspective that can only increase your investment results.

Bad News and Opportunity

Don't look at bad news as frightening. Look at it as a possible opportunity. Markets tend to plunge on bad news. Stock prices are often low after some adverse political or economic development. That is the time to buy, when prices are low. The major stock markets always recover. If you buy after bad news has driven prices down, you will have significant gains when the market recovers.

French stocks, for example, plunged in May 1981 after the victory of François Mitterrand and the Socialist party in national elections. Investors were afraid that France was on the road to Communism. That was a major buying opportunity. French stocks gained 85.5 percent in U.S. dollar terms between the postelection plunge and the end of 1984. The U.S. Standard and Poor's 400 Industrials gained 27 percent over the same period. In terms of French francs the French stock market gained 209 percent. The Mitterrand victory and above-average French inflation, however, took a toll on the French franc. It fell against the dollar, reducing the gain for American investors. Nevertheless, the gain, even in the face of a strong dollar and declining French franc, was impressive. This story of French stocks is not only an example of profits that follow from buying on bad news; it also is an example of substantial gains in U.S. dollars even though the foreign currency is weak.

During the Mitterrand period, most investors had the impression that the French economy was in serious trouble. The usual reaction to the statement that there was a substantial profit opportunity in French stocks at the time is shock and disbelief. The key to success in French stocks during the period was buying low, after the bad news of a Socialist political sweep in 1981.

If you had not only bought in 1981 but held on past the end of 1984, the gains in dollar terms became spectacular. In 1985 the dollar fell from its peak. That added a substantial currency gain to all French stock positions. In dollars, French stocks gained an additional 78.4 percent in 1985. Buying in May 1981 and holding until the end of 1985 produced a total gain of 231 percent. Stepping in, taking advantage of the bad news in France in 1981 and investing $10,000 in French stocks was a route to extraordinary capital gains. Your $10,000 in May 1981 became $33,093 by the end of 1985.

When this example of profits in French stocks is added to the story of German stocks in 1985, you have solid proof of the fact that there is a world of opportunity. You can add significantly to your personal wealth by expanding your investment horizons. Using common sense and basic strategies, you can not only add materially to your fortune but increase your level of confidence and objectivity. It is much harder to be a bitter monger of gloom and doom when you are busy looking over a world of opportunity.

The Possibilities of a Worldwide Bear Market or Another Crash

The Great Crash of 1929–1932 was devastating. At the 1932 low the Dow Jones Industrial Average stood at 41. That is one side of the story of the crash. There is another side, one that is usually overlooked. Between 1932 and 1934 the Dow Jones Industrial Average rose from 41 to 100 for a gain of 144 percent. The market paused for a while at the 100 level before continuing its climb. Before a significant correction set in, the Dow rose to 194. Investors who missed the low and bought at 100 nearly doubled their money. From the 1932 low to the next peak the Dow rose an impressive 373 percent.

The first conclusion to be drawn from the Great Crash is that it created a substantial opportunity. A future crash is to be feared only if you expect to be invested in stocks when the market plunges. That might happen if you focus only on the U.S. stock market. Your risk of being caught up in a stock-buying frenzy are increased if your perspective is too narrow. Human beings are drawn into wild, unpredictable markets by greed and the lure of being part of the action. Fighting against these powerful temptations is not easy. It can't be done by mere resolve. Ironically, the investor who "learns a lesson" and stays out of the markets is the one most likely to be brutalized in an economic disaster. Being on the sidelines is only fun while markets are stagnant or declining. Sideliners become irritated when stock markets rise. They become frustrated as the rise continues. Finally, patience gone, they become convinced that they were wrong all along. They take the plunge and buy stocks at exactly the wrong time. They end up losers again, ready to repeat the same dismal cycle.

The best way to assure that you will not be caught in the next worldwide bear market or stock market crash is to be an active participant in the markets on an international basis. It is much easier to be objective after you have enjoyed profits of 231 percent on French stocks and 131 percent on German stocks. Successful investors are not drawn into the depressing cycle of market losses because their greed impulses have already been satisfied by taking advantage of opportunities.

Plunging into French stocks when they are falling after a Socialist political sweep will do more for your sense of real risk than any sideline mental exercise. By taking real risks willingly you will learn the characteristics of trouble. You will be able to tell fact from fantasy, opportunity from pending disaster. Those who sit by and fret about the coming crash are most vulnerable to popular fantasies. They are the ones who will be seduced into the wrong move at the wrong time because reality and fantasy are blended in their minds.

A second way to defend yourself against a worldwide market crash is to sell stocks in overvalued markets. It can take years for a market to swing from being undervalued to overvalued. The process is often so slow that it is easy to become numbed into a pattern of procrastination. The French stock market swing began in the spring of 1981 and was alive and well at the end of 1985. Making money and keeping it demand discipline. You must have clear standards as well as strategies. You need to know when a market is overvalued as well as undervalued. Markets don't crash from their lows and seldom from points in between. They crash from unsustainable high levels. Overvalued markets are vulnerable. You should sell out of an overvalued market as a matter of course. There are no guarantees.

You could get caught in a market plunge while you are fully invested. One way to minimize that risk is to have a clear idea of what an overvalued market looks like and then sell every time those characteristics appear.

Markets become overvalued in two ways. Sometimes the economic fundamentals change, and sometimes crowds of investors bid stocks to unsustainable levels. You must include both in your picture of an overvalued market. The fundamental risk is the opposite of an undervalued market. When it seems likely that the growth in the money supply will be arrested, that is the time to sell stocks. Weak currencies, relatively high inflation, and full employment are characteristics of economies ripe for a pullback. You should sell when those fundamentals appear in the news.

Markets that rise tend to attract investors. They can remain strong for a long time. Bull markets have lasted for years in the past. Knowing when a market has gone so far that it is truly overvalued is not easy. By comparing one world market to another, however, it is much easier to gain a sense of relative value. Comparison is the discipline that detects overvalued markets. An overvalued market is relative. The Dow crashed from 384 in 1929 and reached 1,600 in 1986. Numbers alone are not enough to separate risk from opportunity. Compare one market to the other. Look at both performance and fundamentals. Concentrate on markets that are undervalued. And don't be afraid to sell.

A worldwide bear market can develop, as it did in the mid-1970s, at any time. Any investor, even the most astute and the most fortunate, can be caught. That is one of the risks. The best protection is the confidence to sell. Selling and then watching as the market keeps rising can be disconcerting. Selling requires just as much philosophy, discipline, and courage as buying at a time of bad news. An international perspective will do wonders for your selling confidence. When you look only at the U.S. stock market, you automatically worry about getting in and out at the right time. Timing has become an American fetish. When you step back and look at the timing question from a distance, you realize that it basically is an exercise in frustration. Instead of patiently waiting for an opportunity or selling confidently after a substantial gain, market timers hope to profit by getting in and out of the U.S. stock market as it rises and falls from month to month or week to week. There is no need to worry about market timing when you are looking over a world of opportunity. There is no need to try and catch every upswing and downswing of the Dow industrials if you are confident of finding major opportunity.

Money is made by applying simple, straightforward, age-old principles. Hold on to your cash until you see a clear opportunity. Then buy and wait patiently until profits begin to develop. Let your profits run as far as they will. Finally sell when the crowd rushes in.

Don't try to create opportunity where none exists. Don't confuse trading and investing. Trading is a legitimate route to investment profits, but it is far different from investing. Trading is the subject of the next chapter on currency markets.

When to Be in and When to Be out of Stock Markets

In an ideal situation you arrive on the investment scene with a bank account full of cash and begin looking for opportunity. More often, however, you start out with a list of existing investments and are faced not with the problem of what to do with cash but with what to do with a long list of respectable investments. The question always is, Should you sell everything and start fresh, or apply some less drastic strategy? The tough, hard-boiled professionals want you to sell everything and start with cash. I don't agree. That approach is too arrogant. It assumes that the past decisions are wrong and that the future decisions will be right. The world of investing is seldom that clear-cut. Most investors have a good deal of common sense and do not invest in situations that are obviously wrong. I advocate gradualism when switching to a new investment approach. While there is no doubt that the representative-stock approach to international investing will not only work but will produce significant capital gains, the correct execution of the strategy depends on your ability to apply the principles. The more you understand, the more comfortable you will feel with the international approach and the more likely you will maximize your profits.

Go slowly. As the first step, sell only those present investments that seem unattractive. Consider selling 10 percent or 15 percent of every holding. Establish a goal. Convert 10 to 15 percent or $10,000 worth of your present holdings to cash (whichever is greater). Start your international investment program with that portion. Over the following year or two you will naturally and sensibly convert your old thinking and your old portfolio to the new approach.

The second step, after raising cash, is to wait. This is a very important step. The natural inclination is to rush into a foreign market so that your cash will "begin working for you." The international approach requires a different attitude. You have to be accustomed to holding cash for long periods while you patiently and carefully search for opportunity. Some investors go so far as never to sell one stock or bond until they have found another to buy. They leap from one investment to another, never taking the interim step of holding cash. That, too, is the wrong approach because it is based on insecurity. Investors hang on to old stocks because they are afraid that they will go up after they are sold. Perhaps they will. Another rule for successful investing is to sell and never look back. Mistakes and even outright failures are a part of investing. You must be tough and disciplined to beat the markets. There will always be another major investment opportunity. It is far better to wait until you find it than to rush ahead and be constantly looking over your shoulder. Accept your mistakes as part of the process and move on. Look at your cash position as a ticket to future wealth. Study the five major markets. Apply the concepts of value to each and then make your forecasts. List the markets in order of your performance expectations. Which one do you think will be the best market in the coming year? Which one will be second? and so on. Are there elections coming up in the near future? They often bring uncertainty, falling stocks prices, and opportunity for an investor with cash like yourself. Do any of the five look to you like a clear opportunity for a profit in the coming six months? If the answer to that is yes, take the plunge and buy ADRs in the representative stocks for that market.

We are all gamblers. Like a player at the race track, we hope that the investments we select will rise immediately after purchase. When they don't, we often have reservations and wonder if the market knows more than we do. Once you have made your decision, develop the habit of ignoring the market for a few weeks. This will counter the gambling instincts. If after six months the market is not performing as expected, then you should rethink your decision.

Be patient; give your decisions time to develop. Some will develop quickly, while others may take a year or more. Remember that investing goes on for decades. The objective is not to get in and get out, as if the financial world, like a television set, could be turned on and off. Finance is part of living and surviving. You will be practicing your skills for decades to come. The objective is to beat the markets year in and year out. That is done by anticipating their next move and having the patience to wait for others to see things your way.

Let your profits run. It may take a year before you see a significant gain in a market. Under those circumstances there is a natural tendency to take profits. Don't be too quick to sell. Market trends, once under way, can last for years. Let the market give you all the gains it can. Sell only when you have a clear reason to think that the profit run is over. Apply the same clear-headed discipline to selling that you do to investing. When you sell, don't switch into another market immediately. Get in the habit of selling, sitting on your cash for a while, and reviewing all five markets just as you did in the first instance.

There will be times when none of the five markets is attractive. In that situation hold on to your cash and wait. Opportunities have to develop. You can't create them.

There are no guarantees in financial markets. There are no sure-fire formulas that will allow you to be a robot, automatically buying and selling on given signals. There is always risk, and you will always be making mistakes. Success in investing comes from understanding, patience, and the careful application of a disciplined approach.

The Representative-Stock Approach: Principles, Opportunities, Keeping Score, and Problems

Principles of Investing by the Representative-Stock Approach

1. Limit your selections to the five major stock markets: The United States, Japan, Germany, France, and Britain.
2. Buy predetermined representative stocks in the markets of your choice. Stick to ADRs.
3. Buy into markets only when there is a clear opportunity.
4. Hold on to your positions until there is a clear reason for selling.
5. When sale is indicated, do not hesitate.

6. Be willing to hold cash indefinitely while waiting for an opportunity.
7. Plan to be involved with this approach for years if not decades.

How to Find Opportunity

1. Look for these three characteristics in one or more of the five countries: low inflation, high unemployment, and a strong currency.
2. Always ask yourself, Is the government under any pressure to expand the money supply? If the answer is yes, then you have found an opportunity.
3. The opposite, economic setbacks, can also mean opportunity. The major markets always bounce back.

No doubt you could go a lifetime with this representative-stock strategy. But there may be times when the five major markets are too dull and you yearn for a more exciting opportunity. Once you have learned to use the principles described in this chapter, they can be taken and applied to the other markets. You can, with experience, venture into such markets as Holland, Hong Kong, Mexico, etc. Once you have mastered the tools and the discipline, you can use them to profit in any of the world's markets.

Keeping Score

In addition to watching the fundamentals, you will also want to keep track of the major markets and their performance. There are indexes for all of the major markets. They can be found in the usual financial publications such as *Barron's,* the *Wall Street Journal,* and the *New York Times.*

There is no need to chart the daily action of the five major markets. Keeping score on a monthly or twice-monthly basis is sufficient. Choose any of the available indexes for each market and then stick with your choice. Monitor market action month by month to see the overall trend as well as individual market performance. Individual markets tend to follow the course set by the majority. If you see one market lagging behind a world trend, you can expect that, sooner or later, the lagging market will move up or down to catch up with the world trend. Keeping score can add a new dimension to your international strategy.

Some of the ADRs for the representative stocks are listed on various U.S. markets. They can be found on the New York Stock Exchange as well as in the Over the Counter listings. Others are not listed on any U.S. market. For those you will not find a price for the ADR in the popular financial papers. Instead you will find the price for the underlying foreign share in the "Foreign Market" section of the paper. To convert the foreign price to the U.S. ADR price, you must adjust the foreign price by the current exchange rate.

Dealing with Practical Problems

Trading in foreign stocks is still the province of professional money managers and a minority of individual investors. Brokers tend to respond to the majority of the clients and for that reason may not be familiar with foreign stocks and ADRs. Most brokers are familiar with South African gold stocks, but when you ask about ADRs for stocks in other countries there can be practical problems. Most of the problems you will encounter, from trouble obtaining quotes to checking on the dividends, can be resolved if you know the cusip number for the ADR. Cusip numbers are assigned to every stock traded in the United States. The number becomes the stock's official indicator of U.S. status. The cusip number is used by computers at banks and brokerage houses to track down information about the stock. Armed with the cusip number you can handle just about anything.

The cusip number can be found by asking your broker or adviser for a list of all available ADRs. The banks publish these lists and provide the cusip number as well as other basic information. If you are stumped and can't find any other source for the information, call the ADR departments of the three banks listed below; they will be glad to help.

The Bank of New York
90 Washington Street
New York, NY 10015
(212) 530-2321

Citibank, N.A.
American Depositary Receipts Dept.
111 Wall Street
New York, NY 10043
(212) 558-5657

Morgan Guaranty Trust Company of New York
Corporate Trust Department
30 West Broadway
New York, NY 10015

Chapter 4

Currency Markets: The Worldwide Poker Game

YOU CAN BECOME VERY rich in a short time if you are on the right side of the currency markets at the right time. The leverage is enormous. When the markets move, your investment can be either wiped out or multiplied many times over. The ordinary reaction to currency markets is either to be seduced by visions of riches or turned away by lurid images of wild speculation. Everyone wants to be wealthy. No one wants to live in despair. Few are able to tolerate the pressure of the high-leverage currency game. Fewer still thrive on it. It is safe to say that most investors shy away from the currency markets. They find currencies too risky or too complicated. They think that currencies are a market like others, that you can decide to be in or be out. That is the problem. In fact, you have no choice. You can't escape the long reach of the currency market. You can make believe that the dollar's fluctuations don't matter—and find yourself puzzled, confused, and frustrated by seemingly impossible financial trends.

The value of the dollar on foreign-exchange markets affects every financial and economic trend. Interest rates dance to the dollar's tune. American business can be battered by foreign competition when the dollar soars. Inflation often runs wild when the dollar plunges. And the currency markets frequently veto official U.S. government policy. Those few investors who have been willing to tackle the mysteries of the currency markets have enjoyed an enormous advantage. To them the wild ride in U.S. stocks and bonds has made sense. They have been able to take meaningful positions and enjoy above-average gains.

The basics of the currency markets are within the reach of every investor. You don't have to move to Zurich or London to develop a base of knowledge and experience. Whether your interest is in trading currencies or just improving your general investment profits, the currency markets have a lot to offer.

Most investors will never bother to learn about currencies, but a small minority will always beat the crowd. Some people are willing to learn new concepts. Others find the task too dull, too hard, or just plain boring.

Einstein said it: "Everything is relative." The problem is that human beings still find that idea difficult to incorporate in everyday living. We like certainty and fixed ideas. We need a place to stand, a constant perspective, continuity, and visions of immutable values. Imagine a world like the one that Einstein portrayed in his essays. It is a world where every point of view is both different and correct. Einstein told about an imaginary train traveling through a town at the speed of light. To a person on the station platform, the clock in the town hall tower showed one time; to a man on the train, it told another. Both readings were correct. Einstein was trying to point out that even time is relative. Most find his observations puzzling. If time is relative, what can you count on? How can it be one o'clock for one person and two o'clock for another person at the same place?

For hundreds of years, people thought that the world was flat. The idea of a round globe was considered impossible. We imagined that people would be constantly sliding down around the surface to the other side. So desperate are we for fixed points of view that some people, still today, refuse to believe that the world is round. For most of us who have seen the beautiful photographs taken from outer space, it is hard to cling to the old notion of a flat earth. When it comes to financial markets, however, there are no guiding photographs to define reality. Artificial concepts like the flat-earth idea live on in the minds of investors. Even otherwise intelligent economists sometimes embrace ridiculous notions about financial markets. They act as if the world of finance were fixed, as if their point of view were the only valid perspective.

What we can't have in the physical world we try to create in the financial world. We live, work, and think in a single currency, as if one form of paper money defined all financial reality. How much are you worth? How much do you make in a year? What does it cost to go to college? Is the value of your house appreciating? These are common, everyday questions. In the United States they are always quickly answered with confidence in terms of U.S. dollars. Instinctively we react as if the dollar's value were constant. If our net worth is higher in dollars in 1985 than in 1975, we assume that we are ahead. We do the same when it comes to financial markets. Seldom, if ever, is the U.S. stock market expressed in terms of anything but dollars. The view of a foreign investor looking at the U.S. stock market is ignored.

The 1970s taught us a little about relativity in the financial markets. Most people now understand that inflation eroded the value of a dollar. Few can tell precisely how much the dollar declined, but most would not be shocked to know that a dollar in 1985 was worth exactly half of what a dollar was worth at the end of 1975. Nevertheless, we remain fond of valuing everything in today's dollars alone. When the Dow Jones Industrial Average broke above 1,600 in early 1986, there was a cry of wonder. The stock market made all the major news networks for the evening news. Not one mentioned that the Dow had reached 1,000 in 1976 and that adjusting for inflation, a Dow of 1,600 was really only a Dow of 800 in 1975 dollars. In real terms the market had not reached a new record high. Yet, everyone acted as if a new record had been attained.

That view is comfortable. We have no choice when it comes to accepting the changes that time brings. We grow older, like it or not. But by making believe that a dollar is a dollar, by jumping for joy in 1986 when the Dow hit 1,600, we cling to fantasies just like the flat-earth idea. We fool ourselves into believing that our fantasy is the truth. Unfortunately, the world in which we live is a vast and confusing mix of relative values. Dollars can be exchanged for German marks, Swiss francs, or Japanese yen. Real estate in New York is valued in dollars for Americans, but a German businessman looks at the same property in terms of marks. Worse, from the point of view of multiple values, the exchange rate for currencies is constantly changing. The chain of relative values goes on and on, round and round. The process of change never stops. It is midday somewhere in the world at all times. Markets are open and prices fluctuate twenty-four hours a day. It is impossible to stop the clock and "fix" values. The task of getting your bearings in a modern world of constant change and instant communications can seem impossible.

Early navigators faced a similar problem. As they sailed the globe they were dealing with constant changes in time. An artificial, fixed reference point had to be created and adopted so ships could find their way. The Greenwich Meridian has come to serve not only sailors but landlubbers as well. It was created for sailors and today forms the basis for all timetables. Our wristwatches relate to the Greenwich Meridian.

The old standard for money was the financial equivalent to the Greenwich Meridian. As long as paper currencies were fixed rigidly to gold, all values could be expressed in terms of gold. Once the financial world left the gold standard, the full weight of relative values fell on investors' shoulders. Some sit, lament the loss, and exhort governments on the necessity of returning to a gold standard. In time, there is little doubt that the world will either return to the gold standard or create a new form of Financial Greenwich Meridian. It may be dollars or European Currency Units (ECUs) or some yet-to-be-created financial standard. In the meanwhile, you have an opportunity. We live and operate in an ever-changing world of relative values. Those who learn how to cope will be a step or two ahead.

There is no profit in wishing for the past, a return to the gold standard. There is no point in trying to ignore the present reality. The currency markets may be wild, wooly, and unpredictable in the short term, but you can adjust. Nothing really has changed. We may be off the gold standard. We may have lost a convenient reference point, but the only thing that is truly different is the method for keeping score. The financial markets always have been treacherous. Returning to the gold standard would not change that.

Barring dumb luck, the odds on long-term financial success are against those who refuse to learn the basics about currencies. You can do it! It is possible to develop a personal Greenwich Meridian, a level of understanding that will give you a competitive edge. Looking at things the other way around, it is close to impossible to earn an above-average investment return without learning something about the currency markets.

Step 1: Reducing the Currency Markets to Manageable Proportions

There are hundreds of countries and currencies. Just as with world stock markets, however, only a few can be classified as major. The six that count most when it comes to world trade and investment are the following:

U.S. dollar
German mark
Japanese yen
British pound
French franc
Swiss franc

Following all six major currencies is time-consuming and confusing. Domestic and international economic forces push and pull currency markets. Japan, for example, has a reputation for keeping inflation down. Britain and France do not. The yen will not always be moving in sync with the British pound or the French franc. The yen was the last to respond to the weak dollar in the 1970s and last again to decline when the dollar soared in the 1980s.

Following all six major currencies means keeping track of interest and inflation rates in six countries. And, knowing is not always a blessing.

Doctors and nurses, when they are sick, know all the possibilities and tend to be difficult patients. They are overly anxious, often fearful, and always demanding. Knowing all the details, all the possible combinations of inflation and interest rates, can put you in a position similar to that of a doctor who is in the hospital as a patient. You can become worried, too intense, and blind to the underlying trend. The classic advice "keep it simple" applies to following currency markets.

What you need is a practical, straightforward, reliable way to determine the dollar's basic trend. Once that is known, the additional detail can be put in a sensible, understandable perspective. The answer is to watch the dollar versus the Swiss franc.

Focus on the Swiss Franc

Switzerland, a tiny country with about 6 million people, is so small that it doesn't count when it comes to world trade. When it comes to investments, however, Switzerland is a world-class competitor.

Investors from every corner of the globe turn to Switzerland for their personal investments. They come from both sides of the Iron Curtain, from developing countries, from industrialized nations, and from underdeveloped regions. Japanese have Swiss bank accounts. So do Germans and French. When it comes to investing and currencies, Switzerland is the world's melting pot.

Sheiks and shahs, kings and captains of industry, manage their personal wealth through accounts in Switzerland. They know what is happening in the world. As people of wealth and power, they have access to critical information. That information is used in the decisions about what to buy and what to sell in their personal accounts. A corporate treasurer may, at times, be casual about what is done with the company's money, but when personal financial security is at stake the decisions will be crisp and well informed.

Swiss secrecy is tight, as previously noted. You can't go and ask the Swiss about their clients' investments. But you can have the benefit of that "inside" information simply by watching the dollar versus the Swiss franc. When powerful people are down on the outlook for the dollar, you will know. When they are bullish on the dollar you will know that as well.

Swiss banks offer multiple-currency accounts as a matter of course. A depositor can easily switch from one currency to another by giving simple instructions. That is different from the average U.S. bank account. There aren't many U.S. banks that will allow you to denominate your account in anything but dollars. The flexibility and secrecy of Swiss banking have made Switzerland the first choice for investors when it comes to their personal funds. It doesn't take long for opinions about the dollar to be expressed in real transactions. There is little time lag between the knowledge and the action. The dollar-Swiss franc exchange rate is both sensitive and informative. You don't have to dig into esoteric statistics such as the "trade weighted" dollar or spend hours analyzing various currencies. All you have to do is keep track of how the dollar is doing versus the Swiss franc.

Currency Mathematics

Currency mathematics can be a source of confusion. The problem is that currencies can be expressed in one of two ways. For example, you can say that one Swiss franc is worth $0.25 or you can say that it takes four Swiss francs to buy one dollar.

The world of international currencies, with one exception, operates relative to the U.S. dollar. American dollars form a base for most currency-market communications. Investors from other countries want to know how many Swiss francs they will have to give in exchange for one U.S. dollar. If it takes four Swiss francs to buy one dollar, the relationship is expressed as 4.00, meaning four to one.

The exception is the British pound. In the case of the pound sterling, as it is called, the international convention works the other way around. The exchange rate is expressed in terms of how many U.S. dollars it takes to buy one British pound. The reason for this exceptional treatment of the British pound is that it once was the reserve currency for the world. Years ago businessmen and traders dealt primarily in terms of pounds. That has changed. Today the most important currency is the U.S. dollar. Nevertheless, the old expression for the exchange rate between dollars and pound lives on. When you see a rate for the pound of 1.40 it means that one British pound costs $1.40.

In the United States there is a tendency for things to be reversed. Americans want to know the value of everything in dollars and cents. Saying that the dollar is 4.00 versus the Swiss franc draws a blank. Saying that one Swiss franc is worth $0.25 brings instant understanding.

We are so unaccustomed to dealing in foreign currencies that we often behave like the tourist in an Irish joke. In a pub near Dublin, an American traveler, weary and thirsty, once asked for a "pint." The barkeep, pleased at the patronage, said, with a smile, "That will be 60 pee." Whereupon the Yank looked astounded, puzzled, and confused. Sensing that the barkeep was asking for money (we all seem to know when we are expected to pay no matter what the language), he blurted out, "How much is that in real money?" The barkeep laughed and replied, "And what might that be?"

We don't know if the traveler understood the reply. Tourists from the states often have a mental block when it comes to currencies in other countries. We just can't seem to accept that strange paper to us is exactly the same to an Irishman as a dollar is to us. Irish pounds are real money too.

Americans want to know the price of everything in terms of U.S. dollars. For that reason, many U.S. markets quote foreign currencies in U.S. dollars. You will see Swiss francs quoted as $0.51, for example. Don't be confused when you see the quotes. Just remember the story of the American in an Irish pub.

In your personal investment work stick with the international standard. Keep your calculations in the same way that a trader in London or Zurich would. Think of the franc as 4.00 versus the dollar and not as $0.25. When you need to make the adjustment between your figures and the U.S. way, divide one by your figures and you will be in line with the U.S. method.

For example, if the current exchange rate is 4 Swiss francs to one U.S. dollar, divide 1 by 4 ($1 \div 4 = 0.25$) and you will have the U.S. dollar value for one Swiss franc. To convert the U.S. figures to international figures simply reverse the process. Divide 1 by the rate in U.S. dollars ($1 \div 0.25 = 4$) and you will have the number of Swiss francs in one dollar.

There is an advantage to the international method. It makes it much simpler to find out how the dollar is doing. When your figures are going up, the dollar is gaining strength. When your figures are falling, the dollar is getting weak. For example, in the mid-1970s the Swiss franc traded at 2.50 to the dollar. By late 1979, the dollar was down and the franc was less than 2.00. When you look at exchange rates in terms of dollars, the picture you get tells what the foreign currency is doing. For example, between the mid-1970s and 1979 the rate of Swiss francs to the dollar went from $0.40 to $0.50. That is a rising trend. It means that the Swiss franc went up.

It may not seem to matter which way you keep score. After all everyone knows that if the Swiss franc is rising the dollar must be falling. While that is correct, you will find that it is far more convenient to have figures that tell you directly what the dollar is doing. When you draw a chart of the dollar in relation to the Swiss franc in international terms, you end up with a graph showing what happened to the value of the U.S. dollar. And that is the single most important piece of financial information you can have.

You will, at a glance be able to see the dollar's trend. You will be able to visit a trading room in London or Zurich and feel at home. You can stay at home and know that your view of the dollar is in tune with major markets around the world.

Applying the Concept in the Real World

During the 1970s the dollar grew steadily weaker. With hindsight we know that the dollar was doomed to decline until 1980, when the U.S. Federal Reserve stepped in and rescued the U.S. currency with record-high interest rates. Looking back, we think that it must have been obvious at the time that the dollar was in a long-term bear market. But that was not true. All along, as the dollar kept falling, there were arguments about the trend. I remember a time in the mid 1970s when chairmen and presidents of major U.S. corporations confidently explained that the dollar wasn't as weak as many feared. Some were "sure" that the dollar would quickly rebound. Of course, they were wrong. The dollar fell for years after their confident predictions of coming strength. People paid heavily for those misguided prognostications. Consider the employees of those companies stationed in hard-currency countries such as Germany and Switzerland. They were being paid in dollars, taxed by the U.S. government, but they paid their bills in local currency. As the dollar fell, their cost of living skyrocketed. Had they known just how weak the dollar was, they might have been able to take steps to protect their personal financial well-being.

All along, during those dismal days for the dollar, the Swiss franc told the truth. Each year, year after year, for the entire decade the average annual exchange rate for the dollar was lower than the previous year. Anyone watching that single exchange rate was able to see the severe weakness in the dollar. Anyone who also realized the significance of the Swiss franc as a barometer of investor sentiment knew that people were selling dollars in favor of Swiss francs at a record rate. Armed with that single bit of information, it would have been common sense to predict that it would take major action by the United States to reverse such a powerful, grass-roots trend. Corporate executives refused to accept the truth. Economists refused to accept the truth. Even the U.S. government refused to accept the truth until there was a crisis in world trade. They all had axes to grind. They all had reasons to hope that things would get better by themselves. They all misread the signals and instead allowed themselves to be lost in the plentiful array of economic statistics from which you can always make any case you wish. Plain, simple, common-sense observations like the dollar-Swiss franc exchange rate don't always tell you what you want to hear.

In 1980 the dollar stopped declining versus the Swiss franc. Late that year the dollar began to rise. The Swiss franc exchange rate signaled an end to the dollar's long decline and began to show the first signs of fresh strength. Talking about a strong dollar in 1980, however, was greeted with the same ridicule as were forecasts of continued dollar weakness in the mid-1970s. Neither the trade-weighted dollar nor a multiple-currency approach to the dollar gave such a clear picture. The crowd, still lost in the array of statistics, never saw the coming dollar surge until it was upon them. Many people in 1980, as the dollar was making a significant reversal, were convinced that the U.S. currency had been crushed and would never fully recover. Once again the dollar-Swiss franc exchange rate told the truth.

The first and most important step to take toward mastering the mysteries of the currency markets is to practice watching the dollar-Swiss franc exchange rate. For a few months check the figures daily. Make notes; keep records of your observations. Once you have become accustomed to the numbers and feel comfortable with the mathematics, you can decide how often to make regular observations.

After a relatively short time the numbers will become second nature; you will be able to pick up a paper anywhere in the world any time, look for the dollar-Swiss franc rate, and know instantly if the dollar is strong or weak.

If you take nothing else from this book, take the dollar-Swiss franc concept. Use it to help make forecasts of stocks, bonds, and gold. Armed with this one additional tool, you will increase your return on your investments. The dollar-Swiss franc rate may not unravel all the complexities of modern currency markets. You may not be able to grasp the significance of swaps, hedging, or forward contacts. That isn't necessary. You will be a step ahead of the crowd. You will know when the dollar is in real trouble. You will see major turning points and opportunities *before* they are obvious to the majority. You will be able to make major changes in your personal investment strategy at critical points. Never again will you look back and wonder why you didn't see high interest rates coming. Through the dollar-Swiss franc exchange rate you will have a practical, easy-to-use tool for watching the most significant financial market in the world.

Step 2: Understanding What Makes Currency Markets Move

Currency markets, especially over the short term, can be difficult if not impossible to predict. That does not mean they are impossible to understand. A soaring dollar, a plunging dollar, and everything in between have a common denominator—transactions. People are deciding to buy, sell, hold, or switch. The human motives behind the transactions hold the clues to understanding the market. We want to know what the traders, speculators, corporations, and other investors expect to accomplish when they buy, sell, or hold the dollar. You could take a survey. But that would be expensive, time-consuming, and frustrating. If you ask people why they bought or sold, you will get their opinion. Many times the decision comes from a "feeling" or an "instinct." How many times have you heard a successful investor say, "You have to have good instincts to make money?" As investors, we need to know the real motive, the basis for those instincts and feelings. Opinions are of much less value. In currency markets, as in any other financial market, you should learn to detect motive not from what people say but from what they do. Watch the transactions, fit them into the fabric of financial trends, and use common sense to reach an understanding of what is happening and why.

The world of currency markets operates as if the United States were a single, giant, global bank. While each currency is independent and can fluctuate based on domestic inflation and interest rates, there is a common denominator, a background of linkage with the U.S. dollar.

For a short time in the late 1970s, there was serious concern that this linkage with the dollar would be broken. It was thought that the Japanese yen or German mark or some fabricated basket of currencies might replace the dollar. That concern was born in the anxious days when the dollar was plunging. Once the dollar began to recover, in the early 1980s, the mood changed. All thoughts of replacing the dollar vanished, and the world picked up where it left off, before the dollar's dramatic slide. The dollar's central role is trade related. In the days following World War II the United States was the principal market for just about everything. The dollar was the only major currency left.

Since the 1940s, Europe and Asia have become significant economies with important currencies. To this day, however, gold, oil, and copper, to mention three of the more significant markets, are priced in U.S. dollars. Their price is converted from dollars to whatever local currency is involved. When Germany buys oil, the local German price is derived from a currency-market calculation that starts with the U.S. dollar price for a barrel of oil. This concept is significant both for understanding how currency markets work and for understanding why dollar fluctuations are so significant in determining the course of the world economy and world financial markets.

For example, when the dollar rises, the price of oil and copper will also rise in terms of other currencies. Between 1980 and 1984, the price of oil rose by 60 percent in France, while in dollars the price of oil declined by 34 percent. Americans rejoiced at lower fuel bills. At the same time, the costs of heat and gasoline were rising in France. A continuing stream of record-high oil prices in France and the rest of Europe depressed demand for oil, intensifying the decline in demand for it and leading to a 1986 plunge in oil prices. If oil had been denominated in French francs or German marks, the oil-price pattern of the 1980s would have been far different.

Think of the United States as a single world bank. That is a simplification, but it makes complex international economic concepts easier to grasp. Looking at the United States that way is not a distorting oversimplification. The image is helpful and leads to an accurate understanding of what makes currency markets move. The basis for the analogy is the underlying fact that so much of world trade is based on the U.S. dollar.

Banks make loans and take in deposits. In the last half of the 1970s, there was a mad rush to borrow dollars. Americans were borrowing, foreign businesses were borrowing, and foreign governments were borrowing. At the time, borrowing dollars to be paid back later looked like a sure thing. Interest rates on dollars were relatively low, and inflation in the United States was rising. That combination meant that today's dollar loan could be repaid later with dollars devalued by inflation. The interest cost was less than the rate of inflation, so the borrowing seemed to make sense.

For example, consider a loan to a German company made in 1976 and repaid in 1979. The interest rate would have been about 9 percent. On a loan of $100,000, the total interest costs for three years would have been $27,000. During the three years, the dollar fell from 2.50 to 1.71 versus the mark. The original dollar loan was worth 250,000 German marks. The cost of repayment in 1979 was 217,171 marks, including interest. Thus a German borrower made a substantial profit on a dollar loan between 1976 and 1979. The same was true for an American borrower when inflation was included in the calculations. The "real" cost of a 9 percent loan worked out to be less than zero after inflation. Loans were taken out with the expectation of paying them back with "cheap" dollars. No wonder there was a worldwide rush to borrow dollars.

The situation was too one-sided. The great bank called the United States was in trouble. There were no incoming deposits, but billions were going out in the form of loans. The money was flowing in one direction, out of the bank. The dollar was in trouble. Something had to change or else the entire U.S. financial system would become vulnerable. The great bank called the United States was suffering a destructive run in the form of a global borrowing scheme. Notice that the problem was not the decline of the dollar itself. The dollar fell because of the capital outflow. The capital was flowing out because interest rates were too low and inflation rates were too high. The threat to the country came not from economists calculating the possible mathematical consequences of a decline in the dollar but from real transactions, a massive outflow of capital.

The strategy that stopped the dollar's devastating dive proves that the analysis is correct. Interest rates were raised to record-high levels. The cost of borrowing dollars skyrocketed. In 1980 the U.S. prime lending rate peaked at near 22 percent. Loans that were once bargains became extremely costly. The massive borrowing of dollars abruptly stopped, and so did the dollar's plunge. Capital no longer flowed out of the global bank called the United States. High interest rates had another effect. They made holding dollars on deposit in our symbolic bank attractive. Not only did the borrowing stop, capital began to flow the other way, into the United States. Not surprisingly, the dollar began to rise. Once that happened the situation in the 1970s that made borrowing so attractive reversed and made it imperative that dollar loans be repaid to avoid extremely high borrowing costs. In 1984 the dollar rose by 12 percent versus the German mark. In that year the U.S. prime rate was down from its peaks to about 11 percent. The total cost of borrowing, including the cost of an appreciating currency, was 23 percent for a German borrower. The cost to an international borrower of dollars remained very high for a long time. The cycle came full circle. Borrowers rushed to buy dollars to use in repaying dollar-denominated loans. In 1984 and 1985 the combination of capital flowing in to repay loans and investors bringing capital in to take advantage of attractive U.S. interest rates produced a soaring dollar.

By late in 1984 there were early signs that the mad dash to repay loans was nearing an end. After all, not all borrowers were flush enough to repay loans even if they wanted to. The number that were credit worthy enough to raise cash in other markets was finite. The massive inflow of cash in repayment of loans had to come to an end. By spring of 1985 the dollar had risen so far that the entire U.S. economy was threatened. It was at that point that central banks from the five major industrial nations joined together in an effort to bring the dollar down. The United States reduced interest rates and all these countries began a program of selling dollars. The tactic worked. The dollar began to fall. The significant point, however, is that the strategy worked because conditions were ripe for a dollar decline in any event. It is doubtful that the central banks could have brought the dollar down had they moved much sooner. They wisely waited until the rush to repay dollar loans and the associated flood of capital had subsided.

This story of the dollar, interest rates, and borrowing shows that the pivotal issue in the movement of currency markets is the flow of capital. It is money on the move that makes one currency rise and the other fall. The reasons for money moving internationally are the same as the reasons for money moving in and out of your local bank. The story also shows the power of interest rates and particularly borrowing in influencing the flows of capital.

When borrowing is in vogue, the affected currency will be weak, and when borrowing is too dear the currency will be strong. The combination of currency movements and interest rates can be self-intensifying. It is common to look at a trend, especially one that has been established for a year or two, and think that it will go in forever. When the dollar was approaching the major 1980 turning point, few people thought it would ever recover. Fewer still realized that a soaring, overvalued dollar was just a few short years away. The gloom-and-doom crowd, at the time, correctly recognized that the dollar's plunge, if not corrected, would ultimately lead to disaster. Investors rushed out of dollars into gold for protection. Their logic and fear were correct, but their forecasts were completely wrong. They paid for their lack of understanding with painful losses.

The bank analogy helps us to understand what happened. Put yourself in the position of a bank president. No bank management wants their institution to collapse. They will, under pressure, take action to save their bank. We don't usually look at the United States as a single, huge entity. Up close it looks more like a horse with many heads. Congress, the president, the Federal Reserve, and consumers all seem to be going their independent ways.

When crisis approaches, however, the heads of the horse line up and the beast leaps away out of the path of danger. At times the United States can and does act as a single entity. In 1979, it was the Federal Reserve that showed the way, saved the dollar, and averted the disaster.

By late 1984, when the dollar was excessively strong, the same problem surfaced. Again many thought the horse would continue to wander aimlessly into disaster. It looked for a while as if the dollar would remain strong too long, that the U.S. economy would be swamped by a flood of imports. Instead the logical thing happened. Interest rates fell. The forecasters of ever-higher interest rates were wrong again. The horse moved out of the path of catastrophe.

Currencies have two enemies. One is failure and the other is success. In 1979 the United States was plagued by failure. Inflation rose and the dollar fell. Success as a threat to currencies is a lesson yet to be learned in the United States. The problems of success can be seen in Japan. Low inflation and a high savings rate depressed the yen for years. The reason is simple enough. A nation that has an excess supply of capital is like a bank with lots of deposits and no borrowers. The bank looks for places to invest the surplus funds at a profit. The excess savings produced low interest rates in Japan, and investors looked elsewhere for attractive investments. When the capital left Japan, it pushed the yen down. Remember the lessons from Japan and the bank analogy. The day may come when the dollar is weak because there is too much prosperity and too much cash in the United States.

In the short run, a few weeks or even a month or two, traders and speculators can affect the currency markets. For example, in February 1986 the dollar was weak; it fell below 200 yen to the dollar and 2.0 Swiss francs to the dollar. As the dollar fell, concern increased that the U.S. currency might be suffering from the same disease as in the

1970s. Some warned of a dollar free-fall, an out-of-control destructive plunge. The tip-off was the action of the gold market. In 1985 and 1986 gold did not rise as much as the dollar fell. Capital was not fleeing from inflation; there was no rush out of the dollar. Instead there was posturing. Investors, traders, and speculators were trying to switch into the "right" currency to make a profit. That is far different from a currency-market move driven by basic capital flows. Speculation can produce wild, unnerving markets. When a market moves on thin volume and with no basic fundamental support, economists, bankers, and business executives worry. They don't like uncertainty; they fear rapid change and can become hysterical over irrational markets. You can be sure, however, that "irrational" markets, moved by speculation and posturing rather than capital flows, will emerge from time to time; they will always be frightening and will always turn at some unpredictable point.

In the long run, international capital flows will determine the trend. Speculators can move markets only so far; there is a limit beyond which the power of moving capital will be unleashed. Capital flows always have the final say in setting the exchange rate between the major currencies.

By 1984 some people had come to doubt this conclusion. The foreign-exchange market doubled in size between 1979 and 1984, from approximately $75 billion a day to more than $150 billion a day. Worldwide investment activity and extensive trading in new financial instruments were the principal sources of the growth. Financial activity grew so fast that it far outstripped world trade. Logic might indicate that a doubling of a market would mean that it would take ever-larger transactions to move the markets. The opposite was true. By 1985 the currency markets had lost their resiliency. The size of the transaction that could be absorbed grew smaller and smaller. And most disturbing, there was a noticeable decline in the level of competency of the dealers playing the currency-market game. The currency market had grown in size and become more fragile. That fragile condition in late 1985 is further evidence of the conclusion that currency markets are moved basically by capital flows. When the amount of capital flowing slows down, as it did after the massive debt repayments of the early 1980s, the markets lose power, no matter how much trading is being done in clever, new financial instruments. Investors who keep a steady eye on the facts bearing on capital flows will always have a clear view of conditions in the currency markets.

Step 3: Trading Currencies for Profit

It is possible for a private individual to make millions trading currencies. But doing it requires a commitment most people are not willing to make. We all dream of having millions and will sometimes dabble in speculative ventures, hoping for the best. Making a fortune in currencies is far more demanding.

Trading is different from investing. The usual distinction is time. Traders deal from hour to hour. Investors deal for much longer periods of time. The time distinction, however, is only half right. Traders also make a commitment. They are in for the long pull. They suffer enormous strain as they watch markets from hour to hour. But few set out to make a quick killing so that they can run away to their chosen paradise. Most are traders for life. A more useful distinction is to realize that good traders don't care what they are trading. A person with the right instincts can make a fortune dealing in stones from the road if there is a moving market. Their mind and instincts focus on the movement of the market itself rather than the underlying asset. Of course, they have to understand the market and must know a lot about the object of their trading. But don't confuse necessary knowledge with caring. Good traders are totally absorbed with the mechanism of the market. They are a part of the process. They are pitting their skills not against economic fundamentals but against the other players in the market. Their profit comes from outwitting the other traders. Trading requires split-second decisions. There is no time for quiet reflection. The decision has to be made immediately. Tuning your mind to that tempo demands total commitment to the market itself. You have to blot out everything except the market's movements. Trading demands living with a high level of constant strain day after day, week after week. Traders know that they can lose all if they are on the wrong side of a market. Ordinary people will borrow $15,000 for a new car, but they find borrowing $5,000 to invest too much of a risk. Out the window of their new vehicle they will explain that they can't afford to "play" the markets. A trader has to have the exact opposite attitude. Traders must be willing to take enormous risks in the midst of uncertainty. They must be able to lose huge sums and bounce back to try again the next time.

Suppose you start out with $10,000 and have a string of good fortune. You find yourself with $100,000 and then run into a bad period and lose half of it on a single trade. Suppose also that you are not rich and work for a relatively modest salary. Suppose that $100,000 was more money than you ever expected to have in your lifetime. Would you be willing to try again? Would you be willing to lose it all and still bounce back to try and try again? That is what good traders do.

Every investor should test his or her skills in trading. You may have the basic instincts and skill and not know it. You may be a successful trader. You owe it to yourself to find out. Even if you discover that trading is not your route to financial success, you should know how to trade, understand what it is, and do it from time to time to stay sharp. Currency markets didn't used to be an appropriate market for the average individual investor. The sums involved were too large and the positions frequently too open-ended to make the risk affordable. Being willing to take a risk is not the same as foolishly embracing a risk that is clearly beyond your limit. In recent years an options market for currencies has developed. Options are interesting trading vehicles because you can limit your loss. The option can end up worthless. You can loose 100 percent of your investment, but you are not obligated to keep coming up with more and more capital just to maintain the position until its natural conclusion. Options in currencies are particularly attractive for trading because the underlying market is large and liquid and can be very volatile. A few points or "pips" one way or the other can make an enormous difference in the value of your options.

A Basic Currency Trading Philosophy

Timing is everything in trading. You don't want to be in the market when it is quiet and not moving. Making money as a trader means taking risks in an active market.

First look at the markets and ask yourself, Are they thick or thin? A thick market is one where the trading volumes are large and the market is able to absorb millions without budging. Thin markets move on light volume. There are times, as in the early days of 1986, when very small transactions will move currency markets through a wide swing. Thin markets are the most treacherous and the most interesting for traders. You never know which way a thin market will move next. In a thin market you are pitting your wits against the other players, unencumbered by economic fundamentals and huge capital flows. The object of trading is to anticipate what the others will do next and beat them to it. It is that simple and that difficult. You have to be a crowd follower one moment and a nonconformist the next.

You have to be a technician looking at charts today and an economist studying the fundamentals tomorrow. There are no rules and no formulas and no guidelines that will help. You should forget all about investing, look at the market, and see if you can guess which way the crowd will jump tomorrow.

Trading can be costly and it can be profitable. Investors who trade to stay sharp should expect to break even over the long pull. Only good traders make money trading. All others are lambs to be sheared. The biggest losers are those who win first and then can't handle the larger sums. They either become overly cautious or reckless.

Use your notes and charts on the dollar versus the Swiss franc as your base line, or frame of reference. The Swiss franc will tell you the current trend and where the action is. If you see that the British pound or German mark is more volatile than the Swiss franc, you will know that there is more potential trading profit in the more active market.

Keep your trading simple and straightforward. Don't get into complex situations such as straddles unless you have become practiced enough that those concepts are simple to you. Take positions that you fully understand. If the markets don't look right to you, then stay out. In fact, as a part-time trader, you should plan on being out of the markets much of the time. There aren't that many times when the profit opportunity is clear to an average investor. Traders, because of their total commitment to the markets, will see opportunities that are anything but clear to others. Don't overestimate your skill. There is a wide gap between what you can do and what you are prepared to do. No one can jump cold into a volatile market and expect profits from anything other than luck. Gamblers should stick to the $2 window at the race track or buy lottery tickets. There is no way you can change the odds on winning a megabucks state lottery. Investors and traders can tilt the odds in their favor by applying discipline, skill, and commitment to the task. Traders engage in a risk-taking practice that is far more than simple gambling. They practice with the same dedication required of an Olympic athlete. They trade every day. They love taking risks and calculating what you, their opponent, will do next.

Currency markets thrive on fear, greed, and rumor. A fabricated rumor can panic markets and send a currency up or down in a few minutes. The daily fluctuations defy rational analysis. The dollar is almost always at the center of the frenzy. It is the currency against which all others are measured. It is also the currency against which skilled traders love to test their mettle. Conditions in the currency markets are further complicated by the fact that corporations, banks, pension funds, trading companies, and portfolio managers do not stick to their respective basic businesses. They join the daily trading frenzy and try to beat the short-term swings. It seems to matter very little that they often take huge losses in the process. When it comes to trading currencies, hope springs eternal.

The currency markets have become so large and so turbulent that the central banks are no longer the absolute powers that they once were. They are no longer able to force markets to go the way the banks choose. At times the currency markets act as powerful, independent forces, capable of vetoing central bank policy. There is a two-way relationship between the central banks such as the U.S. Federal Reserve and the currency markets. Traders understand these facts of modern currency-market life. They prefer today's conditions. The less regulated and the more volatile the markets, the better the chances of a huge trading profit. Traders thrive on the uncertainty, the risks, and the opportunities provided by modern currency markets.

Fortunately, you don't have to be a trader to profit. Currency markets are valuable to patient, long-term investors.

Step 4: Using Currency Markets to Increase Investment Profits

There is a connection between the U.S. stock market and the dollar that can help you to increase your stock market results. During the 1970s, when the dollar was steadily declining, the price-earnings ratio on U.S. stocks also declined. Investors lost confidence. They no longer were willing to pay high prices for stocks in the hope that future earnings would justify the current price. They became increasingly short-term oriented. In 1979 the dollar reached its low point. At the same time the price-earnings ratio for U.S. stocks reached a low point. Once the dollar began to recover, investors felt more confident and the price earnings ratio on U.S. stocks followed the dollar to higher ground (see the chart on the next page).

During the 1970s the dollar was falling because of economic failures. Rising oil prices, rising inflation rates, and higher interest rates affected both stock prices and the dollar. This does not mean that stock prices follow, in lockstep, the dollar's travels on world exchange markets. Don't start programing your computer in hopes of a new formula for sure profits in U.S. stocks. The relationship is long term and related to the nation's economic fundamentals. The point is simply to show that there is a connection. It is possible to improve your stock market results through an understanding of the currency markets.

There is also a connection between the currency markets and corporate profits. Stock prices rise and fall based on corporate profits. We live in a world of intense international competition. The currency markets operate to establish the price of goods from one market to another. For example, a computer made in Japan might sell for 500,000 yen in Tokyo. But how much would that same Japanese-made computer sell for in the United States? The answer depends on the exchange rate. If the yen-dollar exchange

THE U.S. STOCK MARKET AND THE DOLLAR

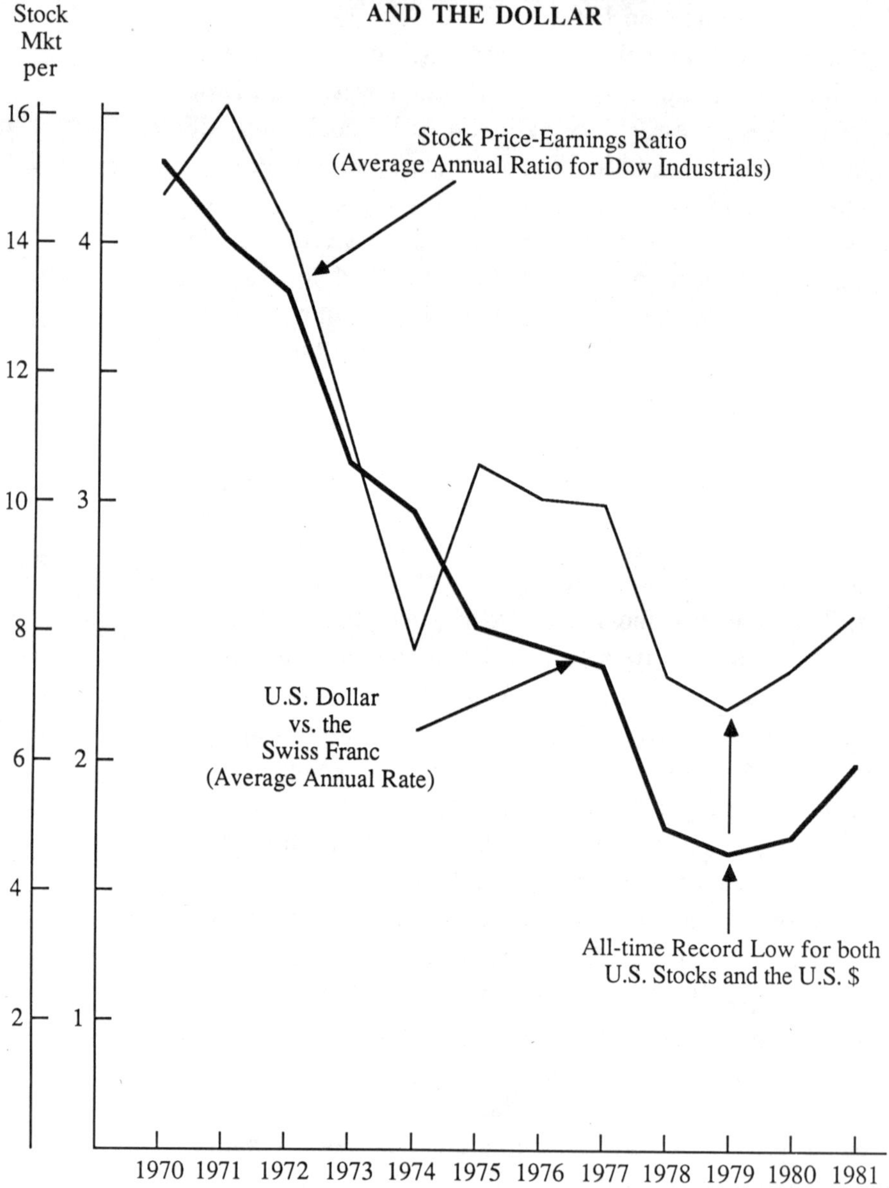

1982 per = 14.3 1983 = 14

Source: Compiled by the author.

rate is 250 to 1, the equivalent price in dollars is $2,000. If the yen rises, however, the dollar falls, the exchange rate becomes 190 yen to one dollar, and the equivalent price becomes $2,632. The cost of a Japanese-made computer or automobile or television set will rise by 30 percent as the dollar falls from 250 yen to 190 yen. An American computer company would be delighted to see the dollar fall. Their costs and selling price are not affected by the currency market. If an American computer sold for $2,200, it was too high priced compared to a Japanese product when the dollar was at 250 yen and extremely competitive when the dollar was down to 190 yen. More Americans would buy U.S.-made computers at $2,200 than Japanese equivalents at $2,600. The rise and fall of the dollar has a significant impact on the ability of U.S. companies to compete at home and abroad.

In the spring of 1984 the U.S. Federal Reserve became concerned that the U.S. economy was growing too fast. The Fed feared that demand would be too strong and that inflation would rise again. To counter the threat, the Fed, following the economic theory called monetarism, raised U.S. interest rates. Higher U.S. interest rates made the dollar more attractive to international investors. They enjoyed the high yields they could earn on U.S. dollars. As a consequence, the dollar began to rise. The dollar's upward move intensified through the summer of 1984. By fall the dollar was so strong that U.S. exports dropped sharply while imports rose just as sharply. U.S. businesses were priced out of markets at home and abroad. At one point in late 1984, it was cheaper to import apples from South America that to go around the corner to a local grower. U.S. corporate profits declined as sales were lost to foreign-made goods. The Federal Reserve was finally forced by the strong dollar to reverse course and bring U.S. interest rates down.

Once the dollar began to fall from its destructive peaks, the U.S. stock market began to move higher. The stock market correctly reasoned that a lower dollar would make U.S.-made products more competitive and produce rising corporate profits. Investors with an understanding of the currency markets watched the battle between the U.S. Federal Reserve and the currency markets. Once it was clear, from the skyrocketing dollar, that the Fed had lost, the U.S. stock market soared and bonds rose to new highs. There was a significant opportunity to profit in both stocks and bonds.

Bonds fall when interest rates rise. That much is a matter of mathematics. When the Fed increased interest rates in early 1984, the bond market declined. Bonds remained at attractive prices through the summer as the dollar rose. An investor willing to make a judgment that the dollar would drive U.S. interest rates back down had a chance to buy bonds low. Bond prices rose when the Fed lost and interest rates fell.

Currency Markets and Interest Rates

For years it was standard practice for European bankers to look with scorn on their American counterparts. They said that the Americans were the only bankers left in the world who could talk about interest rates without mentioning the dollar, and still keep their jobs. The criticism is still valid. All across the United States, in thousands of banks, decisions are made about deposits, loans, and interest rates. The bankers involved literally never mention the dollar. They don't think there is a relevant connection. They operate their businesses as if U.S. interest rates could go up or down completely independent of the dollar's fate. They are wrong. The Europeans are right. But don't be too hard on the U.S. bankers. After all, the Federal Reserve made a tremendous error in underestimating the power of the dollar in 1984. That mistake cost all American banks and all American businesses a heavy loss. If that august body of

U.S. economic thought in the Fed can err so badly on the connection between the dollar and interest rates, it is not right to be too hard on ordinary bankers in middle America. The fault lies not with individual banks or bankers but in U.S. economic thought. That is the reason that the entire U.S. savings industry was caught completely unprepared when U.S. interest rates soared in the late 1970s. The savings bankers were holding billions in long-term, fixed, low-rate mortgages. When interest rates soared, they were caught. On the one side, their cost of funds rose sharply, but on the other side of the profit-and-loss statement, they could not raise prices. They were stuck with fixed incomes and skyrocketing costs. Worse, as interest rates rose, the true market value of their mortgages declined. Had the savings bankers, at the worst of the interest-rate spiral, been required to report mortgages at market values, much of the U.S. savings industry would have been technically bankrupt. In fact, at times there was serious concern that the back of the savings industry would be broken.

There also was economic strain in Europe when U.S. interest rates rose. The degree and extent of the problem, however, was far less. The Americans had been caught totally by surprise. They never made the connection between the long, steady decline of the dollar and the potential for record-high interest rates.

You might think that by the end of the 1970s the U.S. banking and economic community would have discovered the connection between currency movements and interest rates. You might expect that no responsible economist would have made an interest-rate forecast without taking the dollar into account. That was not true, however. Well into the 1980s, prominent, respected financial leaders repeatedly predicted higher interest rates. They ignored the dollar's recovery. And of course, they were repeatedly wrong. In addition, there was the Federal Reserve's disastrous move to raise interest rates in the spring of 1984. Paul

Volcker, chairman of the Fed, used the awesome power of the U.S. central bank to drive U.S. interest rates up when the currency markets were driving them down. The result was considerable damage to the U.S. economy. Farmers in particular were battered. In 1980 one out of every three planted acres in the United States was planted for export. The dollar's dramatic rise, in the wake of the Fed's high interest-rate policy, made U.S. agricultural products more expensive on foreign markets. U.S. farm exports plunged. Farmers lost export sales, and farm income plunged. Before the crisis ended, farmers were faced with new competition from imports in addition to a loss of exports. The Federal Reserve ignored the strong dollar, and the entire economy paid the price.

Volcker, one of the nation's top international bankers, the man who saved the dollar in 1979, fell prey to the American interest-rate disease. He was not able to resist the temptation of believing that the United States could go its own way in ignorance of the currency markets. He wanted to drive inflation down, kill it once and for all. He thought the strong dollar would wait. His anti-inflation power play failed. He learned the lesson about the connection between interest rates and the dollar the hard way. There is no better example to demonstrate what has been known for hundreds of years—interest rates and currencies go together in a global balancing act. They are inseparable.

Investors who understood the relationship may have been awed by the prolonged slide of the dollar in the 1970s and the lack of immediate U.S. response. But they weren't surprised when U.S. interest rates soared to historic high levels in the early 1980s. Likewise, in 1983 and 1984, international investors may have been amazed that Volcker would try to raise U.S. interest rates while the dollar was so strong. But they bought billions of dollars' worth of U.S. bonds anyway. They knew that the currency markets would win in the end. They enjoyed enormous profits when U.S. interest rates fell and the value of their bonds rose.

The basic rule is this: interest rates and currency go hand in hand. A weak currency begets higher interest rates. A strong currency begets lower interest rates. That rule applies to the U.S. dollar and U.S. interest rates no matter what the Federal Reserve or the U.S. banking community may choose to believe.

It also applies to all other currencies. And that presents the most difficult aspect of calling the turns in the currency markets. When the Swiss franc is strong, calling for lower Swiss interest rates, the dollar will, by the numbers, appear weak. The challenge is to know when the dollar is weak and when it is strong. Not every swing in the dollar, up or down, triggers a corresponding move in U.S. interest rates. If the dollar goes down because of a strong Swiss franc, for example, the consequence will be lower interest rates in Switzerland. The key to the connection is that a *strong* dollar produces economic pressure that brings interest rates down. "Strong" in this instance does not mean higher than yesterday or last week. "Strong" means accompanied by capital inflows or so strong that imported goods present unfair competition at home. "Strong" in this sense is not a technical but a fundamental term. You can't tell a strong currency from a weak currency by charts alone. You must add common sense and a legitimate perspective on the world around you. When farmers are suffering, exports are lagging, and business is complaining about foreign competition, you know that the dollar is strong. Likewise, "weak" means an outflow of capital, rising prices for imported goods, upward pressure on inflation, and a flood of foreign tourists at your favorite vacation spot.

Always ask yourself this question, Is it more likely that U.S. interest rates will change or is the better bet that interest rates in Switzerland, Europe, or Japan will change? Is the dollar weak? Or are other currencies strong? There are two sides to every currency movement. By concentrating on the dollar versus the Swiss franc, you have narrowed the field of inquiry to manageable proportions. Your task is to look at those two and judge if investors are fleeing the dollar or discovering attractive qualities in the Swiss franc. Is the market moving because of conditions in the United States or because of conditions in Europe?

There are always some investors who want to call every turn in the interest-rate road. They ask for a formula or set of rules or script to follow that will tell them which way interest rates will go this month and next. The fallacy in their thinking is that they don't recognize the difference between trading and investing. On the one hand, traders call the turns, try to out guess the Federal Reserve's next mistake, and match wits with all the other players in the market. Good traders don't need rules and formulas; they understand how the game is played. Others, who want to remove the risk from trading by searching for cycles, rules, and correlations, are simply afraid of the risk and looking for fantasies to calm their queasy stomachs. On the other hand, investors are willing to wait for a clear opportunity. They are not concerned about what interest rates will do next month. They are concerned about staying in tune with the markets so that they will recognize the next major investment opportunity. The currency markets are one of the more useful tools for assisting to recognize major opportunities. When you see that the dollar is becoming weak, you should begin to expect higher interest rates. When the dollar is growing strong, you look for lower interest rates.

The Great Opportunity

Years ago the United States was on the gold standard. In those days the dollar was fixed and did not provide help and guidance in dealing with financial markets. It is the free-floating dollar, the wild and sometimes volatile currency markets, that provide the information, the clues that can help you to spot an opportunity or sell in time to prevent a loss. Eventually, the United States will learn. In time, the currency markets will be integrated into U.S. financial thinking and policy making. When that happens, the currency markets will become more stable and less informative for investors. But that process probably will take much longer than you would think. In the meantime there is an opportunity for patient investors, who understand the relationship between the currency, interest rates, economic fundamentals, and the financial markets, to increase their profits. No matter what your investment preference—precious metals, bonds, or stocks—the currency markets are critical.

You can count on ignorance and exaggerated swings in the markets. In late 1979, for example, after U.S. interest rates had shot to new highs, there were still popular forecasts of gold at $1,000 an ounce. The new trend to lower gold prices was already determined. The weak dollar had precipitated higher interest rates. Gold's run was over. Still, many people refused to heed the basic message of the dollar and interest rates. In late 1984, when the dollar was soaring and interest rates were already falling, there were forecasts of higher interest rates emanating from sophisticated analysts with Ph.D.s in economics. There was plenty of time and opportunity to buy bonds or stocks and profit from the continuing fall in interest rates.

The Path-to-Profits Rule

The obvious strategy, based on the currency markets, is a contrary one. *Do the opposite of what the crowd is doing—but do it only after a major change in official monetary policy.* When U.S. interest rates rise, look for lower gold prices, lower inflation, and a dollar recovery. When everyone is convinced that interest rates will stay high forever but the dollar is gaining strength, buy bonds.

Take advantage of the cycles. The dollar swings from being overvalued to being undervalued and back again to an overvalued condition. Don't force the cycles into any specific time frame. It can take a long time for one swing, or it may take place within a year or two. Remember that at each new extreme it will be very tempting to fall prey to the common wisdom that the present trend will go on indefinitely. The visible trend that has been around for a while is the one that everyone can see and believe. The coming change is always a surprise for most people. Learn your currency lessons well. Follow the rate of the dollar versus the Swiss franc. Be an informed investor and prepare yourself for the next major opportunity.

To make a fortune, you only need to take full advantage of one or two major opportunities. When government bonds paid 15 percent in 1981, there was a major opportunity. An investor willing to borrow for investment could have turned a modest equity into a not-so-modest fortune. To make such a fortune you need to recognize the opportunity and have the courage of your convictions. The currency markets can provide the information you need to see a major opportunity. Only you, through diligent application of the concepts, can provide the experience that builds confidence. Be patient but always be involved in the markets. You can count on the cycles. There will always be another major opportunity.

Graphic Illustrations of Currency Concepts at Work

Most of the time we carry investment tools in our memory. When it comes time to make a quick decision, we are prepared. Along the way, however, it is useful to stop and review the past, look at it graphically in order to refresh our memory, and keep our current perceptions as sharp as possible.

The first two charts show a long-term view of the 1970s and early 1980s. The chart below is a plot of the dollar's average annual exchange rate versus the Swiss franc. In 1970 one U.S. dollar bought, on average, slightly more than four Swiss francs. By 1979 one dollar no longer bought even two Swiss francs. The dollar had come tumbling down from its lofty peak. The chart is all the more significant because it is both long term and based on annual averages. All of the short-term movements have been absorbed in the annual averages. (An annual average is computed by first

THE DOLLAR VS. THE SWISS FRANC
Average Annual Exchange Rate

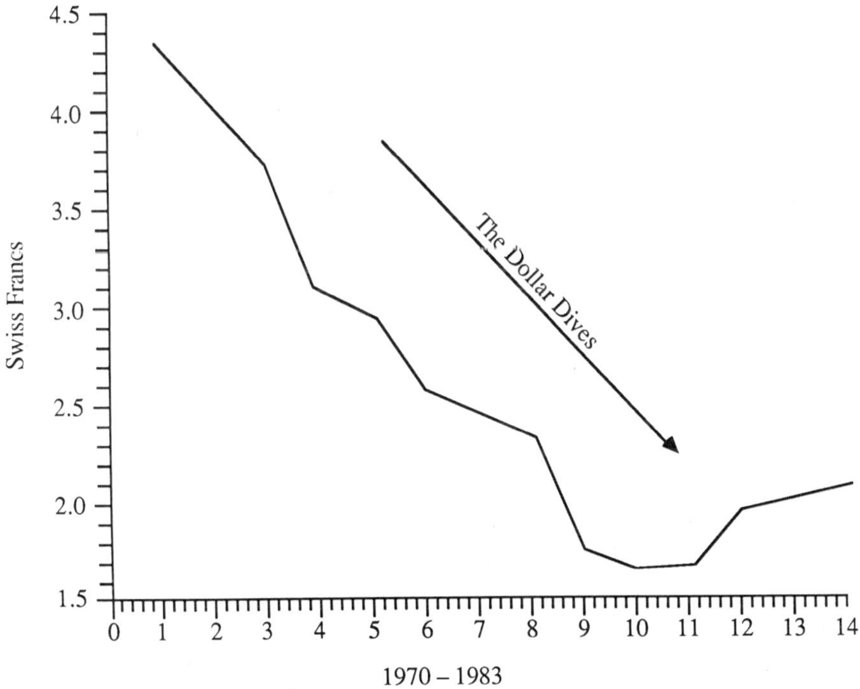

Source: Compiled by the author.

adding up all the daily figures and then dividing the sum by the total number of business days in the year.) The obvious conclusion from the chart on page 175 is that the dollar was in serious trouble in the 1970s. The chart below shows the consequences. Interest rates rose. Finally they rose to record-high levels. This is a plot of long-term interest rates. Specifically, it shows the yields on long-term corporate bonds rated AAA by Moody's. When the two charts are placed side by side, there is no doubt that the dollar's slide was followed, fairly quickly, by a significant rise in U.S. interest rates. It is important to recognize that the advance in interest rates did not follow the dollar's decline precisely. The upward move in interest rates was compressed near the end of the period. Higher interest rates tended to

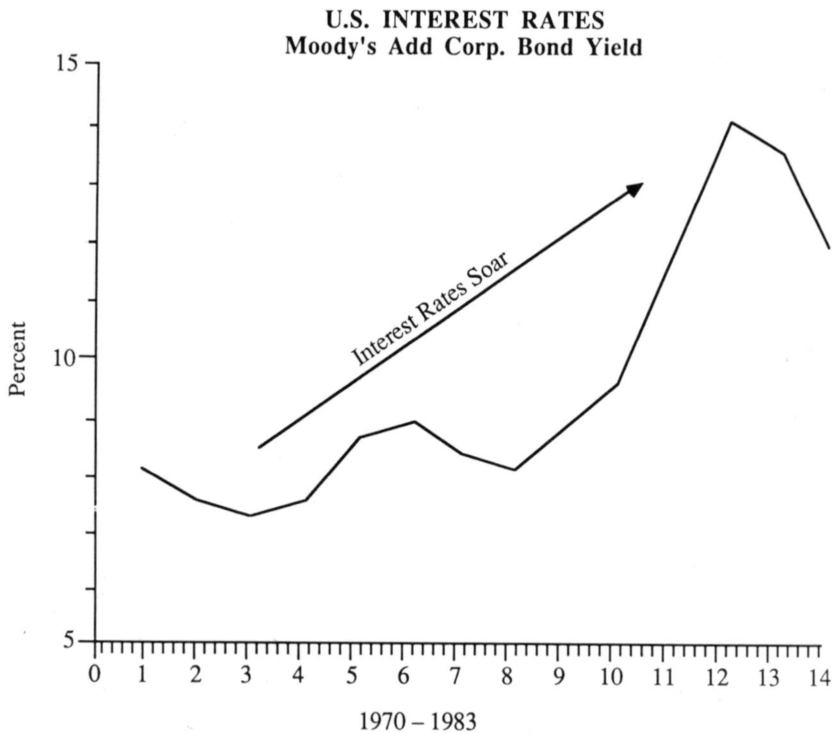

Source: Compiled by the author.

follow the dollar's decline. In the 1970s there was ample time, years in fact, to adjust your investment strategy to the sinking dollar. It is quite common to feel a sense of urgency when managing investments. Markets move from hour to hour. Prices are constantly changing. In fact, more often than not, there is plenty of time. You do not have to rush. You can sit back, watch the markets, make your calculations, do your analysis, and be able to buy or sell at attractive prices. Charts like these two, showing how the dollar and interest rates moved over more than a decade, support that point. It isn't often that markets move as rapidly as gold did in 1980. Gold's rise and fall from a lofty peak developed in less than a month. That kind of market is definitely the exception. You will have to be lucky to get the timing right when markets move so quickly. You can't count on that kind of action.

The charts on the following pages show that the dollar can also have the opposite effect. Between 1980 and 1983 the dollar not only recovered but shot ahead to destructively high levels. By 1984 the dollar was so high that U.S. farm products and manufactured goods were priced out of world markets, and the U.S. domestic economy was being inundated by a flood of imports.

This time the chart of the dollar versus the Swiss franc is a plot of the monthly average exchange rate. It shows much more detail than the chart based on the annual average exchange rate. It also highlights the fact that short-term movements in the currency market, even those from month to month, can be misleading. If you use your hand to block out that portion of the chart from mid-1981 on, you will get the impression that the dollar was heading back down after a brief period of strength. That conclusion would have been completely wrong. When 1981 was over, the dollar averaged an exchange rate versus the Swiss franc higher than in 1980, in spite of the severe mid-year correction.

Currency markets can temporarily reverse, sometimes for several months, before resuming the basic trend. Of course, you never know at the time, from the charts, if the reversal is the start of a new trend. You need both a long-term perspective and a heavy dose of economic common sense to sort out the temporary from the genuine reversals. A guiding principle is, Don't be in a rush. Remember the lessons from the charts on pages 175 and 176. There usually is much more time for evaluation and decision making than you think. You can afford to wait several months to find out if a reversal is the beginning of a new trend that calls for a change in basic strategy.

THE DOLLAR VS. THE SWISS FRANC
1980–1984

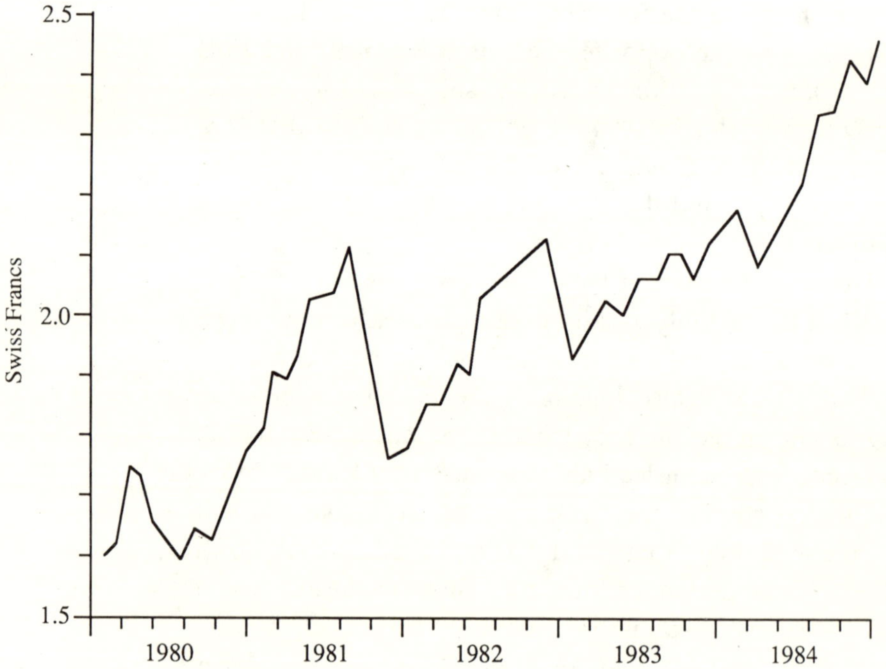

Source: Compiled by the author.

The chart on page 176 shows that the relationship between the currency markets and interest works both ways. The strong dollar forced interest rates down. The chart is again a plot of long-term interest rates on U.S. corporate bonds rated AAA by Moody's.

The chart below shows the dollar versus the Swiss franc from 1983 to the early months of 1986. It also plots the monthly average dollar-Swiss franc exchange rate. If you look at just the last half of the chart, you see that the dollar was in a steep decline. If you saw only that part of the chart, you might be tempted to conclude that the weak dollar would force U.S. interest rates back up to higher levels. When you see the whole chart, however, you can see that the U.S. currency made a round trip and was not nec-

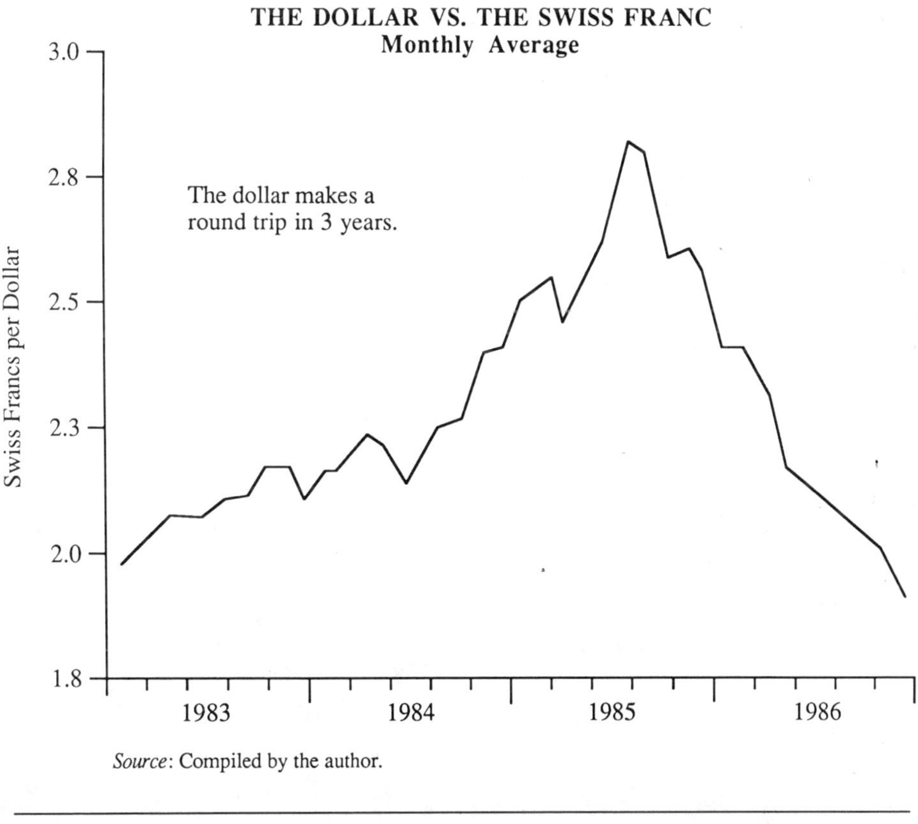

Source: Compiled by the author.

essarily weak in 1985. The test is to look at Swiss interest rates. If the dollar was not to be judged weak, especially in the second half of 1986, then the Swiss franc must have been strong. A strong Swiss franc would force Swiss interest rates down, just as the strong dollar had forced U.S. interest rates down in 1983 and 1984.

The chart below is a plot of Swiss interest rates. Sure enough, it shows a steep fall in Swiss interest rates. This chart shows that in addition to a long-term perspective and common sense you always must remind yourself that when one currency falls, another is rising. You must always consider the question, Is the dollar weak or are other currencies strong? Will U.S. interest rates rise, or will interest rates in Europe and Asia fall? Are world markets generally

SWISS INTEREST RATES
6-Month Euro Rates

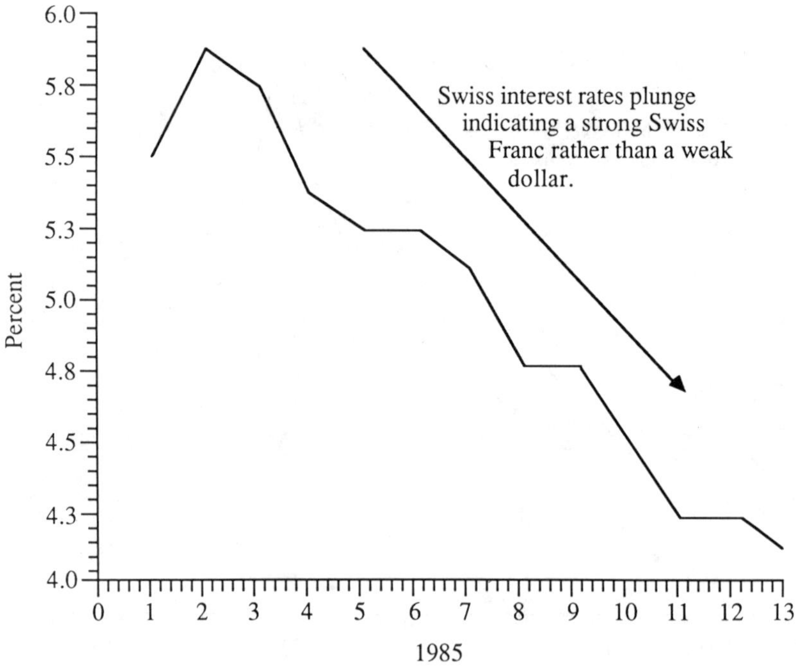

Source: Compiled by the author.

headed for higher or lower interest rates? The dollar is, like all other U.S. financial markets, a part of a global economy.

The correct interpretation of the dollar's movements will always make sense when considered against the broader background. The greatest mistakes come from looking at only one side of the markets. The currency markets force you to apply an international perspective. They help you to internationalize your thinking. They open a new awareness of both risk and opportunity. They frighten many people who don't like to be reminded of the risks. Hiding from the financial truth in order to make risks seem acceptable is just as treacherous as exaggerating risks and forecasting gloom and doom. The truth almost always lies somewhere in the middle. Great catastrophes don't come every year. In most years there is a significant opportunity for you to increase your personal wealth, and that, after all, is the best insurance against the possibility of a future economic catastrophe.

Chapter 5

New Tools for Increasing Profits in the U.S. Stock Market

BETWEEN 1966 AND 1982 the U.S. stock market was not able to rise above and stay above 1,000 on the Dow Jones Industrial Average. The market hit 1,000 for the first time in 1966 and over the next sixteen years made repeated attempts at climbing above that mark. Each time the market fell back. It wasn't until the great bull market that began in 1982 that the market was able to climb and stay above 1,000. An investor who bought stocks in 1966, held on, and waited the sixteen years had a gain of 29 percent by the end of 1982. An investor who sold every time the Dow reached 1,000 and bought back at the market's lows had a gain of 620 percent over the same period. Of course, few, if any, investors would have been fortunate enough to catch the lows during those sixteen years. The peaks, at 1,000, were clear enough, but the lows were much harder to choose. There is no doubt, however, that any investor who at least tried to sell at the peaks and buy back at the lows enjoyed a far greater capital gain. Trying to choose market tops and bottoms is called timing by many professional U.S. investors.

Whenever timing is mentioned, an argument follows. There is another group of U.S. professional investors who apply the principle of selectivity. They point out that even in a bear market there are some stocks that rise. They claim that no one can time the market and that all emphasis should be on choosing the right stocks. The arguments center on the question, Is it a market of stocks or a stock market? The obvious answer is that it is always both.

The representative-stock strategy explained in chapter 6 takes this basic dilemma into account. The strategy of choosing the right markets at the right time combines market timing with stock selection. The stock-selection aspect is simplified by choosing "representative" stocks in advance and then concentrating on comparing world markets. Buying representative stocks when a market looks right is not what is commonly meant by the U.S. expression "timing."

Market timing in the U.S. sense is fairly new. The collapse of the U.S. stock market in the mid-1970s brought about profound changes in U.S. investment thinking. In the rising markets of the 1950s and 1960s it paid to focus on stock selection. The market's broader moves were not great enough to warrant trying to get in and out at interim tops and bottoms. The greatest profits were made by investors with the ability to choose the right stocks. When the Dow Industrial Average fell to 570 in 1974, virtually all stocks declined. The choosers of individual stock lost, no matter how skillfully they had made their selections. Stunned by their losses, investors searched for answers and new techniques. Timing became fashionable. As often happens, the U.S. investment crowd applied logic to the challenge and then took the concepts to extremes. Instead of being satisfied with the conclusion that it would be wise to pay more attention to the overall market, the U.S. investment crowd tried to go to an opposite extreme and eliminate all stock selection. Index funds emerged as the "perfect" solution. An index fund is one that is constructed with a computer. The objective is not to buy representative stocks but to buy an exact slice of the market. The fund, with a large pool of capital, buys and sells stocks in an effort to have as mathematically precise a cross section of the market as possible. Investors can buy and sell the units in such funds with confidence that they are buying and selling "the market."

Index funds were not the end of the timing story. Stock market indexes were constructed and made available through options. By taking a position in options on a particular stock market index, an investor could try to profit from the market's rises and falls or hedge an existing stock portfolio. It is easy to get lost in the myriad of investment alternatives. The basic question of timing versus selection of individual stocks can be forgotten. The truth is that there are swings, cycles, in this regard just as there are in so many other aspects of the financial markets. There are times when individual stocks go their own way in a true market of stocks. Under other conditions a genuine stock market appears, and the herd of individual stocks rushes en masse, first in one direction and then the other.

The challenge is to understand the conditions that produce each kind of behavior. The greatest profits come from anticipating and adjusting your strategy as each new trend emerges. When the herd behavior dominates the markets, you can pay a heavy price by stubbornly sticking with individually selected issues. There are times when it pays to sell even those stocks that appear to have the best long-term promise. Likewise, market timers can find themselves sitting idly by waiting for an expected correction while the market refuses to follow their script and pushes individual stocks to new highs.

By 1982, at the beginning of a new, prolonged bull market, market timing, as you might guess, was at a zenith. Charts, graphs, and technical technique designed to help choose market tops and bottoms were the most popular approach to investing. The time was ripe for the selection of individual stocks to reemerge from the background. Buying individual stocks for their fundamental merit and holding them proved very rewarding over the next several years.

Flexibility is the key to stock market success. You have to be both a timer and a selector of individual stocks. Never let one approach or the other dominate your thinking. Select the stocks that you buy as if selection were 100 percent of the task. Watch the market as if timing were 100 percent of the challenge.

The representative stocks identified in chapter 3 are not cast in concrete. The selection will have to be changed from time to time to be sure that they are truly representative of the market. After a strong surge in the U.S. market, when the representative stocks have produced solid gains, you may want to broaden your participation in U.S. stocks. That will be especially true at times such as early 1986, when the U.S. market was up significantly but still lagged comfortably behind the world trend.

The U.S. stock market is the largest in the world and offers a wide variety of investment opportunities. American investors may find the representative-stock approach too confining. Investors who follow world trends to assist with their U.S. stock market performance surely will find that approach too confining. This raises the challenge of how to go about finding attractive individual stocks. There are several methods that work. Some investors concentrate on developing technologies. Others look for bargains, and still others apply trading techniques to the task of choosing which stocks to buy and which to sell. In the right hands all methods will work. The important thing is to try several and find out which is the most comfortable for you. Once you have a technique, apply it with discipline. Don't be a trader today and a bargain hunter tomorrow. Applying one investment discipline with consistency is the best route to substantial, long-term profits.

Confidence is the foundation for the kind of profits that can change your life. There is little profit in being too nervous to take meaningful positions. Anxiety can cause you to sell too soon. When any investor looks back over the years, one of the classic errors that appears is selling too soon. Who would have thought that American Airline's stock would rise from $9 in 1980 to $48 in 1985? Who could resist the temptation to sell at $18 or $20 along the way? Likewise, all investors live with the fear of holding on too long. Painful memories of markets like 1974 always lurk in the back of your mind. No one wants to be caught when the market takes its next steep plunge.

When the market is down, you have to have tools that will let you know it is time to buy. You also need tools that will give you confidence that the market will rise again and not stay down or go lower. Fear of another stock market crash like that of 1929 kept most individual investors out of the market in early 1982. Even after the bull market had advanced to 1,300 on the Dow, many watched and wondered if the crash would be next.

It is possible that the United States will ignore the lessons of the 1970s and 1980s. We might keep running our nation's fiscal and monetary policies as if the international dimension didn't count. The stock market could crash. It is also possible that the United States will find the route to a long period of economic prosperity. The stock market could go up and stay up for a long period of time.

Against this background of fundamental uncertainty and ever-changing market conditions you need new tools to help develop confidence, tools that will broaden your perspective.

Tool Number 1: The Dow in Swiss Francs

There is a major difference in the stock market before and after 1971. The difference is well known. Before 1971 the United States was on a form of official gold standard, and after 1971 it was not. It is also well recognized that the move away from gold was one of the most significant financial changes in decades. The amazing thing is that so few people take that change into account in their everyday economic and financial thinking.

Before 1971, U.S. financial assets such as stocks and bonds had the same value to an American as to a foreign investor. A foreign investor might have counted wealth in British pounds or German marks, but that didn't matter. Because of the gold standard, the value of the pound and the mark did not change much or often. As a practical matter, values remained stable from one country to another. After 1971, when paper dollars were separated from gold, that changed. Suddenly the dollar was free to fluctuate on world markets. A dollar could be worth four German marks in 1971 and two a few years later. A foreign investor had to begin taking the currency markets into account in assessing the value of holdings of U.S. stocks and bonds.

During the 1920s there was one variable, the price of financial assets such as stocks. The dollar was fixed. Any event, change of sentiment, or economic swing had to appear in stock prices because it couldn't appear in the value of the dollar. From 1921 to 1929 the Dow industrials rose from 64 to 381, a gain of 495 percent. The number 100 was, back then, in some ways similar to 1,000 in recent years. The Dow stood at 100 in 1920, fell to 64, and then recovered to 100 in 1922, where it remained until 1925. At that point, a great bull surge gathered its initial strength. The Dow leapt off from 100 in 1925 and did not stop until it more than tripled at 381 in the fall of 1929.

As the Dow rose, there was increasing concern about imported farm goods taking their market share away from U.S. farmers. Farming was to the U.S. economy in the 1920s as the auto industry was in the 1970s. Just as U.S. automakers lost their market share to imports in the 1970s, American farmers had lost their market share to imports in the 1920s. Congress was just as upset in the 1920s over farm imports as it was in the 1970s over auto imports. In the 1920s Congress enacted the Smoot-Hawley Tariff Act, and foreign investors became terrified. They feared that isolationism and protectionism would spread, causing an official devaluation of the dollar. They decided to take their financial assets home. They withdrew money from U.S. banks and sold U.S. stocks. That sudden wrenching of the capital markets came when stocks were vulnerable. All markets are vulnerable after a major upward move. The 1920s bull market had carried stocks to four times book value. U.S. stocks were particularly vulnerable. They could not withstand the outflow of foreign capital. Pyramid margin debt triggered margin calls, and the selling intensified until it brought about the Great Crash.

The bottom came in 1932 when the Dow stood at 41.2. Through it all the dollar never budged. Foreign investors only had to sell their stocks and then switch at official exchange rates into either their home currency or gold. We will never know what might have happened in the 1920s if the dollar had been officially and sharply devalued *before* the crash. Foreign investors might not have rushed out of the U.S. in the wake of huge losses on the currency. A decline in the dollar in the 1920s might have materially changed the situation, the crash might have been moderated, the depression might have been less severe. We will never know. The dollar was not devalued in the 1920s, and there was a stock market crash and depression. The financial markets took the full brunt of the problems in the 1920s.

That was not true in the 1970s. In 1971 the dollar was cut loose and allowed to fluctuate on world currency markets. Foreign investors were able to sell dollars independent of stocks, bonds, bank accounts, or real estate. There was a new route for financial energy to be dispersed. The

DOW JONES INDUSTRIALS IN SWISS FRANCS

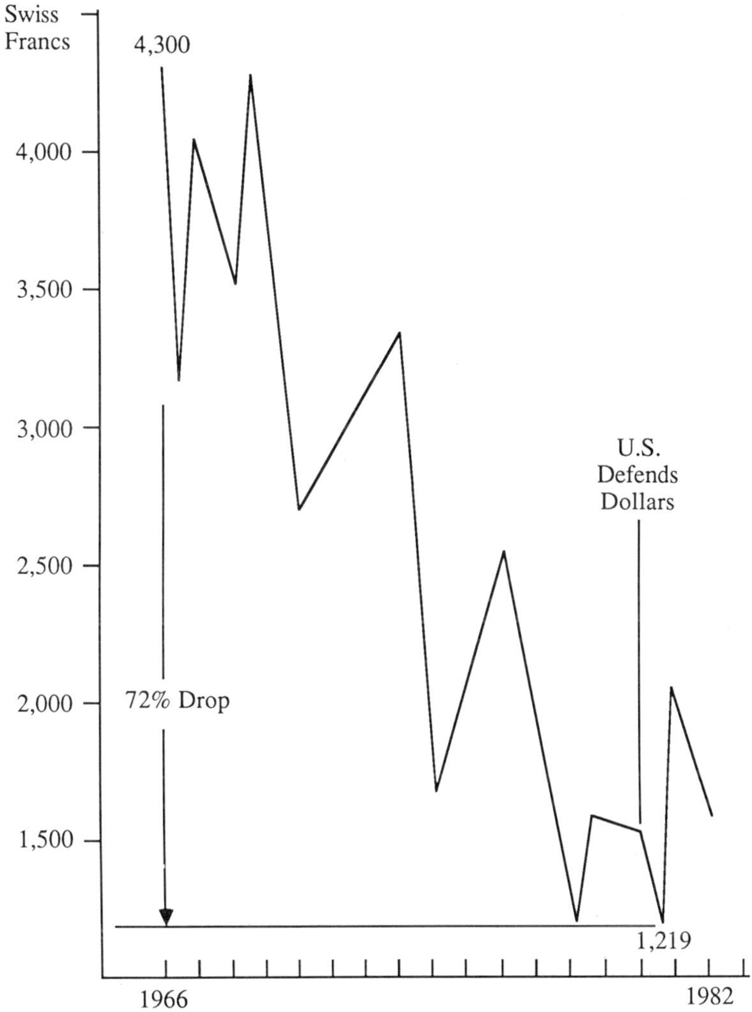

Source: Compiled by the author.

true state of world financial conditions was expressed in both the currency and financial markets. If you looked only at U.S. stock prices, you missed half the story. An accurate view of the U.S. stock market could only be obtained by including the dollar in the analysis.

An effective way of including the dollar in an analysis of the stock market is by expressing the U.S. Dow Jones Industrial Average in terms of a foreign currency, the best choice being the Swiss franc. When this is done the picture of the U.S. stock market in the 1970s changes dramatically. As can be seen from the chart on page 189, the Dow in Swiss francs plunged in the 1970s. Instead of a market going nowhere, falling in 1974 and then recovering, we see

DOW INDUSTRIALS
50 YEARS AGO

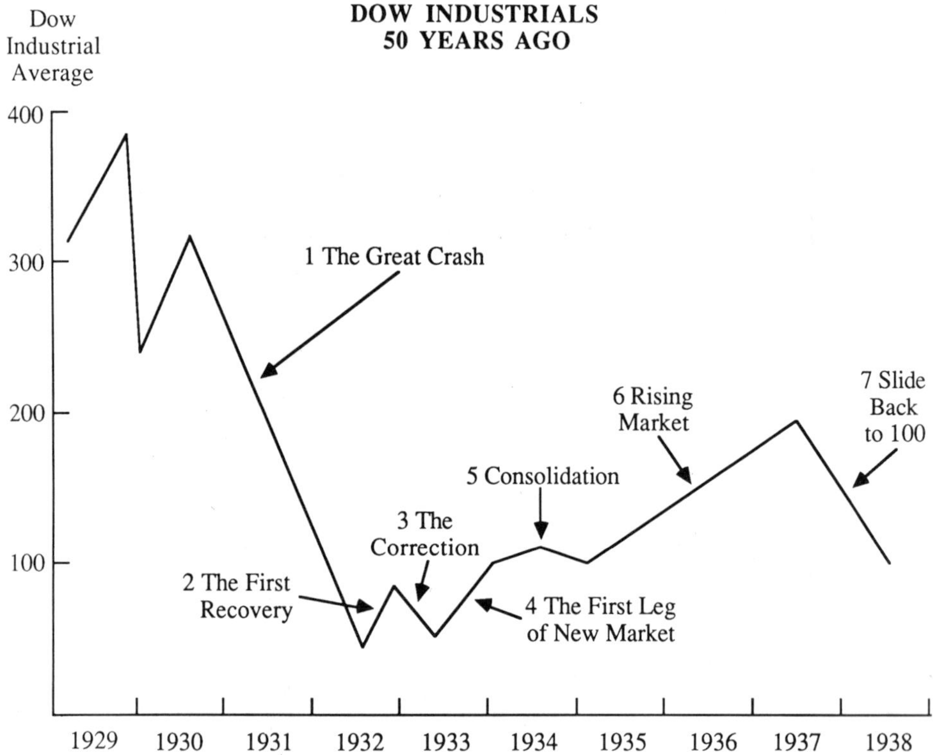

Source: Compiled by the author.

a genuine stock market crash similar to the great crash of 1929–1932. The similarity doesn't stop there. The chart on page 190 shows the Dow's 1929 collapse and the jagged recovery that followed. The following chart shows the Dow in Swiss francs through 1979 and into the early 1980s. By 1983 it was clear that the old history of the 1920s and 1930s was being repeated, but with a significant difference. To see what was happening in the 1970s and 1980s you had to include the dollar in the analysis. Once that step was taken, the U.S. stock market began to show familiar patterns. History had adapted to the new conditions in the

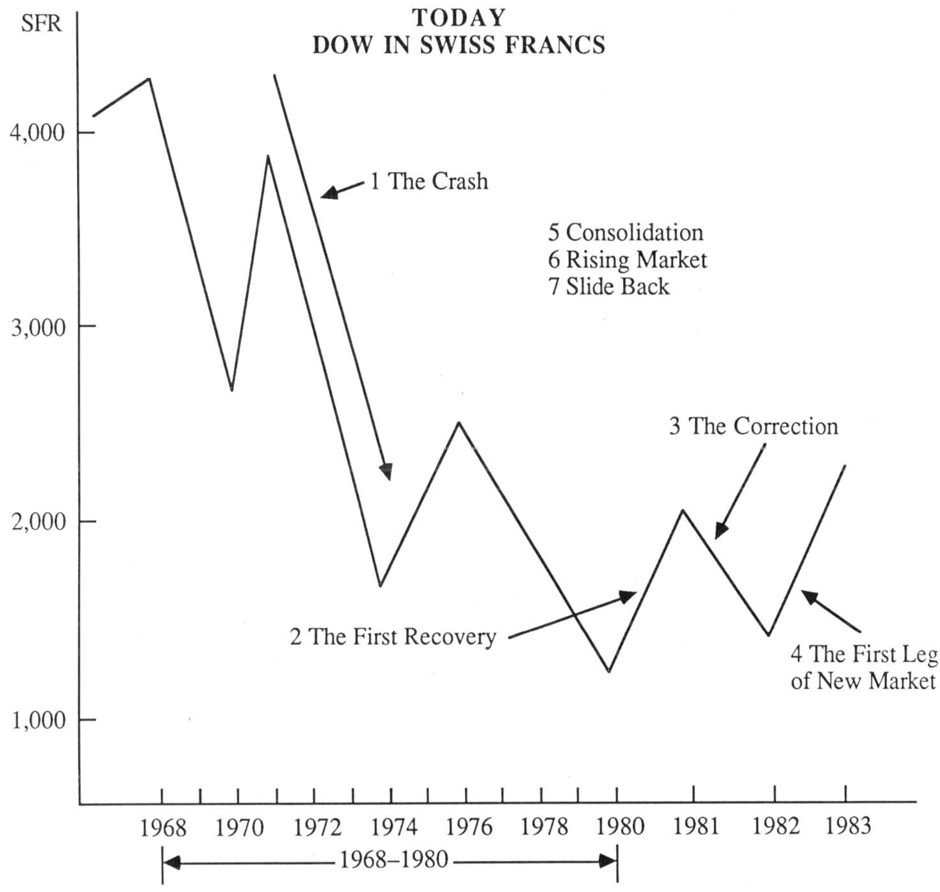

Source: Compiled by the author.

currency markets, but otherwise it was being repeated. After a 72 percent drop, the Dow in Swiss francs first recovered, then corrected, and then began a new upward leg, just as it had in the 1930s.

Time will tell how long the old patterns will keep being repeated. In the 1930s the U.S. economy ran into the early developments leading up to World War II. In 1937, as war clouds were gathering in Europe, the U.S. stock market stalled and then fell back to 100 on the Dow. This time there are no war clouds in Europe. In fact, the economies of Europe were gathering strength even as the U.S. Dow roared over 1,600. It is possible, on the one hand, that the United States will find the path to a longer period of prosperity. On the other hand, the nation may run out of economic fuel just as it did in the 1930s. The answer, for investors, is to be a careful observer of actual conditions, taking advantage of opportunities as they arise.

Many investors were disappointed that the crash of 1979 did not seem to take place on schedule. They had expected the normal Dow, the one they were used to seeing in the paper every day, to collapse in 1979 exactly as it had in 1929. They continued to live in fear of a crash well into the 1980s. They would have been far better off if they had looked at the Dow through the eyes of foreign investors. The Dow in Swiss francs told the story of the crash of 1979 eloquently.

The first obvious benefit of combining the U.S. stock market and the dollar in Swiss francs is to obtain a clearer picture of the actual condition of the U.S. stock market. In one chart you can see the internal and external value of U.S. stocks combined. All the complexities of inflation, interest rates, and currency markets appear in a single chart. No stock market decision should be made without first looking at the Dow in Swiss francs.

A Practical Everyday Market Tool

The Dow in Swiss francs during the 1970s shows how different a picture can result when the dollar is included. That isn't always true. At times the Dow in Swiss francs and the Dow in dollars will march hand-in-hand. When the dollar is stable, the two will follow parallel paths. No news can be valuable news. When the dollar is stable, you will be immediately alerted to that favorable condition by the chart of the Dow in Swiss francs. Since the only good dollar is a stable dollar, similar patterns for both charts can be positive both for the U.S. stock market and for the economy.

At other times the two charts will go in different directions. The dollar is a messenger of financial truth. A weak dollar can precede rising U.S. inflation or rising U.S. interest rates or both. When the U.S. stock market languishes or does not rise as the dollar weakens, the chart of the Dow in Swiss francs will show a decidedly downward trend. The decline will be steeper in the case of the Dow in Swiss francs. In fact, the normal Dow can show a relatively flat chart even as the early clouds of trouble are gathering. When the dollar and U.S. stocks are combined, you can often get an early warning of a coming U.S. stock market slump.

To a degree, stocks are a good hedge against inflation. Corporations are able to manage their costs and prices to assure profits. When inflation rises too high, however, and too fast, corporations are not able to keep pace. Costs rise faster than revenues, and stocks become vulnerable. A sinking dollar is an early warning signal of potentially destructive future inflation. U.S. corporate profits may hold for a while. U.S. stock prices can be remarkably firm for a long time. The normal Dow may not give warning of a pending stock market slide. The Dow in Swiss francs, by combining the performance of both U.S. stocks and the dollar, is more likely to give you the early warning that you need.

The Dow in Swiss francs does much of the work for you. By combining the dollar and stock prices you are quickly and simply informed when the situation has passed reasonable limits. The Dow in Swiss francs will tumble if the dollar becomes so weak that unacceptable inflation and interest rates lie ahead. Conversely, the Dow in Swiss francs will provide an early "all clear" signal when the inflation and interest rate dangers are over.

The chart on page 195 shows the normal Dow compared to the Dow in Swiss francs in 1982. For the first eight months, the normal Dow was weak and growing weaker. In August, the normal Dow fell below the earlier low, and many stock market technicians sounded the alarm. They warned of a coming U.S. stock market plunge. Instead, the U.S. stock market, on a burst of foreign buying, exploded on the up side, catching most investors completely off guard. A new, long-term bull stock market had begun.

The Dow in Swiss francs showed a different pattern. In terms of Swiss francs the Dow did not fall back below the earlier low. Instead, it advanced through June and July, providing two months' early warning of the coming bull market.

When the normal Dow and the Dow in Swiss francs show different patterns, that is a signal for closer study. Usually, as in 1982, the Swiss franc Dow will be showing the correct pattern. At the least, the Swiss franc Dow will give you a basis for not following the crowd. Watching the Dow in Swiss francs in 1982 was one of the best strategies. As it became increasingly popular to be bearish and sell stocks, the Swiss franc chart pointed in the opposite direction. The Swiss franc chart alone might not have been enough to convince you that it was time to buy U.S. stocks in the summer of 1982. The power of the crowd should not be underestimated. In the summer of 1982 the bearish, gloomy stock market scene was very convincing. The Swiss franc chart, however, would at least have formed the basis for doubting the crowd's wisdom. Once the market moved in August, you would have been alert and prepared. You

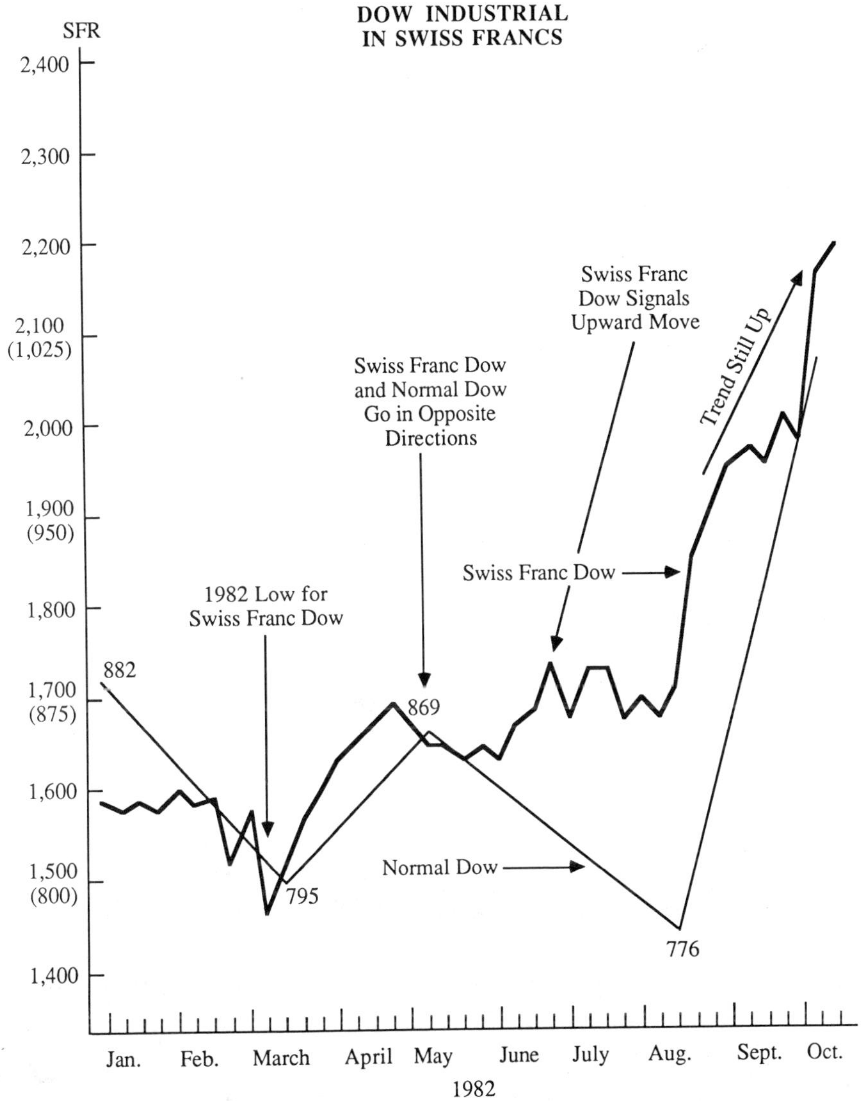

Source: Compiled by the author.

might not have bought at the bottom, but you probably would have been among the first to buy into what became a powerful, new bull market.

The Dow in Swiss francs also gave an early warning at the market bottom in 1980. From an early 1980 low of 730 on the normal Dow, the U.S. stock market rose to 1,030 in 1981. As is so often the case, the bears were holding court as the turn approached. Every investor knows that it pays to be contrary, but it, nevertheless, is difficult to put contrary thinking to work in everyday practice. When the market is down, there are always too many good reasons for stocks to be down, and it is compelling to believe that they will sink even lower. You need a tool to help sort out the conflicting evidence and sharpen your personal contrary instincts. In early 1980, the Swiss franc Dow surged to a new high. The normal Dow showed only a weak and unconvincing uptrend. By May the Swiss franc Dow had fallen back and then reversed. The normal Dow did not show a similar reversal until one month later. The combination of the strong early surge and early reversal shown by the Swiss franc Dow gave an early warning of the strong market to come.

The Fundamentals behind the Dow in Swiss Francs

A long-standing stock market rule is that falling interest rates are positive for stock prices while rising interest rates are negative. That is basically correct. The interest rate connection, however, is indirect. The direct connection is to growth in the money supply. When the money supply is growing at a vigorous pace, stock prices will rise. When the money supply is inadequate, stock prices will decline. That is true not only for U.S. stocks but also for stock markets all around the world. One of the best things to watch in assessing the outlook for stocks is growth in the money supply.

The problem is that watching the money supply in the United States has become complex. The figures published by the Federal Reserve are essentially domestic. They do not, for example, take full account of Eurodollars. Since its birth in the 1950s, the Eurodollar market has grown to significant proportions. The billions in Eurodollars are like an external or second supply of dollars. It is a simplification, but a useful one, to look at the United States as if there were two money supplies, one outside the country and one inside. In the 1970s, when the internal money supply was growing at 10 percent a year, the external money supply was growing at more than 20 percent. That is one reason the dollar was so weak and why the United States was so slow in reacting to the inflation threat. Watching only the domestic money supply did not tell the whole story. Money growth at home of 10 percent did not appear excessive. The 20 percent growth in Eurodollars on top of the 10 percent domestic growth, however, was extremely inflationary.

Conversely, in the early 1980s, the growth in the external money supply dropped to next to nothing, while the domestic figures were showing growth considered to be excessive. For a quarter or two in 1983, the domestic money-supply figures showed growth of 15 to 20 percent. The Federal Reserve's alarm bells rang and monetary policy was tightened. Later, in 1984 it became clear that the tightening had been a mistake.

The 1983 spurt in the domestic money figures remained a mystery for many. The monetarists had warned that the "clearly excessive" money growth would mean higher inflation in 1984. But the expected inflation did not appear. If the monetarists had been able to take proper account of the Eurodollar market, they might have had more accurate inflation expectations. If the Eurodollar market had not been underestimated, the U.S. economy might have been spared the consequences of the Fed's tight money policy.

This is not to say that the economists at the Fed or in private businesses don't know about Eurodollars. They do. But watching the U.S. money supply has become so complex that even the best-informed and best-educated economists can make terrible mistakes.

Obviously, investors who want to avoid confusion and error should study the external money supply, or Eurodollar market, as well as the published domestic statistics. The problem is that the Eurodollar markets are not as well regulated as the domestic U.S. money markets. The kind of figures that would help investors are not available. You have to look at the evidence, the markets, and draw your own conclusions about the underlying state of the money-supply figures. When the dollar is surging, you can feel comfortable with a conclusion that there is a shortage of dollars and that the growth of external money is inadequate. Under those circumstances, the domestic money-supply figures must be tempered. For example, when the headlines were full of reports of a threatening surge in the U.S. money supply (as they were in late 1982 and early 1983) but the dollar was strong, you would take the warnings with a grain of salt. The strong dollar would point to a conclusion that the domestic money figures were overstating the true state of money-supply affairs. Conversely, when the dollar is weak, there is a presumption that the domestic money-supply figures are understating the total growth. Watching the dollar as well as the domestic money-supply figures will give you a much more complete picture of money-supply growth in the United States. When the true, total money supply is expanding at a reasonable rate, you can expect higher stock prices. When growth is excessive, you can expect higher inflation and eventually higher interest rates and lower stock prices. Conversely, inadequate total money-supply growth is negative for stock prices but often leads to a later expansion and subsequent upswing in the stock market.

Money-supply watching takes practice and study. An easier way to "compute" all the complex international money-supply data and apply them to the U.S. stock market is through the Dow in Swiss francs. By combining the stock market and the dollar, you automatically include both domestic and international financial forces. The Dow in Swiss francs won't satisfy an economist's need for precise statistics, but it will act as a usable proxy for investors. Watching the Dow in Swiss francs is far easier than trying to collect data on the money supply, interest rates, and currency markets. You may never fully understand the Eurocurrency markets or why the money supply expands as it does. You don't have to. If you can learn to "read" the markets, you don't need to know the why of every economic principle. Reading the markets isn't new. Investors have been doing that for decades. Reading the entire market, seeing the U.S. stock market through foreign eyes as well as in the usual domestic way, will add to your base of important information.

The Dow in Swiss francs isn't published in the newspapers. You won't find it in popular chart books either. In fact, you may never have seen such a chart before. That is both good and bad news. The good news is that not many investors are using this new tool. That means you will have an advantage, which is important in modern competitive markets. The better tools frequently are those that are used by few investors. The bad news is that you have to do your own homework.

Some investors like keeping data and making charts. If you have a computer, the task is much easier. Others abhor the process of plotting and calculating. If you don't have the time or inclination to draw your own charts, don't give up hope. There are two things you can do. First is to find a publisher who does provide the charts, and second is to apply the broad principles of the tool without charts.

There are charts available of the dollar versus the Swiss franc and also charts of the Dow Jones Industrial Average. Just put the two close together and look at them. If both the dollar and the Dow are rising you know you have a very strong Dow in Swiss francs. If both are falling, you have a weak Dow in Swiss francs. When they go in opposite directions, you want to "see" which chart is winning the race. When the dollar chart is winning, that is the one to heed. With a little practice you will be able to construct a picture of the Dow in Swiss francs without having to go through the exercise of actually doing the plotting. For those times when you are not sure your observations are correct you can always check by drawing an occasional chart.

Whether you draw careful and meticulous charts or use the comparative method, you will benefit. A new dimension will be added to your perception of the U.S. stock market. You will begin to see the effects of the dollar on the behavior of U.S. stock prices. The chances of your getting caught by an unpleasant surprise or missing a major opportunity will be reduced. You will be among the few who see the U.S. stock market from two sides. You will understand how American investors view their own market. And in addition you will know how the U.S. stock market appears to a foreign investor.

The latter view has grown ever more important since the early 1970s. Foreign investors have become an increasingly significant factor in determining the direction of the U.S. stock market.

Foreign Investors and the U.S. Stock Market

The major changes that swept the world's financial markets in the 1970s and 1980s altered the character of the U.S. stock market. For the first time in decades foreign investors became a force to be reckoned with in the U.S. financial world.

For example, British investors have been leaders in diversifying assets in markets around the world. From £12 billion in 1979, overseas investment expanded to £58 billion in 1984. By the end of that year, British overseas holdings of stocks and bonds totaled the equivalent of $84 billion, rivaling the $85 billion of foreign stocks held by U.S. investors. The British have become a powerful international investment force. Their impact has been felt in the United States. In 1984, when many U.S. investors shunned long-term bonds out of fear of higher interest rates, British investors bought $8.5 billion in bonds. There is little doubt that the British purchase, which persisted month after month right through 1985, had an impact on the U.S. bond market and the level of U.S. interest rates. Those experts who had so confidently predicted higher U.S. interest rates and lower U.S. bond prices were amazed at the "mysterious" strength of the U.S. bond market. When long-term U.S. government bonds rose to the point that interest rates fell below 9 percent, the pundits of gloom were hard to find. They had failed to take into account the power of foreign buying and had missed an entire interest-rate trend.

By the end of 1984 foreign holdings of U.S. securities totaled $155 billion and were rising. That is a sum large enough to move markets.

When you pick up the newspapers and check stock prices, you no longer know who is buying and who is selling. The motives of an investor in Germany, Japan, or Britain could be very different from those of an American investor. You may think that stocks should go up or down, but they may do the opposite as foreign investors increase or liquidate their U.S. stock holdings. Foreign investors may find the dollar too risky or see a better opportunity in another market or simply have different ideas about how to manage money. No matter what their motives, foreign investors have become a significant factor in determining both the level and the direction of the U.S. stock and bond markets.

In 1982, the Dow Jones Industrial Stock Average sank for eight months. In August there was a sudden and explosive upward move. It was no coincidence that the rise came on a surge of foreign buying. For a long time there had been a growing sense that U.S. stocks were too cheap. But American investors, individual and institutional alike, sat waiting for someone else to make the first move. Once foreign buying moved stock prices higher, there was an institutional stampede to buy. Institutions live or die based on relative performance figures. Being left out of a bull market can be just as devastating, in terms of lost clients, as losing money through poor selections. The institutions with the best records attract the largest number of new clients. Ironically, it was this same performance drive that kept the institutions out of the market earlier in 1982. No one could afford to be first. Interest rates were too high. If you bought stocks and had to wait months for the market to move, you would fall behind. The other institution with cash at high interest rates would move ahead. Someone else, other than the U.S. institutions, had to make the first move. It could have been individual U.S. investors or foreign investors. In 1982 it was foreign investors.

In September 1984 there was a virtual buyers' strike in the U.S. bond market. Institutions feared higher interest rates and would not buy bonds, not even U.S. government bonds. The federal government persisted in trying to sell fixed-rate, long-term bonds as if there were no problem. At one point the dealers and brokers were faced with a near crisis. They held bonds that they could not sell, and the government was ready to sell more. Then almost mysteriously the crisis passed. The bond market did not collapse. Interest rates did not rise. Several months later when the official government statistics were released, it became known that foreign investors had purchased $1.421 billion in U.S. bonds that month. Foreign buying had prevented a crisis in the U.S. bond markets. The foreign investors were right. By February 1986 when interest rates on U.S. government bonds fell below 9 percent, they had enormous capital gains and had enjoyed high interest rates in the meanwhile. Not only had the different view from overseas prevented a bond market catastrophe, it had provided its beneficiaries with substantial profits.

Foreign investors are not charitable, and they don't have any special insight or foresight that allows them to profit at the expense of U.S. investors. They simply act in their own personal interests just as U.S. investors do. The difference is that they operate from a broader perspective. They have been through wars, and lost. They have experienced the catastrophes that we worry about. They look at the dollar as "another currency." And they compare one market to another. They have earned huge gains in U.S. stocks and bonds. They bought when U.S. investors were selling.

The British pound had been in a steep decline in 1984. British investors were selling pounds and buying dollars because that was a logical strategy for any U.K.-based portfolio. High U.S. interest rates offered an attractive opportunity for profit if the dollar strengthened or if U.S. interest rates declined. In September 1984 the U.S. reluctance to buy bonds raised the level of U.S. interest rates to 12 to 13 percent. At that level there was little risk for a U.K. investor. If the dollar fell, it would be because U.S. interest rates declined. Lower interest rates would lift bond prices, and the British investor would have a profit on the bond to offset any loss on the currency. If U.S. interest rates had gone higher, as so many U.S. investors wrongly feared, the dollar would have risen, offsetting any loss on the bonds. High-yielding U.S. bonds were an excellent hedge for British investors in the fall of 1984. That fact had not been taken into account by the economists and market experts who had predicted with such confidence that U.S. interest rates would climb. Even long after their forecasts had been proven wrong by the market, few looked back to study the situation. Few ever recognized that foreign buying had come into the U.S. market at just the right moment.

Popular forecasts at the time took no account of the foreign perspective. The pundits in Washington and New York based their erroneous forecasts exclusively on domestic U.S. activity. In the 1960s and early 1970s, there was no reason to pay attention to foreign investors. Their buying and selling of U.S. stocks and bonds was small compared to that of U.S. institutional and individual investors. Conventional analysis was all that any investor needed. By the late 1970s, however, it was clear that things had changed. Americans found it ever more difficult to cope with volatile markets. The markets seemed to have a life of their own. Old and trusted techniques and methods failed. Confusion abounded. Foreign investors had arrived on the American scene and become a force large enough to produce unexpected twists and turns in U.S. stock prices.

Initially the buying came from the oil-rich sheiks of OPEC. Rising oil prices transferred billions of dollars from the United States to oil producers in the Middle East. Several OPEC countries had no debt, primitive economies, and low production costs. Rising oil revenues quickly became giant surpluses available for investment. American investors were unimpressed. American bankers and brokers visited the deserts of OPEC countries and found that most were not sophisticated investors. Some had investment experience, but the majority liked bank accounts and fixed income. The idea that foreign investors would soon have a significant influence on the direction of U.S. markets seemed ridiculous at that time. How could these newly rich people from so far away have an impact on sophisticated U.S. markets? When part of the OPEC billions began to come back to the United States in the form of stock buying, analysts did take notice. They completely misinterpreted the OPEC phenomenon, however. Some analysts went so far as to forecast a collapse in U.S. stocks when the OPEC surpluses ran out and oil prices fell. In 1985 and 1986 when the OPEC surpluses were gone and oil prices tumbled, U.S. stocks surged to new record highs. The analysts were right that the OPEC oil profits wouldn't last forever. They were even right to worry about falling oil prices. But when it came to foreign investment in U.S. stocks and the consequences for U.S. stock prices, they were completely wrong. The OPEC surpluses were a trigger that brought down exchange-control barriers. Capital began to flow freely from one market to another. Foreign investment activity in the U.S. markets grew, even as the OPEC surpluses diminished.

The U.S. Stock Market, Never the Same Again

Stock prices in the United States are now pushed and pulled by three powerful groups of investors:

1. Individual American investors
2. U.S. institutional investors
3. Foreign investors

In 1983, total foreign buying and selling of U.S. stocks rose above $100 billion for the first time in history. Foreign activity remained at those lofty levels in 1984 and 1985, solid evidence that foreign involvement is not a passing phenomenon.

Foreign buying can ignite a stock market rise or prevent a crash even when U.S. investors are pessimistic. Conversely, foreign selling can limit any move upward. When foreign and domestic investors are on the same side, buying or selling together, the results are nothing short of spectacular.

Foreign Selling: A Significant Factor in the Great Crash of 1929

The straw that broke the back of the rising U.S. stock market in 1929 was foreign selling. In those unregulated, freewheeling days, money moved easily and quickly from one market to another. As the day of the Great Crash approached, Congress was preoccupied with protectionism and finally passed the Smoot-Hawley Tariff Act, a restrictive trade law. Foreign investors were quick to react. They feared that the next step would be a massive devaluation of the dollar. They wanted to be out of the dollar before it tumbled. In those days there were no free currency markets and no opportunities to hedge. The only way out of the dollar was to withdraw funds from U.S. banks, to sell stocks and bonds, and to take the proceeds home. The sudden outflow of capital sent interest rates soaring and stocks plunging.

On March 25, 1929, the *New York Times* headlined: "Stocks Break Heavily as Money Soars to 14%." John Kenneth Galbraith, in his book *The Great Crash,* identified the cause of spiraling interest rates. He wrote that money tightened "largely as a result of the withdrawal of funds by foreigners."

In 1929, the Dow had been rising for eight years. It opened in 1921 at 72. By March of 1929, it had reached more than 300. It was at that point that the *New York Times* reported the withdrawal of funds by foreigners. Those who understood the significance of that news and recognized the danger were able to sell near the top. Even those who missed the first opportunity had a second chance.

On October 28, 1929, the Dow closed at 260, well down from the peak but far above the ultimate low of 41. As the stock market broke, the *Times* reported: "Selling by Europeans and Mob Psychology Big Factors in Second Big Break." Investors who followed in the footsteps of foreign investors in 1929 were spared the worst of the financial devastation in the Great Crash.

The same thing *could* happen again. Foreign investors hold more than 15 percent of all U.S. government bonds. Foreign holdings of U.S. common stocks exceed $40 billion. In 1985 alone, foreign holdings of U.S. bonds grew by more than $30 billion. If foreign investors suddenly sold their U.S. stocks and bonds, a panic and crash could develop. The U.S. stock market could soar to unsustainable heights. The entire market could become vulnerable. Congress could do something foolish. It wouldn't be exactly the same as 1929. History never repeats itself in a precise duplication. Congress might, for example, enact a law requiring that foreign investors register all their U.S. holdings. Such a bill has been proposed at least once. Foreign investors will not register. They fear the long reach of government more than they are attracted by a profit opportunity. It is conceivable that onerous laws could chase foreign investors out of the U.S. markets again, just as they did in 1929. If such a law were passed when the U.S. markets were high, foreign investors would have an opportunity to flee the U.S. markets with substantial profits in anticipation of undesirable U.S. legislation. It could all come together again—a high stock market and a sudden outflow of foreign capital.

If there is one single reason for watching foreign activity in the U.S. markets, it is for insurance against another disastrous market crash. There are other compelling reasons. Watching activity by foreign investors in U.S. markets can help to strip away confusion, deepen your understanding of the underlying forces that drive stocks higher and lower, and improve your market timing.

The Never-Ending Tug-of-War between Optimists and Pessimists

A seasoned professional stock trader is frequently asked this question, "Why did that stock go up (or down)?" He always answers, "There were more buyers than sellers (or vice versa)." He deliberately leaves the question of why unanswered. He simply states the fact of everyday market activity. For every buyer there must be a seller. Stocks rise or fall "on the margin." If there are more buyers, the sellers quickly sense an opportunity to raise their asking price. If the buyers keep buying, the price will keep rising. But it is always a fragile situation that can change at any time.

Optimism and pessimism are infectious. When a stock or an entire market is rising, it is because the optimists hold the margin of influence. People are more willing to believe in the positives than the negatives. Conversely, a sinking market means that pessimism is ruling the minds of investors.

The answer given by that trader always seems to grate on the nerves of the questioners. They feel cheated, as if he had a great secret truth that he wouldn't reveal. They are never satisfied with the simple facts. That trader and his answer are actually far more helpful than all the misleading but more satisfying explanations of why the market does what it does.

The first step in successful stock market investing is to be constantly and acutely aware of the basics. Are there more buyers or sellers? That is always the right starting point. You want to know who is winning the tug-of-war between the pessimists and optimists. Then you want to look at the three groups of investors and think about tomorrow. How are individual investors acting today? What are they likely to do tomorrow? What about the institutions? Are they just trading or genuinely apprehensive? What will it take to turn the institutions into optimists? And foreign investors, are they buying or selling?

The amazing thing is that there is so little attention paid to foreign investors. The federal government keeps statistics. The problem is that they are published two months late. But you can find out what foreign investors were doing two months ago by looking at the figures in the monthly bulletin published by the Federal Reserve. Few investors even do that. Fewer still look at the figures with a sense of what they mean. Some of the major brokerage firms, such as Merrill Lynch and Brown Brothers, also keep track of foreign investors. They have huge custody departments and act as custodian for billions in foreign holdings of U.S. stocks. When foreign investors are buying or selling, they know because they are receiving the instructions on what to do with the stocks they hold. The problem for an individual investor is that the information from the big brokers is too expensive. In one instance the information is part of a package that costs $25,000 a year.

Tool Number 2: The First-Hour Volume Indicator

There is a practical solution to the challenge of watching foreign investors in the U.S. stock market. I call the technique the "First-Hour Volume Indicator." It was developed while I was living in Switzerland, working in the investment business. The indicator is based on the fact that foreign orders tend to be concentrated in the first hour of trading in New York. By watching activity on the New York Stock Exchange during the first hour, it is possible to tell what foreign investors are doing on a day-to-day basis.

There is a significant time difference between New York

and foreign financial centers. For example, when New York opens, European traders are ready to go home for the evening. Foreign traders, like all others, like to be at their desks when orders are executed. They want to be sure that they buy or sell at a good price. As a practical matter this means that foreign orders for U.S. stocks are bunched during the first hour of trading.

At one time I had responsibility for a large investment department in Europe. In my first days on the job I was dismayed to find the traders going home when the New York Stock Exchange was just opening. I naively thought that European traders would slavishly stay at their desks long into the night to stay in touch with the "action" in New York.

Those European traders gave me an education. They weren't just going home for the evening because it was quitting time. They were disciplined, knowledgeable, international investors. They had studied the New York and other world markets in great detail. They knew that more often than not it made little difference if a trade was executed during the first hour or later in the trading day. On those few occasions when the trading in New York was particularly hectic or when their trades were particularly difficult, they would stay as late as necessary to get the job done. But ordinarily they could trade during the opening hour and then go home for a peaceful supper. They had a perspective broader than mine. They were watching trades in markets all around the world. If they stayed at their desks until all markets were closed, they would, literally, never sleep. International traders have to develop techniques and disciplines to cope with the world's time zones.

The most important thing was to get the order executed quickly and at a reasonable price. That could usually be done in the opening hour. On occasion they would use limit orders or transfer the responsibility to a colleague in the United States. But the bulk of the trading was done in the first hour and with above-average results.

The First-Hour Volume Indicator was initially based solely on that practical experience. Later, a poll was taken of twenty-five large European institutional traders and European offices of eight U.S. brokers. Of the thirty-three firms, fifteen said they placed most of their orders before the opening in New York for execution when the market opened. Six said they waited for the opening and then placed their orders. Some said they insist on execution at the opening price. There is no doubt that tired European traders, anxious to leave for the day, execute as many trades as possible during the opening hour.

That doesn't mean that all foreign trades are executed during the first hour. Some traders use limit orders that could be executed at any time during the day. Others feel that the first hour is not representative of the day's activity and insist that orders be executed later in the day.

In the Far East, Tokyo in particular, the time difference is so great that there is no practical time window at all. Orders for investors in the Far East are executed by their brokers in Europe or the United States.

If all foreign orders were executed during the first hour, it would be easy to keep track of foreign activity. There would be no need for my First-Hour Volume Indicator.

The indicator is not a perfect statistical measure of foreign activity. Neither the government nor economists would dare rely on such a proxy in their analysis of foreign activity. That makes it all the more attractive. It is a useful tool or proxy for watching foreign activity in the U.S. stock market. Understanding the principles involved will enable you to know what foreign investors are doing on a day-to-day or week-to-week basis. With that information you will be among the few that know how buying and selling breaks down into the three major investor groups. You will be able to buy with confidence when others are selling and sell when the market reaches an unsustainable peak.

Because financial markets, including the U.S. stock market, have become so international there is discussion of keeping the New York Stock Exchange open twenty-four hours a day. That would allow investors in all corners of the globe to execute orders at their local convenience. It would not destroy the First-Hour Volume Indicator. Local investors are the dominant force in any market. The size of the United States means that this is especially true in New York. Successful trading demands being in tune with the local market. Unless Americans start staying up all night to trade stocks, the basic trading day will remain the same. The normal business hours in New York City will always determine the fundamental trading patterns on the New York Stock Exchange. Investors in Europe will still wait for the opening in New York to take the temperature of the U.S. stock market. The First-Hour Volume Indicator will continue to work even if the New York Exchange is open twenty-four hours a day.

In 1985 the New York Stock Exchange began opening one half hour earlier, at 9:30 A.M. That made little difference when it came to the First-Hour Volume Indicator. In fact, it seemed to increase the indicator's effectiveness. The earlier opening made it more convenient for European traders. They had one-half hour more of regular business hours to watch New York. The change made it a little more difficult for analysts like myself who had a long collection of statistics on the first hour from 10:00 A.M. to 11:00 A.M. The new first "hour" ran from 9:30 to 10:30, requiring an adjustment in the statistics to be sure that all the numbers remained comparable. For someone just starting to watch the first hour's trading the change makes no difference at all.

The principles of the indicator are:

1. When the first hour's volume rises significantly you presume that foreign investors are active.
2. As a check on whether the first hour's volume is significant, a daily percentage is calculated. When the volume rises and the first hour's trading is an above-average percent of the total for the day, the presumption of increased foreign activity is solid.
3. A rising market during an active first hour means that foreign investors are net buyers.
4. A falling market on above-average, first-hour volume means that foreign investors are net sellers.

It's that simple. You watch the first-hour volume. When it surges, take special notice. If the surge drives stock prices higher, foreign investors are buying. If the volume surge sends stock prices lower, foreign investors are selling.

A word of caution: Don't draw far-reaching conclusions from a single day's information. Collect observations and make judgments after looking at a full month's data.

A word of encouragement: The First-Hour Volume Indicator is not widely followed. By using this technique, you will have a competitive advantage over the investment crowd.

Watching foreign investors is commonplace in Japan, Germany, Britain, and many other countries. In other countries stock market analysts always want to know who is buying and who is selling. They regularly separate foreign activity from trades by local investors. In the United States many people still refuse to recognize the power of foreign investors. Some day that will change. When it does, there will be more precise data on foreign activity in the U.S. stock market. Then the First-Hour Volume Indicator will be less important. Meanwhile, it offers a practical solution to the challenge of watching the newest powerful force in the U.S. stock market.

Everyday Use of the First-Hour Volume Indicator

You can use the First-Hour Volume Indicator as a casual daily tool for watching the U.S. stock market or as a serious statistical study of foreign influence on U.S. stock prices. The choice is yours.

The starting point is the same either way. You begin by looking at the inside back page of the *Wall Street Journal.* There you will find a table entitled, "Breakdown of Trading in NYSE Stocks." Starting in 1985, the table provides trading figures by the half hour. Before the New York Stock Exchange began opening at 9:30 A.M. the table was hourly, making your task easier. Someday the exchange may revert to a 10:00 A.M. opening, and if it does the *Wall Street Journal* table will go back to being hourly. The table shows the trading for the previous day, the day prior to that, and a week before. Look at the figures for each half hour from 9:30 to 11:00. What you are looking for is an increase in volume. Sometimes there will be an enormous increase from one day to another. Those are the days you are waiting for. On days when the volume figure are more or less unchanged or decrease, pay no further attention. The ordinary day tells you nothing about foreign investors. The extraordinary day when trading volume increases tells you that foreign investors were active. The increase in volume is the signal.

When the alarm sounds, volume is up, look to the next table showing the hourly fluctuation for the Dow Jones Industrial Average. How did the market behave on the increased volume? Was the Dow up, down, or flat? If the market was up, then foreign investors were buying. If the market was down, they were selling. If the market was flat, they were buying and selling in about equal amounts.

The casual user of the First-Hour Volume Indicator need only watch for the spectacular days. There will be days when the volume during the first hour or hour and a half surges by 10, 15, or even 20 million shares. Those are the days that tell you the most about what foreign investors are doing. Keep a notebook or diary. Note the days when volume surges and whether the market was up or down. At the end of a month you will have a solid indication of what foreign investors have been doing in the U.S. stock market. A daily glance at the *Wall Street Journal,* a few notes, and you will know as much as the experts about this important group of investors.

If you prefer a more serious approach, you can keep a daily log of the volume, the market action, and your conclusions. You can, as a check, calculate the first hour's volume as a percentage of the day's total. When both the absolute volume level and the percentage rise, you can be sure that you have an exceptional day worth special note. The degree of detail you accumulate is a matter of available time and personal choice. For basic investment information the daily scan and a few notes will give you enough information to be well ahead of the investment crowd.

The Federal Reserve publishes a monthly bulletin; buried in the detail are statistics on foreign buying and selling of U.S. stocks and bonds. The figures can be used as a periodic check on the accuracy of your notes and conclusions.

Keeping an Open Mind

Investors, myself included, seem to have an above-average desire to find order in the markets. We love to discover rules and formulas that help make decisions. The quest for order and reason is important to a successful investment strategy, but it must be balanced with a fair amount of open mindedness. Stock market technicians, those followers of charts and graphs, refer to this attribute as "letting the market tell its own story."

Tools such as the First-Hour Volume Indicator lead to information, not to rigid rules and formulas. You have to put the information to good use.

Between 1972 and 1983, if you simply bought U.S. stocks when foreign investors were buying and sold when foreign buying declined, you would have increased your U.S. stock market profits by a significant amount. After eleven years there was a natural temptation to begin applying history as a rule for the future. It seemed easy. Just watch the First-Hour Volume Indicator; when it showed an increase in foreign buying, you jumped into the market. When the indicator showed foreign buying falling off, you sold. As with so many investment rules that are applied rigidly, that practice would have led to losses in 1984.

In 1984 foreign investors didn't just stop buying; they sold substantial amounts of U.S. stocks. The selling persisted through much of the entire year. Month after month foreign investors were net sellers. The U.S. stock market did not collapse. Instead, it gathered strength. The initial reaction of a follower of rules and formulas would have been, "Following foreign investors doesn't work any more." That would have been the wrong conclusion. Watching foreign investors and the U.S. stock market produced some of the most valuable information in a decade. The correct conclusion was that a fundamental change was developing. The apparent breach of the "rule" was not a breach at all. The market was telling a story of future profits to any one willing to listen.

During the 1970s foreign investors accumulated billions in U.S. stock holdings. There were few new issues. That meant that U.S. investors were net sellers. Americans were reducing their holdings of U.S. stocks by selling to foreign investors. That alone was important information. The tendency for U.S. investors to sell accounted for the long period when the Dow was not able to rise above 1,000. There simply weren't enough U.S. stock buyers to support a sustained rise in the U.S. market. Persistent net U.S. selling also explained the popularity of forecasts of stock market gloom. Americans were genuinely afraid of another devastating stock market crash and backed up that pessimism with sales of stocks. Foreign investors were less afraid. They were willing to buy U.S. stock market bargains. All the while that U.S. investors toyed with fantasies of a coming depression, foreign investors accumulated U.S. stocks.

Followers of popular market theories saw the long selling periods, the dismal stock market performance of the 1970s, and thought the gloom would last indefinitely. At least they felt confident that it would take a full-blown depression to cleanse the economy and make way for a new bull stock market. When the bull market exploded in August 1982, they were shocked. To them, the burst of buying that carried the Dow to a 1983 high near 1,300 was a total surprise. Even after that surge the warnings of a coming crash persisted. The idea of a Dow at 1,700 within four years was beyond belief.

Observers of foreign buying and selling were not only alerted to the 1982 bull market in time to profit, they were informed of a significant 1984 change in the very foundations of the U.S. stock market, one that warned of a stronger bull market ahead.

In 1984 foreign investors were net sellers of U.S. common stocks for the first time in years. The U.S. stock market did not collapse in the face of the selling; instead it held firmly and showed periodic signs of fresh strength. Foreign investors sold $2.924 billion in U.S. common stocks in 1984. That meant that U.S. investors, for the first time in ten years, were net buyers of their own stocks. That was a clear signal of new U.S. investor optimism. American investors did not step aside in 1984 when foreign investors sold. They did not wait for the Dow to drop back below 1,000 or fall to even lower lows. American investors, the same people who had been so pessimistic for so long, were willing to step up to the market and invest cash in U.S. stocks when the Dow was well over 1,000. This kind of watershed change in sentiment should have attracted attention. There should have been articles in all the popular financial papers trying to answer the question, Why had Americans changed? There were no articles. The question was not asked, never mind answered. Hardly anyone followed foreign investor activity in the U.S. stock market. Almost no one knew that a major change had occurred. The U.S. stock market had become a powder keg, ready to explode into one of the greatest bull markets in U.S. history, and few even recognized that basic attitudes had changed for the better.

You didn't have to have a computer. There was no need to keep meticulous, detailed journals on the First-Hour Volume Indicator. All that was necessary was the most basic awareness of the plain fact that after ten years of American selling and foreign buying, the tables had been reversed. Americans were buying stocks again.

Likewise, there was no need for studious economics or complex market forecasting. A little common sense was the best stock market tool. If foreign investors had been net buyers of substantial amounts of U.S. stocks for ten years, then there was reason to wonder if they might not eventually stop selling and begin buying again. The Dow in Swiss francs would have added some intriguing details to this stock market picture. It showed a market that crashed in the 1970s and recovered in the 1980s. By 1984 both the market and the dollar were up sharply, and foreign investors had huge profits on their U.S. stocks. Foreign selling in 1984, in view of the Swiss franc Dow, had all the earmarks of profit taking. Once the profit taking ran its course, foreign investors might become buyers again. This time foreign and U.S. investors would be on the same side for the first time. Buying by U.S. and foreign investors could have but one effect, a series of new record U.S. stock market highs.

The combination of the Dow in Swiss francs and the First-Hour Volume Indicator provided all the information needed to make a credible forecast of the coming U.S. bull market years in advance.

The same tools and ordinary common sense will keep you informed of the underlying tone of the U.S. stock market through good times and bad. If you worry about the possibility of a stock market crash, then remember 1929. The best defense in 1929 was watching foreign investors. The best insurance against another crash is being aware of who is buying and who is selling U.S. stocks.

Tool Number 3: The World Stock Trend

Stock markets and horse races do have something in common. They tend to run together on the same track, and the horse behind often catches up with the pack before the race is over. During a bull market you want to know which of the world's stock markets are ahead and which are behind.

U.S. Stocks vs. the World

By mid-1983 the U.S. stock market had pulled out ahead of the world stock trend that was ignited in 1982. Then, like a horse growing tired of leading the pack, U.S. stocks cooled and fell behind. By 1985 the U.S. stock market had fallen far behind the world trend. Not surprisingly, U.S. stocks surged ahead in a catch-up move that carried the Dow Jones Industrial Average to a long series of new record highs. By watching world stock markets and comparing the U.S. market to others, you will be able to monitor both the world trend and the U.S. market's relative position.

Comparing world stock markets is based on modern economic fundamentals. Investors communicate with one another through their transactions. The difference in the last half of the twentieth century is that those transactions are carried by electronic communications to every corner of the globe. Trends can start in one corner of the globe and spread, seemingly unannounced, to markets everywhere. There always has been a degree of interdependence from nation to nation. Today that interdependence includes currencies, money-supply management, inflation, and financial markets. The recession of 1982 affected all countries. Likewise, the recovery from the 1982 downtrend faltered until the major countries began to cooperate in efforts to stabilize currency markets, bring interest rates down, and accelerate real growth. The world has grown smaller, and no where is that more evident than in financial markets.

Buyers will bid up stocks in one market. When they become fully valued, the same investors will look for similar situations in other markets. Each nation's stock market has individual characteristics. Each can, within limits, go its own way. But within the fabric of a global economy and relative values, all major stock markets will move along the same general path. If the world trend is up, all the major markets will tend to rise. If the world trend is down, the majors will follow one another to lower levels.

The U.S. stock market can go its own way, be out of step and independent, but only for a while. When the U.S. stock market goes in one direction and other markets the opposite, one or the other must be right. Sooner or later they will come back together. Super U.S. stock market patriots like to believe that the United States is the only stock market that counts. They argue that U.S. stocks will always lead the way. That may have been true in the 1960s. It is far from true in the 1980s.

The U.S. stock market roared ahead in the early days of the 1982 bull market. By the end of 1982 Standard and Poor's Corporation Index (a broader measure of stock performance than the Dow Industrials) was up 13 percent. That was right in line with world market leaders such as Britain, whose stocks were up 16 percent, and well ahead of the laggards, such as Japan, up a modest 3 percent. By mid-1983 the U.S. stock market was showing signs of falling behind. In June Standard and Poor's Index was up 33 percent, while stocks in Germany and Britain were up 36 percent and 35 percent respectively. During the last half of 1983 and throughout 1984 the U.S. stock market moved sideways. The strong dollar depressed U.S. corporate profits, making investors nervous. The United States fell gradually farther and farther behind. At the end of 1984 the score was U.S. stocks up 36 percent, Japanese stocks up 50 percent, German stocks up 71 percent, British stocks up 82 percent, and French stocks up 192 percent.

At year end 1984 it was clear that the world and the United States were going in different stock market directions. Some investors, in effect, tried to argue that the United States was right and the world wrong. They didn't say it that way. Instead they made a case in favor of higher U.S. interest rates, a deficit crisis, and a fall in U.S. corporate profits. Those were the foundations of a conclusion that the U.S. stock market would fall, not rise in 1985. U.S. market observers did not compare the U.S. to other world markets. They ignored the booming bull market in the rest of the world. They didn't realize that they were arguing that the worldwide bull market was wrong, that other world stock markets were going to plunge, because that is the only way that those 1984 forecasts of a plunge in U.S. stock prices could become true. In the small modern world of finance it would not be possible to have a major market such as the United States first fall behind and then plunge without dragging the whole world of stock markets along in its wake. In 1984 the only logical approach was to look at the disparity between U.S. stocks and the world trend and wonder which would prove correct. Democratic principles suggested that the majority would prevail. Since all but the United States were advancing, the United States seemed the least likely choice for leadership. Even if the gloomy forecasts for U.S. stocks were correct, however, there would be ample warning. Before a decline in U.S. prices could carry very far, other world markets, so far ahead of the U.S. market, would come tumbling down. By watching all major world markets you would know how the trends were developing. You could buy U.S. stocks in 1984 with confidence.

In 1985 it became clear that the world trend had been setting the pace. Stocks in Europe and Asia moved vigorously higher, and the U.S. stock market rose sharply, breaking new record highs in late 1985 and early 1986.

To improve your U.S. stock market results you should always compare the United States to the other major world stock markets. Never make a U.S. stock market judgment without first looking at markets in Europe and Japan.

Don't look at all markets, however. Keep it simple; confine your international stock market watching to the major markets: Japan, Germany, Britain, and France. Start your comparisons at the last major turning point. For example, after the bull market of 1982 you would make all comparisons from 1982 forward. Prior to 1982 the measurements would have started in 1979, the previous major, world, financial turning point. Those turning points are like starting gates at the races. Whether up or down, a new trend has developed, and all major markets will continue advancing in the same general direction until the next major turning point. At the races you keep track of the horses race by race. In the world stock market, each new trend is a new race. What you want to know is the relative position of the U.S. stock market. All the major markets try to reach the finish line at the same time. When the U.S. market has fallen behind, you should look for a catch-up move. When it is ahead of the pack, you should expect U.S. stocks to slow down and wait for the rest.

Prior to 1980 calculating the relative performance of the major world stock markets would have been difficult. The U.S. financial press did not carry much information on foreign stock markets. That has changed. All the major papers—the *Wall Street Journal, Barron's,* and the *New York Times,* to mention three—now carry tables showing the performance of the major foreign stock markets. Take your pick. Simply be careful that you always compare apples to apples. Don't pick up one index for 1983 and another for 1984. Choose the indexes that you can find most easily. Make notes. The papers don't offer much historical data. If you don't keep the figures for last year or the year before, you will find yourself heading to a library to dig out the data. You don't have to write down the various market indexes every day. Once a month is almost too often. Quarterly, twice a year, or even once a year will do. As long as you have some data going back to the beginning of the last trend, you will be able to take the current temperature of the world's major markets. Investing always deals with the uncertainties of tomorrow. Yesterday and last year are only interesting insofar as they help with the decisions of today. Don't spend too much time gathering old data. Collect just enough to let you know where the markets stand today. Then march ahead with confidence.

The *Wall Street Journal* publishes the Capital International Country Indices on a daily basis. To save you having to go and dig through old copies of that respected daily financial paper, here are a few figures to get your notebook started:

	1/31/81	*1/31/82*	*1/31/83*	*1/31/84*	*1/31/85*	*1/31/86*
USA	116.5	134.2	156.4	158.0	201.1	201.7
ENGLAND	186.5	226.3	281.6	354.3	416.7	424.2
JAPAN	332.3	346.9	420.6	528.2	599.1	591.8
GERMANY	82.0	92.3	127.1	136.4	246.8	248.5
FRANCE	97.9	104.3	165.2	194.5	272.0	286.6

Note: All the indices started at 100 in 1970.
Source: Morgan Stanley Capital International Perspective, 1633 Broadway, New York, NY 10019, created these country indices in 1970.

A quick glance at this table shows that with the exception of Japanese stocks, the 1970s were hard on stocks in the industrialized countries. Rising oil prices imposed a burden on manufacturing. The Japanese were able to weather the storm of the 1970s better than most because of their relatively modern plants and a strong emphasis on exports. During the first five years of the 1980s, the performance gap began to narrow. Lower oil prices boosted all the major stock markets, while resistance to Japanese exports began to slow the pace of growth in Japan. As you can see from this note, watching stock markets around the world offers almost limitless opportunities to increase your awareness of underlying investment trends.

Selecting U.S. Stocks

Armed with these three tools—the Dow in Swiss francs, the First-Hour Volume Indicator, and international comparison—you will be able to improve your U.S. stock market profits no matter what method you use for selecting U.S. stocks.

You can invest solely in U.S. mutual funds, deciding when to be mostly in stocks and when to cut back, based on these three tools. You can also apply the representative-stock approach, buying preselected U.S. stocks when the U.S. market looks relatively attractive. For example, you could pick the following as representative of the U.S. market: Exxon, General Motors, IBM, General Electric, and Citicorp. They are all leading companies in their respective fields. When the three tools indicate that the U.S. stock market is attractive, you divide your funds into equal amounts and invest one portion in each stock. When the tools indicate that the U.S. stock market is vulnerable, you would sell all the stocks and wait for another buying opportunity or move the proceeds into another, more attractive market in another country.

Stock market futures and options have become popular. There are trading profits to be made by buying and selling these futures at the right time. Trading options or futures can help your overall stock market profits by allowing you to take highly leveraged positions with relatively small amounts of money. Trading can keep you alert and sharp. Trading based on these three tools will at least assure you of breaking even in the long run with a part-time trading practice. Because of the leverage inherent in the options themselves, there is always the chance that you will hit the timing more often right than wrong. In that event, these three tools will have assisted you in adding trading profits to your overall investment program.

No matter what your strategy—buying and holding, trading, picking contrary stocks, or buying growth and high-tech stocks—these three tools will be of immeasurable value in establishing a basic strategy, understanding the market, and increasing your confidence at the right time. It is one thing to have a good investment idea. It is another to have the confidence to invest a substantial amount in that idea. It is still a third to have the patience to wait until the investment matures bringing you substantial profits.

In early 1986 the Dow Jones Industrial Average broke above 1,600 and was incredibly strong. But hundreds of stocks were left languishing behind. Investors lost patience and began to sell the laggards and buy into the "hot" stocks. They were afraid that the bull market wouldn't last. They wanted to "cash in" and "get the profits while the getting was good." That created another opportunity for those few investors with the confidence to buy the lagging stocks. They were selling at low prices. When the bull market continued, those low-priced stocks would rise, providing the best future profits. But to buy low in 1986 you had to have the confidence that the bull market was real. That confidence came from having an international perspective.

When selecting stocks in any market, especially the U.S. stock market, use a shopper's approach. Every investor knows that profits follow from buying low and selling high. The challenge is in determining when a stock is low and when it is high. Shopping for stocks means comparing one group and one issue to another. Look at stock prices compared to book value, earnings, cash flow, and dividends. Look for groups that appear undervalued compared to the market. Within each group look for the low-priced individual stocks. Buying the lowest-price stock, or at least one of the lower-priced stocks in a group, is a strategy to generate above-average profits. There is ample evidence that there is less risk and more opportunity in low-priced rather than high-priced stocks.

Don't be a crowd follower, rushing along into every new investment trend, hoping to make a few dollars. Use these three tools to help you develop the kind of confidence that will set you on a course designed to change your life permanently. There is a world of opportunity. You can be far richer in the future than you dare to dream today. The difference is always confidence, and that comes from awareness, understanding, and a point of view different from that of the crowd.

Chapter 6

Developing a Personal Investment Strategy

WE ARE SURROUNDED by opportunities. There are daily reports in the financial pages of every newspaper on how you could have made a killing *yesterday*. With hindsight it is easy to see what you could have done to be rich today. That is a source of encouragement. At least you know that it is possible to become rich.

Some people seem to have a knack for choosing the right investments today for profits tomorrow. Others look back, count their losses, and wonder if they will ever get it right. Most willingly admit that they wouldn't mind being rich, but they refuse to take command of their financial future.

State lotteries have become a $3 billion-a-year industry. Their popularity explains why most Americans never will be rich. Lotteries also underscore the reason why there always will be significant opportunity for those few who are willing to learn, study, and take financial risks.

The odds on winning a state lottery are less than the odds on making a fortune in the casinos of Las Vegas and Atlantic City. Nevertheless, long lines will form when the jackpot swells to multimillion-dollar proportions. People hope to get something, a big payoff, for nothing, a dollar bill. There is nothing wrong with trying to make a million in return for a dollar. If all you have left at the end of each pay period is a dollar, then it is better to buy a lottery ticket than to stuff the dollar under the mattress waiting for the banks to collapse.

The popularity of lotteries tells us that while most people want to be rich they won't take real risks in pursuit of that ambition. Instead they will be drawn into a losing proposition, over and over again. They want to be rich but are only willing to risk a dollar. Most people run away from financial risk.

When the news reported the chemical disaster in Bhopal, India, Union Carbide's stock price plunged to $33. Investors were selling, trying to get away from the risk that damage claims would bankrupt the company. The damage claims turned out to be enormous. The risks were real. Nevertheless, General AnaLine Film Corp. (GAF) thought the company was attractive and made takeover moves. By February 1986 Union Carbide shares were selling at $99. Normal human fear of risk created an opportunity. An investor willing to take the risks associated with Bhopal and Union Carbide made a profit of 202 percent in slightly more than a year.

As sure as people buy lottery tickets there will be hundreds, if not thousands, of stories similar to that of Union Carbide, of stocks and other investments that first plunge and then soar. People of the right character, willing carefully to calculate their risks and invest when prices are, for good reason, low, will always find ample opportunity.

Taking risks is never easy. The greatest opportunities are always associated with real risks that most investors find frightening. Plunging ahead and investing without study can lead to financial disaster. It isn't enough to be a risk taker. Driving at high speeds, diving to ocean depths, parachuting out of airplanes, and gambling at the race track are all forms of risk taking. Successful investing demands more than physical courage or gambling on Lady Luck, it demands cool-headed, cold-hearted calculation with a single objective—financial profit.

There are two parts to the challenge. You must learn to deal with your own personal feelings, and you must also learn to cope with the world of volatile financial markets and ever-changing economic trends. For those willing to embrace the challenge the reward is not just profit but financial security.

The Personal Side of Investing

In 1980 when Wang Laboratories' "B" stock was at its low of \$7, an accountant with no stock market experience invested \$10,000 on margin. He was able to borrow an additional \$10,000 and owned a total of \$20,000 worth of Wang shares. The stock rose immediately. He increased his borrowing to buy more stock at \$15. When the stock hit \$23 late in the year, his holdings were worth \$110,000, but he had a debt of \$40,000. Nevertheless, his original \$10,000 equity had become worth \$70,000, a very impressive gain. The accountant then fell prey to one of the common stock market diseases. He looked at himself as one of the lucky few, a born successful investor. With a swollen ego he did the right thing and used his accounting skills to examine the future prospects for Wang. What he saw looked impressive and he decided to hang on and make a real fortune. Late in 1981 the stock retreated to \$12. The accountant's fortune had shrunk to \$17,600. Discouraged, he sold while he still had a profit, paid his taxes, and went back to his books.

During 1982 and 1983, however, Wang stock soared, reaching \$42½ at the peak. Had he held on, he would have enjoyed substantial gains. Had he continued to borrow when the stock rose, he might have made a small fortune. By 1985 when the computer industry was in the doldrums,

Wang shares were back down to $15, not far above the price where the accountant had given up. Nevertheless, had he held on, he would have had opportunities to sell at high prices and in the end been able to sell at a price higher than the $12 of 1981.

The accountant had the right stock and the right idea at the right time, but he failed to take full advantage of the situation. The reason he made only a modest profit and not a small fortune had more to do with his attitudes, his reactions to debts and the swings in the market, than with the market itself. A cold-hearted, calculating risk taker, able to brush aside both the markets and personal good fortune, would have done much better.

Worried Money Never Wins

Money is a major element of modern life. Survival in the twentieth century requires cash. It is fun to dream of a simpler life, planting corn and collecting firewood. Returning to the woods can be a pleasant interlude or vacation. It is healthy to keep in touch with basic, physical survival skills. But returning full-time to a world of firewood and pastoral settings is a fantasy. The world clock cannot be turned back. There are many more people on the earth today. If they all burned firewood, for example, the forests would be depleted and the air polluted. Dismal pictures from famine-stricken Africa tell us the truth. Cutting firewood and living in ignorance do not produce happiness. They produce arid lands and starvation.

Modern man is condemned by circumstances. We have no choice; we must keep the monetary system alive and growing to produce a reasonable standard of living. A depression today would not be like the 1930s. This time, there are so many more people that a major economic failure would mean disease, misery, and starvation for millions. Too few people are living on farms. Long distribution lines lead from the few remaining farms to the great centers of population. How many people could grow enough food in their own back yards to avoid hunger if the system was shattered? If the farmers go bankrupt, we all will go hungry.

The false confidence that prevailed in the 1960s is gone. There aren't many people left who still argue that a depression "can't happen." Oil shocks in both directions, high interest rates, deflation, trade deficits, and a burgeoning national debt have made most people aware that the risks are real. There could be an international economic disaster, and there is nothing that we as individuals can do to prevent it.

These harsh realities leave many investors despondent, preoccupied with disaster as if it were a present reality, and groping for economic shelters. It is easy to succumb and worry. It is easier yet to look at the terrifying possibilities and use them as an excuse for taking no risks. Venturing out through investment into a treacherous and uncertain world can seem foolhardy. The truth is that staying hidden in "safe" investments is the greatest risk of all. The value of your savings will be taken away by the constant erosion of money growth and by government spending. You could lose your livelihood in an economic disaster. Refusing to take risks could leave you hungry and out in the cold even if the disaster never happens.

We live in a world where it is impossible to survive without money and at the same time difficult to have confidence in the long-term survival of the economic system. The real world is one of incredible tension. Try to suppress the reality, attempt to delude yourself into feelings of false security, and the tensions will appear as high blood pressure, hives, aches, heart disease, or some other malady. If you accept the reality of an uncertain future, the level of conscious pain increases. Every risk looks monstrous. You begin to fear losing your money through inflation, government action, or unpredictable markets. There doesn't seem to be a way out of the misery. All options have serious drawbacks. All the tension has a direct effect on how investors behave. They buy and sell based on their feelings about the future. Most spend an inordinate amount of energy worrying about their portfolios in a vain effort to use personal mental power to accomplish something. Worrying about money is a prime cause of poor investment results. Successful investing follows from converting the tensions to a new level of awareness, replacing worry with calculated risks and developed disciplines.

Don't push the realities aside. They won't go away. Instead, take advantage of the fact that so many people are worrying.

Amusement Park Economics

As human beings we must learn to live with fear. We fear disease, injury, war, torture, assaults, terrorism, theft, poverty, death, and a host of other hazards. One of the mechanisms we use to cope with fear is fantasy. We create fear under controlled conditions in order to adjust to the feelings. Horror movies are an example. The roller coaster at the amusement park is another. The risks are controlled, but the violence on the screen or the feelings as the roller coaster drops produce "feelings" of fear.

Fantasy is ordinarily useful. It really helps in our lifelong battle to live with fear. When the mechanism is misused, however, we aggravate our anxieties. This is often done in the field of economics and finance. I call the phenomenon "amusement park economics."

Respectable analysts take real possibilities and use them as the basis for making compelling forecasts. In terror, investment strategies are adjusted. Markets are twisted out of touch with real, underlying trends.

In the early 1980s the U.S. money supply was erratic, at times growing for a full quarter or two at double-digit rates. Economists convinced many people that the double-digit inflation of the 1970s was caused not by rising oil prices but by excessive growth in the money supply. Such rapid growth was confidently used to forecast higher future inflation. Gold rose from a June 1982 low of $297 to an early 1983 high of $507. The U.S. bond market was paralyzed by inflation warnings. The warnings were wrong. Inflation stayed in low, single digits for years in spite of rapid growth in the money supply. Gold prices came back down, and the bond market was strong.

Another tantalizing idea in the early 1980s was that the huge U.S. federal deficit would gobble up so much of the U.S. credit market that interest rates would soar to new heights. In fact, interest rates fell even as the deficit rose to $200 billion a year.

Looking back to the 1970s, you can find more examples of amusement park economics and their effect on the markets. Fear of a coming stock market crash, for example, sent U.S. stocks down to their 1982 lows. At the time the warnings of a fifty-year cycle were compelling. There were signs of a coming economic crunch. In fact, the recession of 1982 was the worst recession since the Great Depression. Fear of a never-ending rise in oil prices sent gold to $850 in early 1980.

Investors reacted to the long series of new horrors with a combination of sincere anguish and greed. Some bought gold or stayed in short-term, safe investments such as money market funds and treasury bills in a genuine effort to avoid losses. Others tantalized themselves with stories of disaster to justify speculation, particularly in gold and silver. They said they were buying gold as insurance against disaster (a good idea). In reality, they were covering up an inner greed. They were speculating, hoping that gold would run up to new highs as it had done in early 1980. The long list of possible economic disasters was used in an attempt to make a killing. In the end the economists' forecasts were wrong, and the greedy speculators suffered huge losses.

Worried money and amusement park economics can be expensive.

You can't become superhuman. We are all vulnerable to economic fantasies. To avoid falling prey to treacherous predictions of gloom, you must engage in a never-ending struggle to sort out possibilities from probabilities.

You can deal with uncertainties. You can construct a personal strategy designed to cope with possible disasters and free you to take reasonable risks. You can sleep well at night, balance fear and greed, and increase your financial security.

Be honest about your personal financial circumstances. Put your financial house in order. You need a secure home, life insurance, a retirement plan, and cash in the bank for emergencies. From a solid foundation you can approach the financial markets with courage. That doesn't mean you have to be rich to invest. Far from it. It means that you have to be honest with yourself and able to use common sense before you stand a chance in the markets.

It is possible to start an aggressive investment program, one that can change your financial life, with $1,000. It is impossible to expect to be a cool-headed, hard-hearted investor even with $100,000 if you are worried about meeting your everyday financial obligations.

After setting your personal financial house in order, the next step is to face the fact that the world could fall off the edge into financial chaos. You need to build insurance against that possibility. Gold or silver coins offer an attractive way to build a contingency fund. Take a part of your savings and buy a few gold or silver coins. Put them in a safe place and then discipline yourself to take a part of every future profit and add to your coin-based insurance. It is to be hoped that you will never need to use the coins. If you do, they will serve you well. When fear of economic chaos catches you off guard, when feelings of fear and anxiety grip you, take out some of your coins. Look at them and remind yourself that gold coins have been a source of financial security for ages. Even a modest accumulation of coins can do wonders for your self-confidence. You will know that at least you are doing something to protect your financial future against catastrophe. If the day of economic reckoning waits long enough, you will accumulate enough coins to make a difference. Buy peace of mind with gold or silver coins. Sleep well and then set out to increase your fortune with confidence.

Moving On

When you have made a killing in some investment, sell it all. Move on to something else. The sudden influx of wealth can be devastating. Whole nations have suffered. Saudi Arabia, for example, suffered high inflation, distribution log jams, and rising corruption in the wake of the oil price increases of the late 1970s. South Africa suffered severe economic problems after the gold price shot up to new record-high levels. Nevertheless, as individuals, we assume that we can handle profits even though others cannot.

Our egos can be our undoing. Once we have made a good decision and the profits multiply, our feelings of accomplishment grow. We fall in love with our own ideas. We hang on to a stock or an investment strategy, convinced that we know what we are doing. That is a trap. The markets don't take account of individual personalities. They don't know that you are a successful investor. The markets will take your fortune no matter how you feel.

Feeling successful can be a cover-up. It is hard to sell a stock and start over. It takes a lot of work to find a good investment. Finding a new opportunity can be intimidating. Too often our pride in a particular accomplishment becomes an excuse for not going back to work.

For example, if you were fortunate enough to make a killing in gold or silver in the late 1970s, the best strategy would have been to sell all precious metals (all except that portion held as insurance, that is.) Many people held on, convinced that they had found the secret to the markets and unending fortune. Even after gold and silver had fallen back from their highs, many investors bought more, looking forward to the next rise. Some advisers preyed on these feeling by forecasting gold at $2,000 an ounce. Even if you believed that forecast, after making a substantial amount in precious metals, you should have followed the rule: sell and move on.

If you buy stock in a company and triple or quadruple your investment, sell and start looking for another idea. Never look back. It doesn't matter if the stock or other investment doubles after you sell. This rule is purely personal. It is designed to make sure that you go on to add to your fortune. The important thing is to keep yourself in a position to take advantage of the next opportunity. There will always be another great investment idea, another small company that grows. If you are diligent, open-minded, rested, and confident, the odds will be in your favor.

Bernard Baruch, when asked about his financial mistakes, is reputed to have answered, "I always sell too soon." Reading between those lines we can see that he followed this rule. When he had made a killing he sold for personal reasons and let the market go on without him.

What to Do When You Are Wrong

There are times when nothing goes the way it was intended. The best investors and the most successful traders suffer the doldrums, long periods when losses follow upon losses.

There will be times when your best investment does more than go down. It plunges to near bankruptcy.

Watching a portfolio dwindle is painful. We are not tolerant of failure, particularly our own. We can be hard on ourselves when the number of dollars in our net worth is diminishing. Deep, dark, painful failure can strike at any time without warning. You may work hard, study for long hours, be bright, consult the best advisers, have the best intentions, be honest, obey all the laws, and still wake up to the terrible news that you have lost your capital and your income. The markets don't care.

In the Great Depression of 1929 the reality of failure sent some investors to the windows and suicide. Failure sends many people to alcohol or drugs. Others muddle in despair and look for sympathy from friends. Still others cover up their failure by bragging about their past triumphs. Some "take it like men" and quit investing.

Without risk there can be no gain. And without real failure there can be no risk. Failure is an essential part of investing. It is the real risk that all must be willing to face.

You can't avoid risk. Those who invested in "safe" treasury bills when interest rates were 15 percent saw their incomes plunge when interest rates tumbled. Their capital was intact, but their buying power, the basis for every standard of living, was badly damaged.

Embrace risk willingly but not foolishly. Always be prepared to start again. Set a portion of your capital aside; invest it in gold or short-term securities so you will have the funds to start again if everything goes against you. Accept failure. When it comes, don't keep pyramiding your risks, hoping for the ultimate killing to make up for the losses. Sell out, take a vacation, and then come back to try again.

Some investors try to use traders' techniques to minimize their losses. They will place stop-loss orders below the market or have rules on when assets should be sold. All are worthwhile strategies. But none will prevent you from making the big mistake. Failure is essential not only to the working of the markets but to personal, long-term success as well. The best investors are those that have made a fortune, lost it, and are busy making it a second time. They have confidence born of experience. They have tasted success. They have survived failure.

The Role of Taxes

Americans live in one of the more onerous tax environments. Nevertheless, they insist that the United States is the only place to live. Based on that contradiction, they plunge into all sorts of tax shelters. Sometimes it seems as if Americans are trying to cleanse their homeland by using investments to reduce their tax bills to establish something more in keeping with their visions of what the United States should be.

The best tax shelter is to give up your U.S. citizenship and move to a country where there is no income tax. Second best is to move to a state that has no income tax. If you speak only English and want to remain where you are, then be willing to accept the tax consequences willingly. Many bad investment decisions are made on the basis of looking for lower taxes. Many of those who buy into tax shelters really don't have enough income or capital to make that necessary. They tie up capital in illiquid investments and miss out on taxable opportunities that, after tax, would multiply their fortunes.

Tax shelters have their place in your portfolio, after you have made your fortune.

There are ways to manage taxes. For example, you might regularly sell appreciating investments and buy them back, paying your taxes as you go. That way you would never be faced with one huge tax bill on the final sale after a significant gain.

The best tactic is simply to accept taxes as another part of the process of making a fortune. Make the best investment decisions you can. Disregard taxes until they are a present obligation. Once you are obligated to pay, immediately set the cash aside and pay your taxes promptly. Never invest money that you already owe in taxes. That will create feelings of panic and can easily push you into ill-advised decisions that will cost you more than you are willing to lose.

Just imagine the taxes you are going to pay each year after you have made your fortune. It is to be hoped that the day will come when your annual tax bill is twice or three times your present income.

Establish Personal Priorities

There are two financial building blocks—income and capital. How much you earn or enjoy in income from investments is the first priority. How much you are worth is the second.

You have to live comfortably. If you don't, if you are not at peace with your present standard of living, you will be straining to make profits, impatient with your decisions, and too hard on yourself. Always make sure that your energies and your investments are deployed to ensure that you have an adequate income. That doesn't mean to reach for the highest yields. A basic investment principle is that the higher the yield, the greater the risk. Establishing an adequate income means doing so at reasonable risk and at reasonable yields.

What about people with inadequate capital and inadequate income? Confucius defined a rich person as one whose living expenses were one dollar less than income.

While true, that can lead to the conclusion that personal finance is easy. Just cut back on expenses and all will be well. Unfortunately, that ideal approach to finance is not always realistic. There are lots of difficult situations in the real world. Senior citizens, for example, can easily find themselves in financial difficulties. Their temptation is to reach for the highest yields to lift income to a level as close as possible to their basic need. Too often they reach too far and take huge losses. In recent years we have all seen the television reports of tearful senior citizens who had lost their life savings in a bank that collapsed or in bonds that became worthless or in insurance schemes that failed.

Generating Income vs. Affordable Risk

The drive to generate income must be balanced against affordable risk. It is smarter to speculate in the stock market with a modest sum than to reach for yield with the bulk of your assets. Buy a few shares in a mutual fund that specializes in venture capital or even buy a few shares of a small company that can grow. If you are fortunate, a few thousand dollars could become ten thousand or more, and then you would have enough to invest at reasonable yields to generate enough income to be comfortable.

Balancing the priorities against reasonable risk is a fundamental challenge. The "secret" is to be realistic both about your personal circumstances and about the markets. Never say, "I can't afford . . ." and then invest based on a vision of benevolent markets. The markets are impersonal. They pay no attention to your situation. They are also harsh and will take away the life savings of senior citizens or any other unwary investor.

Live within your means. Invest first to produce a reasonable standard of living. Then, embrace all the risk you can afford and tolerate in an effort to increase your net worth.

Wealthy international investors often keep a large portion, two-thirds, of their net worth in liquid investments such as bank accounts or short-term government securities. They move into stocks, bonds, or gold only when they can "see" an opportunity for a significant profit within the next six months. Once they have realized a meaningful profit, they sell. This is not an ideal strategy for all investors in all markets. But it is a guide, a starting point, for adjusting your personal financial priorities. Whenever you are confused about what to do, consider selling and retreating to a two-thirds liquid portfolio. After a while, you will begin to "see" opportunity and risk more clearly again.

Investing and the Markets

There are significant differences between trading and investing. But they have something in common. Making money is like being a great chef or an artist. To be successful you have to love what you are doing and apply total concentration. The greatest pitfall is loving the end result, riches, and becoming impatient and overly ambitious.

Trading vs. Investing

Good traders can deal in anything from stones in the road to rare coins. They concentrate on the immediate market action and try to stay one short step ahead of the crowd. Trading demands total concentration and dedication. You have to stay in touch with the market at all times. The objective is not to figure out why the market is moving but how far the immediate move will go and what the next move will be.

Currency traders will sometimes try to move the market in a favorable direction. A trader in Zurich might, for example, sell hundreds of thousands of dollars to buy German marks just to throw the other trader off guard. Currency trades are done through banks, and the banks, of course, have their own currency traders and their own trading accounts. The banks, like brokers and all other dealers, will try to use what they know about the trading activity to make a profit. When they see a trade come in from a well-respected trader who is selling dollars and buying marks, they might conclude that the dollar is going to go down and the mark is headed higher. If the bank takes that bait, the bank's own trader will follow that lead and sell dollars against the mark. Others may then notice that the dollar is down slightly and the mark a bit stronger. They might move in to take advantage of the new trend. An entire trend for an afternoon or a day or sometimes longer may have been produced by a single trader trying to move the market by placing orders carefully.

The unaware will read the next day in the papers that the dollar fell "because. . . ." Some plausible explanation will be given. But no one will publish the real truth that a single clever trader in Europe placed an order or several orders in such a way as to give the market a slight push.

Whether you trade currencies, precious metals, stocks, commodities, or bonds, the challenge is always the same; you are competing for today's profits with other clever traders. You had better know as much or more about the market as they do. You had better concentrate on the market so you don't miss a single important detail. If you are a good trader, can stand the pressure, and thrive on the competition, you will make money more often that you lose. You might make millions.

By the early 1980s computers and technical analysis had become popular trading tools, particularly in the United States. A reasonably wealthy older couple became fascinated by some of the new techniques and decided that they wanted to become modern-day traders. They studied the commodity markets, sought help from brokers, learned technical analysis, and then began trading. Within a year they had lost $300,000, roughly half of their entire net worth. At that point they gave up trading and complained about their losses. Trading can be captivating and costly.

Nevertheless, there are more than a few stories of people who started with nothing, learned about the markets, saved a few thousand dollars, and began a successful trading program that over several years brought them millions. What is the difference between a successful trader and an unsuccessful trader? Is it just luck? Or do you have to be born with a specific talent?

The answer comes from learning to know both successful and unsuccessful traders. There is no doubt that you must start off with some special character traits. Anyone can learn the techniques, the tools, the disciplines, and the markets. But those who are not oriented in the right way suffer terribly from the strain. They can end up with high blood pressure, a heart attack, or ulcers. It is one thing to know how to trade, it is another to be able to relax with what you are doing. The secret is to be able to relax with that particular type of strain.

We all change as we travel through life. It is conceivable that at some time in our life we will be able to relax with the strain of active trading. There could be a profit window in our future, a time when we will be able to add significantly to our fortune through trading. You just never know. In any event, trading, because of the stress and the short-term orientation, tends to sharpen our awareness of what is making the markets move. It is a good idea to take trading positions every once in a while. Test the water, not to find out if you can make money or not but to feel the strain and discover your feelings. Even if you repeatedly try trading and do not follow through, you will benefit from keeping your market sense sharp.

Successful investors have a different orientation. They concentrate on the underlying asset and hunt for bargains.

Traders, just as in the example of the deliberate selling of dollars, will frequently move prices too far in one direction or the other. Investors wait for those moves and then take positions with the expectation of making a profit on a major move. When the market moves just 3 or 4 percent, a trader will be satisfied. An investor looks for much larger moves, on the order of 50 or even 100 percent. Traders also tend to be watching for short-term moves; investors frequently are looking for total returns over long periods of time. An investor will count the dividend and price action in determining total profits and may hold a stock through several cycles over several years.

Investors, for example, look at a company's financial statements and market trends in order to make a judgment about the future for the stock. A trader is concerned with the company's financial statements only if they can be expected to have an effect on the market today.

The differences between trading and investing can vanish in the day-to-day task of making money in the financial markets. Traders can become investors and vice versa. Stocks, for example, are often moved not by investors with a business orientation but by "investors" concentrating solely on the market trend. They call themselves investors, but in reality they are traders. They don't care what the underlying business may be; they are just in it for the next market move.

Not everyone understands the difference between trading and investing. Those who do have an advantage. Markets at times will move based on a proliferation of traders. A trend starts and thousands of traders rush in, causing the initial trend to carry far beyond reasonable limits. Gold prices have been propelled upward and sent plunging by traders following an existing trend. The phenomenon occurs frequently in the stock market. Who hasn't bought a stock and then watched over the next several weeks as the stock price drifts slowly lower? Finally we say, "Enough! I must have been wrong," and sell. You may have purchased the stock initially after careful study of the company, but that sell decision was made purely because the stock had declined. That is a trading decision. There may have been scores of others making the same judgment, not because there is anything wrong with the company's financial statements but simply because the stock price went down. That is why, so often, a stock will fall, and then the company will announce good news and the stock will immediately shoot back to significantly higher ground.

In any and all markets you must continually ask yourself, Are today's trends due to trading or are they based on strong underlying fundamentals? The answer is never easy and comes only from experience and the disciplined application of the new tools provided in this book.

It is a good idea to be clear about what you are doing. If you set out to trade a particular investment, then act like a trader. Don't start out buying something for a trade, that is, because you think the market's next move will be in your favor, and then end up holding on for the long pull when the market goes against you. Conversely, if you are investing, don't be frightened by day-to-day price changes.

In the roaring bull market of early 1986, many investors had trouble with this advice. They bought stock in small companies with great promise and then saw their stock stagnate while others on the New York Stock Exchange roared ahead. Holding a stock that doesn't move or goes down while the news reports day after day new record highs for the popular market indexes is extremely difficult. When the market is hot, everyone wants to be a trader. The crowd buys the stocks that are moving and sells those that act dull. Of course, that creates an opportunity for investors. Buying the dull stocks in a roaring bull market can often lead to enormous profits when the market broadens and the overlooked issues make their move.

In a dull market, traders can be tempted to become investors. Suppose you bought gold or silver, looking for a short-term market move, but instead the market sits or drifts lower? Rather than sell and move on to another market, it is tempting to dig in and focus on all the reasons that gold or silver will come back in the long term. Good traders never sit by and accept losses when the market goes against them. They sell and wait for the next market move.

Successful investors, on the other hand, are seldom disturbed by a short-term market move against them. In fact, investors will often add to their positions over a long period of time, taking advantage of dull or weak markets. One way to make a lot of money is to accumulate a large holding over a period of time, even years, and then watch when the market moves as expected. For example, those who accumulated gold on the way down in 1974–1976 made enormous profits when the gold price rose from $103 in 1976 to $850 in 1980.

Keep the concepts of trading and investing clearly in mind. Find out where your talents lie. Seldom is one individual both a good trader and a good investor. Usually you are one or the other. You can find out your basic inclination by trying both trading and investing and discovering which feels more comfortable. You can make a fortune at either. Make up your mind and then concentrate on what you do better.

Borrowing to Invest

Thomas J. Stanley, author of the *National Affluent Study,* discovered that 80 percent of American millionaires are not born rich. One generation will make money and the next will squander the fortune. As a nation we are continually replacing our lost millionaires.

Millionaires, Stanley said, tend to have deprived childhoods. They learn valuable lessons from adversity. They are willing to take risks and borrow substantial sums.

Becoming rich means borrowing for investment rather than consumption. Stanley might have gone further with his findings. A January 1985 report from the Federal Reserve showed that one common characteristic of high-income Americans is high consumer debt. People with good jobs and above-average income not only don't save, they borrow to buy cars, take vacations, and pay for Christmas. That is a financial course opposite to one that will lead to financial security. Anyone can become rich and financially secure, but to do it you have to be willing to borrow for investment.

We are a nation of borrowers. Some are on the road to building fortunes. Others are borrowing for consumption and squandering their own potential.

I am always irritated by people who say from the window of their new car or truck that they "can't afford to invest." On the one hand, they will readily borrow $15,000 to $20,000 for the vehicle of their choice, and on the other hand, they will complain about a lack of financial opportunity. Apparently our natural inclinations run counter to building a fortune and establishing financial security. One explanation for this peculiar borrowing behavior could be the psychology of the crowd. In a crowd we feel no responsibility, we are "free." Crowds are bound together not by physical presence but by ideas. The idea of a new car and a car loan, for example, is so common and so much a part of our society that crowd characteristics develop. People don't feel burdened by the car loan. Of course, they complain about the payment when it comes due, but they truly are not burdened by a feeling of personal responsibility. After all, doesn't everyone have a car loan? If you borrow to buy stock, however, you will definitely feel alone, out in the cold, responsible for your own actions. Instead of the warm greetings when you take out a car loan, you will be warned about the dangers of borrowing to invest. You will have to fill out forms saying that you understand the rules for borrowing to buy stocks. You will be under pressure from the very first moment. Only rugged individuals borrow to invest. You have to stand out from the crowd and be willing to take risk and accept the consequences.

Making money always means breaking away from the crowd. You must stand alone if you want to amass a fortune.

Increasing Your Fortune with Sensible Leverage

There are two basic types of borrowing—speculative borrowing and investment borrowing. On the one hand, borrowing a huge sum to trade in currencies, for example, can produce an enormous immediate profit. On the other hand, it can produce instant financial ruin. You don't have to borrow to speculate to become rich. Instead, you can borrow, apply ordinary investment principles, and increase your fortune by more than you imagined. Benjamin Franklin was impressed by compound interest rates. So are many bankers and investors today. It is logical to conclude that an investment compounding at some rate will grow to a sizable sum given enough time.

Papers, magazines, and investment journals are full of calculations showing how $2,000 a year in a tax-free account like an IRA will grow and multiply until at age sixty-five you will be rich. There is, of course, an obvious fallacy in all that clean, clear logic. In every instance the story is told for you, a specific, single individual. But those high and compounding interest rates work across the entire economy. To see if the interest rates assumptions are correct you have to step back and ask, What will happen if all debts and all savings accounts are compounded at this rate for the next twenty years? You may find that either your interest rate assumptions are wrong or that the value of your savings in twenty years will be seriously eroded by inflation.

Building a fortune through compounding interest rates will work for a short period of time, say a few years. But as an approach to long-term investing it is based on a lottery-ticket, no-risk, something-for-nothing psychology. The idea, after all, is that for very little, $2,000 a year, you will end up automatically rich through the magic of compounding interest rates.

The facts are all around us. People who saved diligently over the last fifty years and took advantage of compounding interest rates are not rich today. In many instances they are suffering financial hardships because over fifty years interest rates were not high enough to keep up with inflation. A savings account that looked huge twenty years ago seems inadequate today. Remember that the inflation factor from 1966 to 1985 was slightly more than three. In other words, a savings account of $300,000 today is the equivalent of $100,000 in 1966. You had to multiply your assets by three just to stay even.

Saving is a good idea. You should have a retirement account. You should take full advantage of both the tax laws and compounding interest rates. That is only sensible. But do not fall prey to the fantasy that saving in an IRA at compounding interest will make you rich. It can mean that you will be comfortable in your retirement years, but it won't make you rich.

To be rich you must be either a successful trader or a successful investor and in both instances willing to borrow large sums to make substantial profits. The choice of style is strictly personal. Successful currency traders borrow in the millions every day. A retired senior citizen struggling for financial survival could hardly afford to follow that style. You can borrow for speculation or for long-term investments. You can borrow large sums or small amounts every once in a while.

One of the most popular excuses for not investing in a retirement account is that when spring comes you don't have any spare cash. That is no excuse. Borrow to invest in your IRA. It is far better to be making payments all year on an IRA funding loan than on a new VCR or television set.

You don't have to get the timing right to make a substantial profit. An investor who borrowed an additional $10,000 to invest in the T. Rowe Price International Fund in 1980 would have been wrong on the timing. First, 1980 was early. The worldwide bull stock market didn't get started until two years later. Second, the dollar in 1980 was at a low, ready for a substantial rise. Nevertheless, five years later that investment would have doubled, and that doesn't count dividends. The $20,000 became $40,000. After paying off the loan, the net gain would be $30,000. An investor who borrowed to invest in that international fund at the wrong time ended up five years later with a 200 percent profit. It sounds so simple. But it isn't. During those five years interest rates went down and they went up. At times the dividends were enough to cover the cost of the loan. At other times they weren't, and the investor would have had to come up with additional cash to make interest payments.

On more than one occasion during those five years respected economists such as Henry Kaufman of Salomon Brothers confidently forecast higher interest rates, so high that they would reach new record-high levels. Hanging on to the mutual fund shares, making the loan payments during those days, took nerves of steel. Or did it? One of the lessons of those five years and the poorly timed investment in T. Rowe Price International Fund is that investing isn't as risky as we sometimes choose to believe.

Consider another example, Citicorp. Citicorp is the United States' largest bank and one of the best in the world. An investor might have decided in 1980 to buy Citicorp shares at the wrong time. By 1982 recession was causing loan losses at the banks to rise. In 1983 the international debt crisis loomed large. Continental Illinois failed, and Bank of America found itself in deep financial trouble. The year 1980 might have been one of the worst times since the depression to invest in bank stocks. Citicorp's stock price was volatile. It rose and fell several times. There were times when an investment in Citicorp looked foolish. But the bank continued to increase the dividend, earnings rose, and so did the stock. By early 1986 an investment in Citicorp would have more than doubled in value, not counting the increasing stream of dividends.

Citicorp was not the only big U.S. bank stock to perform well for investors. You could have selected J. P. Morgan, Manufacturer's Hanover, Chase Manhattan, Chemical Bank, or Bank of New York. In fact, the number of big banks with problems, such as Continental Illinois and Bank of America, were few. The odds were in an investor's favor. When the news focused on the problem banks, all the bank stocks went down, creating a buying opportunity for investors willing to face the risks.

The story of the bank stocks during the five troubled years of 1980 to 1985 indicates that while the investment risks are real, the odds are more favorable than many people realize. You can borrow money to invest. You may have to face a long wait until your chosen investment rises enough to generate a substantial profit, and you can lose everything, but you can also make a fortune.

Borrowing to invest can be terrifying. As the price of your investment goes up and down, the value of your equity can swing wildly. It is even possible that the investment will fall so much that you are stuck with a loan greater than the total value of the assets. There are lots of horror stories about investors who borrowed too much and lost everything.

Thinking Long Term and Including Repayment

People will take out a mortgage loan several times greater than their net worth to buy a home. The only consideration is whether they can afford the payments. That kind of borrowing makes sense.

The fact that borrowing to invest really works is easily seen in the makeup of American family wealth. By one government study, the equity in a home represents more than 50 percent of total wealth for the typical family by the time of retirement. If that strategy works for buying a home, it can also work for investments.

Have a repayment plan worked out from the outset and stick to it. If you had borrowed to buy Citicorp or T. Rowe Price International in 1980, you should have also included in the plan a regular repayment plan to reduce the principal of the debt. Making payments on investment loans has a double benefit. First, it adds to your total net worth; second, it uses up discretionary funds that otherwise might have gone to pay back loans for consumer goods.

Treat loans for investing the same as you would a loan for a car. Have a repayment plan that fits your budget. Don't count on capital gains to pay off the loan. Always be in a position to hold on for the long term. Never allow yourself to be in a position where the loan forces you to make a decision to sell. Don't be afraid to borrow. Use investment debt in an orderly way just as you do a car loan or mortgage. People readily borrow to buy cars, an asset that depreciates. The same people will become extremely disturbed if they buy a stock that goes down. It seldom occurs to them that the stock loan is no worse than the car loan. In most instances, a stock loan works out much better than a car loan. In stocks at least there is a chance of substantial appreciation. The beautiful new car loses value the moment you drive it home.

There are hundreds of ways to borrow and invest. They range from speculation to investment in mutual funds. The only limit is your imagination. If you integrate your investment borrowing into your normal budget just as you do with other loans, the risks will be minimal.

Investing for Profit in the U.S. Stock Market

There are investment opportunities in many markets. You can invest in bonds, real estate, or precious metals. One of the greatest arrays of investment opportunity, however, is in business, particularly the U.S. stock market. Millions can be made by buying the right stock at the right time. There are numerous U.S. stock market strategies, developed over the years, that will lead to extraordinary profits. It isn't possible to follow them all. As in every other aspect of investing, you must narrow the world of opportunity down to something usable and practical.

What follows is one particular method for selecting stocks that will prove rewarding. Some experts argue that the best opportunities for profit lie in stocks in small companies that can grow. They have an array of statistics to "prove" that argument. Others argue that it is too risky to choose stocks in small companies and that you should do your investment shopping among the big companies that are currently out of favor. Some experts say that you should buy and hold for the long term. Others are equally convincing in their argument for selling to take profits before they vanish.

The problem with all these popular, much debated issues is that they are unrealistic divisions of the world of opportunity. There can be opportunities in small companies and large. It can pay to buy and hold or trade.

A more useful approach to dividing the world of opportunity is based on your personal self-interest. You are not going to become president of the company whose stock you buy. You are not going to join the board of directors or have a stake in a profitable division. You are a shareholder, and you make money when the value of the stock rises. As an investor, you are looking for stocks that have some hidden attraction. Undiscovered value that will later be "found" by the crowd is what you are after. In pursuit of that objective it is helpful to divide the world of business into three categories:

1. There are companies that are so prosperous that they don't need outside capital. These are often the most profitable businesses, but because they are, they don't sell stock to the public. Investors never have a chance of participating in this type of business. The profits go to the private owners.

2. There are companies that do need capital. They sell stock to the public in exchange for cash. When a company is selling stock you should always wonder why. Do they have a great idea or are the insiders, the management, selling stock that they bought at low prices years ago? When you buy the shares, will your money be going into the business or into the pockets of the management? You don't want to buy stock unless there is a clear opportunity for you to make a profit. If the insiders are getting out, then you might be better off looking for another situation.

Sometimes companies sell stock to finance growth. Growth is expensive. Even then, however, it pays to be a skeptic. The idea may be terrific, but it may not work out as planned.

3. In the third category are companies that needed capital in the past and sold stock to the public years ago. This category covers the vast majority of stocks traded on all the exchanges. Some are very prosperous companies whose stocks have traded up to high prices. Others are not so prosperous and their stocks sell at low prices. Some will be prosperous companies that have been overlooked by the market. Those are the desirable investment gems.

This division of the world of U.S. stock market opportunity allows you to eliminate categories that are not of interest and avoid wasting time searching for the impossible.

New Issues

A new issue is nothing more or less than stock being sold by a company to the public. Companies seldom handle the sale themselves, preferring to have a broker or underwriter take care of raising the cash. Brokers can make a lot of money in fees and commissions handling new sales of stock. To earn the profit, however, they have to convince the public that the stock is a good investment. At the same time, the underwriter will try to get the highest possible price per share for the company. By definition, a new issue is a balancing act between an attractive price for the investor and the highest price for the company. More significantly, a new issue has been closely scrutinized by professional investors. The odds on finding a bargain in the new-issue market are slim.

You can make money in new issues. In the right market environment the price of the stock will soar after the offering. That is due to trading, however, not investing. New issues are interesting trading vehicles in the right market, but they are not what you are looking for as investments in a long-term program with borrowed money.

Fantasy Stocks

One way to get rich is to own your own prosperous business. That fact of economic life often confuses investors. Make no mistake, investing is an entirely different proposition than owning your own business. There is an enormous difference between being a shareholder and being an owner.

The most significant difference is that you can't buy stock in the ordinary, small, prosperous business. That kind of business doesn't need outside capital. It doesn't sell stock to the public. As an investor you are dealing exclusively with companies that at one time or another needed capital and sold stock to the public. Looking for that dream stock, one that has all the characteristics of a prosperous small business, is a waste of time. You can't substitute owning stock for owning a business. If your desire is to be in business for yourself, then go out and look for a business to buy. But don't try to fulfill business fantasies in the stock market.

Solid Investments

If you buy good value, you will both minimize risk and maximize potential. The challenge is to find value and recognize it when you do.

There are all kinds of values to be found in the stock markets of the world. No single investor can be so expert in all fields of business as to recognize them all. When it comes to value you have to narrow the field of concentration, focus on a few standards, and become an expert at applying "your approach." Here are three value tests that you can learn to use to find attractive stocks:

1. Cash flow: This test looks at the questions, How much is this company really earning? and, How much am I paying for those real earnings when I buy the stock? You want to buy stocks at low prices, meaning low compared to the company's earnings. Better yet, you want to buy low into a situation where the earnings in the future will be even greater. Those stocks do exist, and one way to find them is by getting to know the principle of cash flow.

2. Book value: This test addresses the question, How much is this company worth? If you add up all the assets that the company owns and subtract all the debts and other obligations, what is left for the shareholder? The purpose is not just to see how much each share of stock is worth on the company's books but to have a way of becoming alert to those situations where the book value is understated.

3. Capitalization: Some companies do things that have a direct benefit for the shareholders. Others do things that help the company first and trust that in the future the shareholder will benefit as the company prospers. Capitalization is another accounting term. In this test the term means, look carefully at the number of shares and the way the management is treating the shareholder. In the early 1980s the oil price went down. The stocks in most oil companies did poorly. There was one standout exception, Exxon. Exxon was buying back stock in the one market with excess cash. That meant fewer shares left outstanding, basic buying support for the stock, and a rising stock price. Remembering the word *capitalization* might have caused you to look at that aspect of Exxon in your search for value. The capitalization test is designed to look at the number of shares and ask the question, What's in this for me, the shareholder?

These are financial terms. But don't be frightened away. They are not being used in their textbook, accounting definitions. They have been translated into useful ideas as easy to grasp as the terms in your family budget.

Cash flow is a term that describes how much a company is really earning. You have heard about tax shelters. There are earnings shelters too. Sometimes the accounting just works out in such a way as to "hide" some of the earnings, and other times the management deliberately wants to hide earnings in order better to prepare the company and the stock price for the future. It is not unusual to find a company reporting very little in earnings per share but enjoying a time of increasing prosperity. One way to find these hidden values is by looking at a simplified version of cash flow in order to find out (a) Is the stock risky? and (b) Is there a chance that this stock will rise by a substantial amount?

There is an old stock market adage that the price of a stock will follow earnings. The problem is that the price-earnings ratio for stocks varies widely. Sometimes the price of a stock will soar, rising much faster than earnings. At other times earnings will rise, but the stock price will stagnate. The problem is that too many people understand what earnings mean. When they hear that earnings will be up by 35 percent next year, they automatically assume that the stock is a good buy. Once something becomes widely understood and applied in the markets, it loses much of its usefulness as a stock market tool. The better tools are those that few investors understand and use. Cash flow is in that category.

Cash flow is simply the amount of cash earnings that pass through the company's books each year. Suppose a company invests money in a lot of new equipment. Each year during the useful life of that equipment the company will be able to take a deduction for depreciation. Depreciation is not cash. Once the machines and equipment are paid for, there is no more cash being paid out. Businesses pay for equipment only once. They don't keep paying for it over and over again each year. Depreciation is an accounting or book-keeping entry. If a company has net earnings of $1 million and depreciation of $1 million, cash flow is the combination of the two, or $2 million. That is the idea. In this simplified accounting method you look at a description of the company's earnings, and you simply add net earnings and depreciation to arrive at a useful figure called cash flow.

Some investment services do the mathematics more precisely and do it for you. Valueline, for example, provides figures on cash flow per share in their material. In other instances you will have to do your own math. It isn't hard. Just look for earnings and then look for depreciation and add the two together.

The next step is to compare cash flow to the stock prices. For example, in 1984 a company called Smithfield Foods reported net earnings of $3.46 million and depreciation of $6.99 million. Smithfield Foods cash flow came to $10.45 million in 1984. There were about 1.5 million shares of Smithfield Foods outstanding. Dividing cash flow by the number of shares indicates that the company was enjoying almost $7.00 in cash flow for every share of stock in the company. At the end of 1984 and into early 1985, Smithfield Foods stock sold at prices ranging from $7 1/8 to $7 3/4. It doesn't take a degree in finance to realize that paying $7 3/4 for stock in a company generating a cash flow of $7 per share might be a good idea.

Once you find an attractive cash flow situation, the next step is to look at the company and ask yourself, Is the cash flow likely to stay the same for the next few years, rise, or collapse? If you think that the cash flow will collapse because of business conditions or any other reason, then move on to another situation. If you think that cash flow will remain the same or rise, then you may have found a very attractive stock. That certainly was true of Smithfield. The stock rose to more than $20 by early 1986 and at that new high showed no signs of stopping.

Look at the price of the stock and compare that to the cash flow per share to see if the stock is a bargain. As you become familiar with this value tool, you will be able to apply it to whole lists of stocks. In doing that you will discover that investors place different values on different industries and different stocks at different times. In any given month you will find stocks that sell at ten times cash flow and others that sell at two times cash flow. As a value hunter, you want to avoid those that sell at high prices relative to cash flow. They may be good investments, the stocks may stay up or rise higher, but in stocks like that you are dependent on the market and the opinion of the crowd. A stock at ten times cash flow that falls from investor favor can fall precipitously to much lower levels. Stick to your discipline. Buy only stocks that sell at low prices relative to cash flow and even then only those that you think have promising futures.

Smithfield Foods in late 1984 and early 1985 offered another sign of value. The book value of the company was $13.99 at the end of 1984. Book value is what is left after adding up the value of all the company's assets and subtracting the value of all the liabilities. Smithfield had more than $40 million in debts and also $110 million in assets. But for each share of stock there was more than $13 in net assets. By paying $7 3/4 for the shares, you were buying at less than book value.

Cronus Industries was another example of a stock selling at less than book value. In 1983 book value was nearly $10.50. The stock in that year sold from $8 1/4 to $12 1/4, spending most of the year trading at $10. There was plenty of opportunity to buy Cronus Industries at or below book value in 1983 and again in 1984. If you bought Cronus shares in 1983, you had to have patience. The stock didn't do very much in all of 1984. But in early 1985 the stock advanced to $15, and in late 1985 it rose to near $20. In early 1986 the company announced that the managers of one division were proposing to buy that division for a price of $100 million. There were only 4.9 million shares of Cronus Industries. Dividing the $100 million purchase price by the number of shares indicated that Cronus would receive on the sale $20.40 per share. The book value had been understated. A single division had a market value equal to more than twice the stated book value. Buying Cronus Industries based on book value turned out to be an excellent idea.

Be sensitive to book value. Look for stocks that sell at or below stated book value and then take a close look at the company's assets. You may find hidden value, divisions, real estate, or other resources worth more than the stated book value.

The capitalization of the company can provide other valuable clues to the future. Look closely at the number of shares. You will find wide differences. One stock selling at $10, for example, may be in a company that has 10 million shares outstanding. Another company may have 2 million shares outstanding, but the stock may also sell at $10. The one company is being valued by the market at $100 million and the other at $20 million. Comparing the total market value of the shares outstanding to the company's assets and earnings can often lead you to outstanding value. Just look at the business and ask yourself, Do I think that the company is worth more or less than the total market value of all the shares?

In the case of Smithfield Foods in 1984, the stock sold at $7 ³/₅, and there were 1.5 million shares. The total market value of the company was a scant $11.7 million. Cronus Industries had 4.9 million shares, and the stock sold at $10 for a total market value of $49 million. Later a single division turned out to be worth more than twice that amount.

Look for companies with fewer shares outstanding. And be leary of stocks in companies with tens of millions of shares. That is a way of keeping the price per share low to make it appear attractive. It often is, however, a sign of financial weakness, not strength. Better yet, look for companies that are buying back their own shares. That is often a tip-off on a company with excess cash flow and above-average potential. If the company is buying the stock back, you should be relatively safe borrowing money to buy the stock for your account.

Sometimes you will find all the value characteristics present in a single company. When you do, buy and hold on for significant profits. Usually, however, you will have to be satisfied with stocks that show only one or two of the signs of value. In those instances the risks are greater, but the opportunity may still be worthwhile.

Buying low is the first essential step in making money in stocks. There are many ways of judging when a stock is low. This value method is one.

Hanging on to a Fortune

Protecting and preserving a fortune can be as difficult as making it in the first place. Once you have accumulated enough in profits to provide financial security, you won't want to lose and start all over again. You may still pursue greater and greater wealth, but you will want to have enough set aside, invested safely, to make sure that you can live comfortably.

The ordinary answer to protecting wealth is diversification. The idea is to spread your investments so that disaster won't strike all your assets at the same time. The problem is that it can take an expert financial analyst to determine what diversification really means.

Investors deal with the complex task of diversification by dividing the financial world into two parts, risky and safe. The world doesn't fit into that neat pair of classifications. Safe investments are *relatively safe,* not absolutely safe. Investors are risk managers whether they like it or not. A better way is to look at the task of preserving wealth as a balancing act. Always strike a balance; never be one-sided and your investments will be as safe as possible.

The financial world falls into four sets of opposites:

1. Short-term vs. long-term
2. High-yield vs. no-yield
3. Liquid vs. illiquid
4. Foreign vs. domestic

Safety lies in the middle, between the pairs of opposites. You get there by balancing investments. For example, you may have a large holding in a money market account or treasury bills. That holding is vulnerable to a decline in interest rates. Falling interest rates would reduce the income from those holdings. You could balance that position by selling some of the short-term assets and using the proceeds to buy long-term government bonds. They are vulnerable to rising interest rates but tend to appreciate when interest rates go down. They would balance the risk of treasury bills, leaving you with a portfolio in the middle between short-term and long-term investments.

Suppose you were holding a large portfolio of utility stocks and enjoyed the rising dividends but were concerned about long-term risks. Utility stocks would fall into the high-yield extreme and could be balanced by buying a no-yield investment such as gold. If the economy crumbled and chaos swept over the nation, wiping out the value of your utility stocks, the price of gold would soar, providing you with protection. The combination of utility stocks and gold would give balance and safety.

Real estate is illiquid. It cannot be sold readily. To sell a piece of real estate you have to put it on the market and wait for a buyer to come along and offer you the right price. That is quite different from stocks or bonds, which can be sold on a moment's notice simply by calling a broker. Most Americans have a one-sided portfolio. Their home, illiquid real estate, represents the bulk of their net worth. That is fine during the years when you are building your fortune, but there will come a time when holding too much real estate would be wrong. In the event of a real estate market slump, for example, you could be locked in and find yourself short of cash.

Real estate, especially a home, is a long-term, illiquid, no-yield investment. The perfect balance would be an investment that was short-term, liquid, and high-yield. No single investment meets that objective. Real estate has to be balanced by a combination of investments such as treasury bills and long-term government bonds.

Another classic investment error is to ignore the fourth category. It is common to have a portfolio made up 100 percent in U.S. assets. As Americans, we feel safe being one-sided in favor of the dollar. We never think of needing to balance our equity in our home by investments in foreign securities. But being invested entirely in domestic assets can be extremely risky. You need to hedge against the loss of value of the dollar. That can be done by owning gold or by investing in foreign assets or preferably by doing a combination of both.

The objective is to be as balanced as is practical in all four categories. As a practical matter, that usually means holding some gold, some real estate, some stocks both U.S. and foreign, some treasury bills, and some bonds.

A portfolio invested with the objective of balance will be safe. It won't provide the highest possible yield nor will it produce the best capital gains. But it will assure you of financial security through wild and volatile markets and through most of the possible economic catastrophes.

Take a good, honest look at your portfolio and find out how financially secure you really are. If you don't like what you see, do something about it. You know from this book that there is no excuse for not owning some gold and having a part of your assets invested internationally.

Chapter 7

Concluding Thoughts on the Market

The Future

FOR THE NEXT SEVERAL decades the greatest opportunities will be created by the crowd's mistakes. The United States is still a land of opportunity. Converting that opportunity into personal financial gain, however, is a task that few will accomplish.

In the early part of the twentieth century there were opportunities in the United States because the country was still developing. New industries were beginning what was to become a long and profitable period. The nation had enormous future potential. We were "underdeveloped" and had room to grow.

Past opportunity arose out of physical underdevelopment. Growth, while never complete, has advanced to the point that there cannot be, in the coming decades, a repeat of the physical growth that marked the beginning of the century. The next series of opportunities arise out of a different kind of underdevelopment. There is enormous potential for financial development in the United States. For example, investors in Switzerland or Germany can call their broker and easily discuss investments in the United States or a wide range of other countries. That is not yet true in the United States. We have a long way to go in developing our financial potential.

Opportunity comes in various forms. Ordinarily we think of it in terms of specific companies, growth industries, and new inventions. There is also opportunity that arises out of human behavior.

If everyone saw the potential in IBM or any other stock, the price would rise to meet the expectation. The market will always discount what most people expect. Opportunity comes when most people don't see the potential. That doesn't necessarily mean that the crowd is selling. It more often will be that the crowd just didn't notice what was going on. To find opportunity without taking excessive risk you must be looking in a different direction. You must have tools that most investors don't know about. You must be aware of things that are above and beyond what the crowd is considering.

The crowd isn't always wrong. Many investors try to profit by doing the opposite of what the market is doing. Being contrary to the crowd, however, isn't enough to assure above-average profits over the long term. The crowd isn't always wrong. Many times the crowd will be exactly right. Taking advantage of the crowd's mistakes is not simple. It requires the right character, a clear and open mind, and an international perspective.

Making and keeping a fortune in the coming decades will demand enlightened investing. Look where the crowd isn't paying attention. Be aware of markets and trends the world over. Avoid universal rules. Profit from your own individual effort and common sense. Be an independent investor relying on your own judgment. That is the one way you can be sure of having a chance of standing apart, far enough away from the crowd to see things in their proper, international perspective.

The Fear-Confidence Cycle

As sure as the sun comes up in the east, history will be repeated over and over again in the financial markets. The more you study financial markets and the more you compare one market to another, the more aware of cycles you become. Human beings may progress on the road to the ultimate civilization, but the rate of advance is hardly detectable in a single generation. In a decade or two there are few changes in human behavior patterns. Human behavior patterns form the basis for cycles in financial markets. Society's resistance to rapid change means that familiar cycles, with modest changes, are repeated over and over again.

The slow rate at which society changes is an investor's greatest ally. Careful observation of patterns in the markets, combined with judicious study, can lead to considerable success in staying one full step ahead of the crowd.

There are always many aspects to the financial markets. There isn't just one correct way to analyze stocks, bonds, or gold. There are always numerous correct points of view. The important thing is to adopt one at a time and use it logically. One way of looking at the markets is in terms of a fear-confidence cycle. Investors tend to swing from one extreme to the other. At times they are confident, paying high prices for financial assets. At other times they are afraid and rush to the safety of ageless assets such as gold.

When the crowd is full of confidence, nothing can alter the course of the markets. For two decades after World War II, the United States was an independent and dominant economy growing at a comfortable rate. We enjoyed a long period of relative prosperity. Interest rates were low, and there were enormous profits to be made by buying and holding U.S. stocks. The course of events was so powerful that the markets marched higher and higher year after year. Economic, social, and political problems were accepted with understanding and the assurance that they would be solved. Nothing could stop investors from indulging their confidence.

The events of the day were projected indefinitely in a straight line into the future. The growth-stock thesis was one of the logical extensions of that period of super confidence. Investors, professional and individual, all over the country paid forty and fifty times earnings in the confident expectation that future earnings and dividends would fully justify the high price. With hindsight we know that buying growth stocks in the early 1970s was foolish. No one expected the growth stocks to plunge, but they did. From their lofty prices they came crashing down in 1974 and 1975.

The market had been ruled by a series of compelling but incorrect misconceptions. During the time of great confidence those misconceptions were in an overly optimistic direction.

The final indulgence in optimism, the growth-stock buying binge of the early 1970s was the end of a cycle. Confidence that had grown after World War II, matured in the 1950s, and come to fruition in the 1960s, soared to gross overconfidence in the early 1970s. The market's indulgence in popular, self-serving misconceptions produced predictable patterns. Investors became so much impressed by their own ideas that they lost touch with the underlying reality. In the recession of the mid-1970s reality intruded on the comfortable world of the over-confident investment crowd. No amount of logic or influence could alter the fact that the economy had slipped. The markets came crashing down. The Dow fell from 1,000 in 1973 to 570 in 1975.

Looking back on the 1960s and 1970s, we see a pattern emerge. We can see that investment sentiment swung from war-time lows to justifiable highs and finally to unsustainable overconfidence. There is a discernible cycle of confidence. The cycle itself is an investment advantage. You can watch for the progression of the cycle and stay out of the way of financial danger at cyclical extremes. There is another, even more valuable investment tool that emerges from observations of the fear-confidence cycle. During the upward part of the cycle, as sentiment moves toward overconfidence, the process becomes a self-intensifying binge of misconceptions.

The same is true at the other extreme of the cycle. Once confidence in the long term is replaced by fear for the economic future, a gradual transition takes place. Markets become ruled by uncertainty. Stock and bond markets will drop easily and quickly. Gloomy misconceptions replace the old optimistic excesses. The same mistakes are repeated. Investors allow themselves to become convinced of the merit of false assumptions. This time, however, the misconceptions that rule the markets will be negative, pessimistic.

The economic end of the postwar boom came in the second half of the 1960s. After two decades of steady, reliable growth, the foundations of financial optimism were eroded as the United States lost its energy independence, suffered losses in its gold reserves, and faced tough global trade competition. Slow at first, then more rapidly in the latter half of the 1970s, changing economic trends began to shake investor confidence. Convictions gave way to doubts and finally to near-hysterical fear of all sorts of possible economic tragedies.

It was easy to become confused. Interest rates rose to record highs, fell, rose again, and then declined again. The dollar plunged, soared, and plunged again. Half of all the experts warned of pending economic disaster. The other half promised growth and prosperity. How could you know whom to believe? What hope is there for an ordinary investor when the best experts in the world are so divided in their view of the future?

The answer is the fear-confidence cycle. Once you know the state of that single cycle, you will know which experts to believe. When the investment crowd is deep in fear, indulging every gloomy forecast, you know that the fear extreme is approaching and that the gloomy forecasts are based on misconceptions. Under those conditions you can believe the experts with a more optimistic outlook. You can stick with the optimists until their view becomes too popular. When optimism runs wild it will be time to take a closer look at the warnings of coming economic turbulence.

The fear-confidence cycle is a broad measure. Don't look at a single market and jump to conclusions about where the overall financial markets stand in terms of the cycle. Look at the headlines and all the markets, and listen to what others are saying. If this sounds too broad a measure to be of practical help, don't despair. The tools that have been presented in this book will guide you through the process.

The overconfidence that drove the Dow Industrial Average to 1,000 in 1966 was slow to erode. It finally gave way in the mid-1970s to panicky selling of U.S. stocks. By the end of 1974 the Dow was on its way to a low of 570. The rupture of overconfidence spread to the very core of the nation's business and financial markets. A pall of gloom descended on the country. In reality the United States had simply left the cozy, comfortable postwar era and entered a new, more normal era. Most people, however, saw the change not as a return to normal but as a time of financial reckoning.

If you were fortunate enough to have recognized the earlier extreme overconfidence as one limit of the fear-confidence cycle, you would have known that the rupture was coming. You might have been waiting for a buying opportunity.

Another guide to opportunity would have been watching foreign investor activity in the U.S. stock market. Investors in Europe and Asia reacted differently from Americans to the events of the 1970s. They bought U.S. stocks when Americans were aggressively selling. The difference was not that foreign investors were basically contrary. They had been hardened by events. They had suffered runaway inflation and the total destruction of their economies by World War II. They knew all along that the world was a treacherous place for investors. Oil shortages, volatile currencies, and recession did not come as a shock. Americans, spoiled by prosperity and drunk with overconfidence, found the awakening to a "real world" far more terrifying. By watching foreign investors in the mid-1970s you would have seen that they were buying. Knowing that they are not foolhardy investors, you would at least have suspected that you were witnessing an opportunity in the U.S. stock market.

The fear-confidence cycle plus the new tools found in earlier chapters will help cut through confusion and assist you in developing a rational perspective. In 1974 when so many U.S. investors were selling stocks, it was easy to join the crowd, embrace the feelings of panic, and run for the safety of treasury bills or bank accounts. If you understood that American investors were overreacting because of the fear-confidence cycle, it was possible to "see" conditions from the more-objective perspective of a foreign investor. They knew all the possibilities but they came to a different conclusion. Buying U.S. stocks when the Dow was falling precipitously was one route to financial success in the mid-1970s. The courage to go against the crowd, however, does not come automatically. It must be developed through an understanding of the powerful cyclical forces that move markets.

The turbulent markets of the 1970s hardened American investors. By the early 1980s there were signs of change. In 1984 American investors were becoming more optimistic. They were net buyers of U.S. stocks again. The fear portion of the cycle was approaching its limits. Misconceptions ruled the markets. Opportunity abounded for investors who could cut through the cloud of hysteria.

The Evolution of Fear

The farther back you look, the easier it is to "see" conditions in the financial markets. In the mid-1980s there was no problem recognizing the excesses of the growth stock era. Making the leap from the more distant past to the present is always difficult. The reason is that the present is inevitably at a different point in the fear-confidence cycle. The present is caught up with popular misconceptions. Past misconceptions have already been exposed. Dissecting current and recent events is one way to increase awareness of the fear-confidence cycle at work.

The first oil crisis of the 1970s triggered a shattering of confidence. For the next decade, financial markets were twisted and tortured by one financial fear after another. Virtually the entire U.S. investment community lived in fear of one or more of the following:

1. An energy shortage that would crush the economy
2. Runaway inflation
3. A stock market crash
4. A depression
5. A Latin American debt default
6. A U.S. government that couldn't stop printing money
7. A violent devaluation of the dollar
8. An oil price plunge that would wreck the U.S. banking system
9. Huge U.S. federal government deficits
10. Huge U.S. trade deficits
11. Skyrocketing interest rates
12. Deflation

In every item of this litany of fear there was a core of truth. Both inflation and deflation are destructive, and both are always possibilities. The dollar's plunge in the 1970s was accompanied by double-digit inflation and high interest rates. The dollar's excessive recovery in the 1980s nearly swamped the U.S. economy with a flood of imports. Oil prices could have kept rising to $100 a barrel.

As each new fear swept across the financial landscape, the markets were shaken. Investors were not able to distinguish between possibilities and probabilities. They feared that every possible disaster would become reality.

In 1979 when oil prices were rising, some of the nation's most expert oil analysts were convinced that prices would keep rising indefinitely. Few were able to cut through the consequent anxiety and realize that high oil prices would force change, that oil-consuming countries would adapt, and that exploration would bring discoveries of new oil reserves.

Converting possibilities to probabilities may be difficult, but it is also profitable. Extraordinary gains followed from a strategy of buying when the crowd was panicked. The path to profits, simply stated is this: do the opposite of what the crowd is doing, but do it only when the crowd has gone to an extreme.

The past holds clues to the future. An effective way to gain insight into current events and their likely future consequences is careful examination of the past. While tomorrow always holds something new, it also always brings something along from yesterday.

The Oil Panic and the Missing Profits

If there is one thing that investors should have learned from the past, it is the self-limiting nature of market swings. Supply and demand are opposites. Changes on one side of the equation inevitably bring changes on the other. Nevertheless, rising oil prices in the 1970s were treated as a totally new phenomenon.

It is now clear that oil prices were too low in 1970. Demand had begun to exceed supply, and the United States was becoming a major importer of oil from the Middle East. OPEC wanted real gains in oil revenues and chose embargo as a power play to force oil-consuming countries, particularly the United States, into submission. The tactic worked. Oil prices began a climb that did not end until the spot markets reached more than $40 a barrel. Higher oil prices brought logical consequences. Consumers cut back on gasoline and oil consumption, cars became smaller, conservation became profitable, and turning down the thermostat gained in popularity. Oil merchants the world over began to search for new oil. Inevitably the law of supply and demand worked its ageless magic. The balance shifted. Demand dropped and supplies of oil rose. The "impossible" happened. Oil prices plunged in 1985 and 1986.

The first lesson from the recent history of oil prices is the incredible self-limiting nature of markets. Changes in price bring changes in behavior that affect the balance between supply and demand. Oil supplies increased while demand dropped in a direct reaction to OPEC's power play. From the oil experience we have learned in vivid detail how markets behave. The lesson applies to currencies, credit markets, interest rates, stocks, bonds, and precious metals. Rising prices hold the seeds of their own downfall. Falling prices contain the energy for the next rebound.

The second lesson is that the markets will look at events consistently with the fear-confidence cycle. The oil price rise came at a time after confidence had been broken by excessive optimism. Bad news was amplified. Certainly the rising oil prices of the 1970s were bad news. They were not necessarily, however, going to push the world economy into a new depression. The emergence of the fear portion of the cycle had its usual effect. Bad news was exaggerated and projected into the future. Good news or even a more-balanced view of the oil price surge was brushed aside without notice.

The Market Determined by Human Behavior

OPEC learned the hard way that the law of supply and demand respects no master. Cartels can "control" the market in the short run, but eventually the market will be determined by human behavior, not power brokers. Banks and governments have discovered that same truth when it comes to international loans and interest rates. They too thought that it was possible to control human behavior and produce a desired economic result. Their tampering produced the worst recession since the Great Depression. We all would be better off if those in positions of power and authority had a greater respect for basic market laws.

The Great Depression itself might have been avoided if market forces had been allowed to function. Their self-correcting properties were effectively stifled by the combination of U.S. laws to keep out imports and insistence on the rigid gold standard.

A single market, even then the smaller the better, can be controlled and manipulated. Americans' fascination with power and control has often led us into the trap of believing that we (a government, for example) know best. Instead of accepting the messages from the action of free markets, we set out to "correct" the situation or "protect" jobs or restrict growth in the money supply in the name of fighting future inflation. Sometimes we go so far in our attempts at control that we flirt with catastrophe. Sometimes we manage to come away from such encounters with relatively little damage. At other times we pay a price in the form of a market collapse, recession, or depression.

In the 1920s it was widely believed that government could set the "right" gold price and maintain prosperity forever. Fifty years later, in the 1970s, it was widely believed that the U.S. Federal Reserve could control inflation and assure lasting prosperity by determining the "right" rate of growth of the money supply. In the 1930s we paid the price for central economic planning. The price was the Great Depression. In the 1980s we paid again for our recurrent faith in central economic planning. This time the price was the worst recession since the Great Depression.

Along with the fear-confidence cycle, there are reactions at all levels of society including government. Governments go through predictable patterns. At one end of the cycle, they deregulate everything in the name of giving markets the freedom to produce needed economic growth. At the other, extreme governments regulate everything in order to prevent economic disasters. A government's patterns are a reflection of people's attitudes. When we awaken to the disasters brought about by central economic planning, we recoil and reject the entire concept, turning instead to the opposite, unregulated free markets. But markets cannot be allowed to run wild. There is no solution in the extremes. Controls are necessary. It is, as always, a question of balance, moderation, and cooperation between governments and the markets.

If OPEC in the 1970s had followed a course of thoughtful cooperation with the markets, instead of indulging in a power play of price manipulation, the shift in supply and demand would have developed gradually. It would have evolved without the pain and anguish that came to mark the 1970s.

The oil story should act as a hot iron, permanently burning into memory the fact that free markets are self-limiting. Whenever analysts, experts, or investors fall prey to the temptations to make straight-line forecasts, take current events and project them indefinitely into the future, all alarm bells should ring. That kind of fantasy, when popular, will create significant investment opportunities for those who understand the patterns of human behavior.

A Healthy Respect for the Impossible

We become fascinated with the possible and ignore the "impossible." In the case of oil, the Club of Rome had us so indoctrinated with their theories about the limited nature of natural resources that we were convinced that it was impossible to discover significant quantities of new oil reserves. The Club of Rome was obviously wrong. It is, of course, true that the earth as a finite planet has finite natural resources. It is impossible to "make" more oil quickly. There are practical limits beyond which man cannot go. But it was wrong to take that fact and project it onto the oil markets. In the 1970s no one knew the extent of undiscovered oil. That unknown was all too carelessly dismissed. OPEC might have taken a different course if the members of the cartel had had more respect for the unknown. They certainly would have been more moderate in their demands if they had known about the oil in the North Sea, the Gulf of Mexico, and Indonesia. But that knowledge only emerged after billions of dollars had been spent on exploration. OPEC could have been wiser and richer in the long run by simply having a genuine respect for the unknown. Investors can learn from OPEC's mistakes.

Following the first oil shock in the 1970s, the U.S. stock market plunged to a low of 570 on the Dow. The price of a share of Exxon, for example, fell from $26 in 1973 to $14 in 1974. The fact that Exxon's earnings climbed sharply in 1973 and 1974 made no difference. Fear dominated the stock market. Good news was ignored and all the negative possibilities were exaggerated.

It was easy in those days to follow the crowd. The oil shortage was all too real. Long lines at gas stations made

Americans feel politically and economically impotent. The Club of Rome's doctrines and OPEC's power were mesmerizing. The logical thing to do was to sell all stocks, especially oil stocks. But the logic was wrong because its foundation was flawed. The few who bought Exxon at $14 in 1974 were handsomely rewarded. The stock rose to $44 by 1980 for a profit of 300 percent, not counting dividends.

Anyone who claimed in 1974 that you would triple your money in Exxon by 1980 would have been ridiculed. Even today it is popular to assume that big, stodgy stocks like Exxon are too dull under the best of circumstances. Most investors look for excitement and quick profits. They find much more excitement, often in the form of genuine anguish, than profits. Crowd followers are not pursuing large financial gains; they are looking for vague feelings, chasing popular financial fantasies. They don't want feelings of loneliness. They don't want to be responsible for their own decisions. They don't want to have nobody to blame when there are losses, and they don't want to wait patiently, sometimes for years, while an investment develops into an outstanding profit. Standing apart means being willing to accept the dull drudgery of studying financial reports, patiently accumulating assets, taking calculated risks, enduring losses, and waiting for the results.

Buying Exxon in 1974 took real courage. No one looking for security, safety, or excitement would have invested in oil stocks when there were long lines at the gas stations. They would have waited until later, in 1979 and 1980, when buying oil stocks for profit was the rage. They would have bought into oil stocks just as the long climb to a peak was nearing an end. The crowd missed the opportunity in Exxon. But that is the point. The crowd always misses the opportunity. If the crowd had been buying Exxon in 1974, the stock would have gone up, not down. There has to be some cataclysmic event that frightens the crowd in order for opportunity to be created. If you don't stand alone in your investment decision making, you are, by definition, doomed to mediocrity at best.

The only way to triple your wealth and hang on to it is to be in the minority.

Distinguishing between Facts and Fantasy

The crowd is often right about the facts but wrong on the interpretation. The underlying fundamentals and the crowd's perceptions are always separate considerations.

The crowd was right about the first oil shock. Oil prices did continue to climb, there was an outbreak of double-digit inflation, the dollar did plunge, interest rates did soar, and the economy was cast into a deep recession in 1982. But the crowd was wrong to sell stocks in panic in 1974.

If you had written down all the reasons given for selling stocks in 1974, most of them turned out to be correct. The crowd was wrong about the sequence of events and the time table but basically correct on the facts. The crowd took those facts and produced hysterical projections, fantastic summaries of dire consequences, and drove stocks to unwarranted lows.

By the late 1970s the crowd's attention had turned from oil shortages and recession to runaway inflation. Gold and silver prices soared. The fear-confidence cycle was evolving. Almost every professional investor was "overweighting" oil stocks in portfolios. Hedging against inflation was the rage. Few realized that inflation was poised for a collapse or that oil prices would be down to less than $15 a barrel by early 1986.

In the early stages of the new cycle, fear had been based largely on fact. And the facts were basically correct. As the cycle evolved, fear became increasingly based on fantasy. Investors were willing to invest based the assumption that inflation would not only continue but continue to rise.

Gold, for example, was bid to prices that discounted fifteen years of 25 percent inflation rates.

It wasn't too long before the 1980s proved those forecasts incorrect. You might think that declining inflation would have chastened investors, made them cautious and open to a more balanced analysis. Gold fell quickly from the early 1980 peaks, but attitudes did not change significantly. The fear-confidence cycle continued to evolve, as it always does. As investors turned away from the obviously wrong inflation forecasts, there quickly emerged a host of new predictions, equally dire, but in the opposite direction, that of deflation. The crowd was moving steadily away from the facts and becoming ever more involved with fantasy. Misconception after misconception ruled investment thinking and created a string of opportunities.

Money-Supply Madness

As individuals, Americans can be tough, resourceful, proud, and independent. As a nation, however, we have a nearly intolerable penchant for self-criticism. We are quick to find fault with our government, labor unions, corporations, environmentalists, and the system as a whole. We sing of America the beautiful but openly cry out against America the terrible. In the 1970s our national breast-beating led to a perversion of economic thinking, for which we were paying dearly through 1985 and into 1986.

The U.S. inflation rate peaked at 13.5 percent in 1980. Inflation became a source of national hysteria. Senior citizens were terrified that their pensions would become worthless. Others tried to make a killing in gold, diamonds, or antiques. Economic experts searched the statistics for the "true cause" of inflation and for a "sure cure" for this national scourge.

Textbooks define inflation as "Too much money chasing too few goods." The fact that the "goods" in the 1970s happened to be a natural resource, oil, was brushed aside. We decided that the root cause of inflation was "too much money," and we set about to solve the problem by reducing money growth. The Federal Reserve, with the full support of the economic community, investors, Congress, and a majority of the population, drove interest rates up and kept them there to make sure that the U.S. money-supply devil did not grow at an excessive rate. We believed that the inflation of the 1970s was caused not by oil prices, something beyond our immediate control, but by our stupidly allowing the U.S. money supply to grow too rapidly.

As late in the cycle as 1985, the chairman of the U.S. Federal Reserve was able to testify before Congress about the necessity of controlling the risk of future inflation by restricting money growth. Real interest rates in the United States remained high, and the economy, while growing, constantly flirted with recession. Anyone who suggested that the U.S. economy was suffering from too little money was brushed aside.

At one point, in September 1984, the money-supply hysteria had gone so far that there was a virtual buyers' strike in the bond market. Bond prices fell sharply, yields rose, and a major buying opportunity was again created. By early 1986 interest rates were falling and bond prices were soaring. An investor who bought bonds in September 1984, when all the leading experts on Wall Street were forecasting a bond market collapse, had significant profits by early 1986 and rich yields while others waited. British investors, by the way, bought billions of dollars' worth of long-term U.S. bonds in September 1984. The view from London was decidedly different from the view from New York. The more objective view from far away was correct.

The fact was that the United States was not to blame for the inflation of the 1970s. Anyone with a modicum of sense should have realized that the U.S. economy, far from showing signs of excessive money growth, was showing all indications of being strangled by too little money growth. Through the oil crisis the country had managed its affairs too conservatively. An international comparison of money growth in the 1970s and early 1980s would have clearly shown that the U.S. money supply had grown at a rate far less than that of Japan, for example, and only slightly faster than the money supply in Germany. By 1979, the money-supply scoreboard showed that the United States had one of the lowest rates of money growth.

You didn't have to be an economist with access to the international money-supply figures to realize that there was something wrong with the popular money-supply notions. The printing of excess money creates a boom town atmosphere. Demand surges, and interest rates are low. People have plenty of cash to spend, and there is, at least for a while, a general feeling of euphoria. In the United States the economic picture was quite the opposite. Interest rates were high, and the economy plunged into a deep recession in 1982. The symptoms, evident to all, suggested that the real disease was too little, not too much, U.S. money growth. By the early 1980s, the fear-confidence cycle was well advanced. The facts no longer counted. Instead, the crowd created fantasy facts to fit the popular ideas.

The point is not economics, it is investments. After the 1970s rise to double-digit inflation, it was easy to go along with the crowd, believe that the United States had indulged in a wild, money-printing binge, and move all your assets into gold and treasury bills. Not only was the crowd's argument compelling, you could earn high interest rates on short-term investments. Wherever you went—Wall Street, cocktail parties, or bank trust departments—the story was the same, "How can you beat 15 percent on treasury bills?" Bonds were "out." Stocks were for trading. Money market funds and treasury bills were "in." Smug, almost arrogant confidence dripped from every investor's lair.

I remember giving a talk to the board of directors of a small bank in the early 1980s. Interest rates were still high. My subject was the connection between the dollar and interest rates. During the ensuing discussion, I was asked, "What do you think about the long term, three or four years from now? Where will interest rates be then?"

No one "knows" what the future will bring, but you can look at all the possibilities, sort them out, and boil things down to a few probabilities. I said that in my opinion the falling interest-rate cycle would not end until treasury bill rates had declined to less than 6 percent. In my heart I really wanted to be more optimistic and say 5 percent, but I was afraid of the reaction in the audience. I was right. There were rumbles of impolite laughter. One bank officer, sensing the mood of the directors and anxious to be on their side, burst out with, "We will never see interest rates that low again. Those days are gone forever."

My credibility with that bank board was destroyed. The money-supply madness theory and the need for high interest rates had become so ingrained in U.S. investment thinking that the possibility of lower interest rates was categorically ruled out.

There was nothing wrong with enjoying the high yields on treasury bills while they lasted. The investment error was in swallowing the idea that interest rates would never come down. That kind of close-minded thinking kept people in treasury bills too long. They missed several major opportunities in bonds and stocks.

Investors who were able to cut through the crowd's convictions, stand apart, and take advantage of the situation earned handsome profits. Long-term bond yields were 15 percent in 1981. By early 1986 they had fallen to 9 percent or slightly less. Buying bonds in the face of powerful opposition required more than a contrary attitude. It required the right perspective, and one of the best was an international perspective.

Government Debt and Interest-Rate Mania

It is amazing how intelligent people will ignore the past, look at the present as if everything were brand new, and jump to the wrong conclusion. In 1982 and 1983 as the U.S. federal government slipped ever deeper into deficit, a theory was born called "crowding out." It held that monstrous borrowing by the federal government would take so much of the available U.S. credit market that other borrowers, businesses, and private citizens would be crowded out of the market. The punch line was that interest rates were supposed to soar to new record highs. Virtually everyone accepted this reasoning. Investors adjusted investment strategies. Consumers and business adjusted borrowing and spending patterns. The objective was to cope with the expected consequences of a government with a deficit and debts running wild.

The great surprise was that as government debt grew, interest rates did not rise. The economy grew, business borrowed, consumer debt rose to new record-high levels, but interest rates first edged lower and then fell sharply. The economic community and the investment community were shocked. The impossible happened. Interest rates came tumbling down.

Millions of investors lost heavily. Millions more missed out on significant opportunities. In the early 1980s a missed opportunity was as good as an outright loss. Between 1975 and 1985 U.S. inflation cut the value of a dollar in half. To be even, you had to double both income and capital between 1975 and 1985. For a while, when money market rates and treasury bill rates were high, investors were able to increase their income. The safety of treasury bills and money market accounts, however, had a price. The principal did not grow. In fact, it eroded as buying power declined. Then in 1985 and 1986, when interest rates fell, the great investment ideas of the early 1980s were exposed, leaving many in financial trouble. Their capital had not grown and their income was declining. The old, smug, arrogant cocktail party question, "How can you beat treasury bill rates of 15 percent?" had been answered. The inflation that produced high interest rates was eating away at the value of those treasury bills. In the end the smug, treasury bill crowd was left with anxiety and heartache, unable to adjust to falling interest rates.

A quick response, of course, is to remind all those treasury bill addicts that no investment is as good as their claims for treasury bills. There are no truly safe financial havens. Financial security comes from surviving the pounding of the markets. Investors who think they have found the perfect investment are always disappointed. But the story of the federal deficit and U.S. interest rates is more informative than that simple philosophy. There was no need for the economic and investment community to be so wrong. The 1980s were not new times; in fact, they were very close to a repeat of the 1930s.

In 1939 the federal deficit and the national debt were a problem. The total, privately held national debt stood at $33.4 billion. That may not seem like much, but the entire GNP that year was $90.9 billion. The national debt was 37 percent of the GNP. In 1985, after several years of federal deficits of more than $100 billion, the entire, privately held U.S. national debt was 33 percent of the GNP, less than fifty years earlier. Between 1939 and 1946 the United States had to finance World War II. Winning the war in Europe and Asia was expensive. The national debt rose from 37 percent of the GNP in 1939 to 110 percent in February 1946. During the same period the economy grew as well. The U.S. gross national product was $209.8 billion in 1946, up from $90.9 billion in 1939. The United States financed both economic growth and World War II. The punch line is that interest rates did not rise, even as the national debt grew to a size larger than the entire economy.

Moody's AAA corporate bonds provided a yield of 3 percent in 1939 and 2.5 percent in 1946. Interest rates declined as the national debt grew.

Any investor who looked back at the 1930s would have realized that it was possible for interest rates to decline in the 1980s in spite of the huge federal deficits. And sure enough, by 1986 it was clear that, just as in the 1930s, interest rates were falling, even as the national debt and the economy grew.

As if one chance to uncover the fallacies of the early 1980s misconception about interest rates was not enough, there was another perspective that gave the same answer.

The United States was not the only country to run big federal government deficits in the early 1980s. Many countries faced the same problem. By the end of 1983 the United States, in fact, had one of the smaller national debt burdens. Italy, Denmark, Japan, and Britain were struggling with national debts that were a greater percentage of their economies. Nevertheless, in 1983 real, or inflation-adjusted, interest rates were higher in the United States. An international perspective in 1983 exposed the fact that interest rates in the United States were too high. In fact the international data tended directly to contradict the popular views held by U.S. economists. Countries with a relatively high national debt tended to have lower real interest rates. They also tended to have higher rates of inflation. The low rate of U.S. inflation in 1983 alone should have been enough to cause the economists to stop and think. It should have been a signal that the pat, high-interest-rate reasoning could be wrong.

By early 1986 treasury bill rates were down to less than 7 percent. Everyone was pleased to see lower interest rates because the economy needed the boost. But most people were also left in confusion. They had been so convinced that it couldn't happen that they were amazed that interest rates had come so far down so quickly.

You didn't have to have an international perspective or look back fifty years to "see" the underlying truth. Credit markets, like oil markets and most other markets, respond to the laws of supply and demand. The Federal Reserve can, at times, push interest rates in any way it chooses, but eventually the laws of supply and demand will have their way. Every week the *Wall Street Journal* publishes the results of the weekly Treasury Department auction.

Each Monday, the U.S. Treasury goes to market to raise enough cash to pay the government's bills. Uncle Sam raises cash by selling treasury bills. The *Wall Street Journal's* published figures show how much money the government raised and how much money was available. If there were trouble financing the government deficit, it would appear as a slim margin between what was offered to the Treasury and what the government needed. That was not the case. Week after week investors offered to the government far more than what was needed. There was a greater supply of cash than there was government demand for funds. The data from the weekly Treasury auctions told a story the opposite of that which was being argued by the economists.

The government's borrowing needs had grown all right, but the amount of money being offered by investors had grown faster. The economists were half right. They correctly predicted a huge jump in government borrowing. They were wrong in their estimation of what would happen in the credit markets. Investors flocked from all corners of the globe to take advantage of high U.S. interest rates. There was more cash available than had been expected. The law of supply and demand eventually had its way. Interest rates came down. Investors who had been watching the *Wall Street Journal* each Monday saw that the supply of cash was too great to make the forecasts of higher interest rates believable.

U.S. interest rates were high not because of a cash shortage, not because of government deficits, but because of fear, misconceptions, and a Federal Reserve policy that kept the U.S. money supply too tight for too long.

Investors with common sense, a *Wall Street Journal,* an international perspective, or a sense of history were able to cut through the popular ideas and find an opportunity to increase their investment profits.

The Latin American Debt Crisis

Between 1982 and 1986 the investment community did another flip-flop. The recession of 1982 and falling oil prices exposed many international debts as questionable. Countries such as Brazil were faced with slumping exports, owing to the recession. Other countries such as Mexico were faced with falling oil revenue, owing to lower world oil prices. Whatever the cause, the result was the same. Income was coming down, but debts and the cost of servicing those debts remained high. For several years after the international debt problems surfaced, it became increasingly popular to predict a chain of Latin American debt defaults. By 1986, however, when the countries of Latin America for the most part had demonstrated their ability to adjust and cope, the economic community reversed positions, and the "crisis" began to disappear from discussions of Latin American debt.

In the early phase of the international debt flip-flop the case for selling the U.S. money-center bank stocks was very strong. These banks had billions in international loans, particularly to Latin America. A 1930s-type chain of debt defaults would be devastating. If things went far enough, some of the United States' biggest banks would be threatened with bankruptcy.

In the 1930s the chain of default began in 1931 when Bolivia announced that it could no longer meet its debt obligations. Peru, Chile, and Brazil followed with similar announcements. Between September 1931 and September 1932 the list of defaulting countries read like a world atlas. The chain culminated when Germany's new leader, Adolph Hitler, blocked all foreign-debt payments. Yet the news wasn't all black even in 1932. Argentina, Venezuela, and the Dominican Republic continued to make debt payments.

If the dates were covered up and Hitler's name was removed, the litany of debt problems in the early 1980s looked frighteningly like a repeat of the dismal days of the 1930s. American investors were justifiably frightened.

By 1984, the recurring Latin American debt scares had so worn down investors that professional pension-fund managers sold money-center bank stocks just so they wouldn't have to keep explaining the situation to their clients. Pension committees of corporate clients were always asking, "How can you possibly be holding the money-center bank stocks with all the international debt problems? Don't you know what happened in the 1930s?" Consequently, the stocks suffered. Their prices went down. The crowd created another investment opportunity. Buying at that time would have produced handsome profits by early 1986.

The differences between the 1930s and the 1980s were ignored. The fear-confidence cycle was so skewed toward fear that optimistic possibilities were brushed under a thick rug of impressive-sounding but wrong economic reasoning.

The debt crisis in the 1930s and again in the 1980s was not confined to Latin America. Europe was included in the 1930s, and Eastern Europe was a part of the crisis in the 1980s. Fifty years ago both Latin America and Europe defaulted. In the 1980s Eastern Europe did not default. As Eastern Europe recovered from the debt crisis, the good news was all but ignored. At times the headlines screamed the latest bit of negative gossip about possible Latin

American debt default, while news about Poland repaying debts was buried in the back pages.

Leading economists told nightly television audiences that a devastating Latin American debt default was more than a possibility. They forgot to mention as they spoke that thanks to improving balance of payments in Eastern Europe and Latin America, the risk of an international debt collapse was diminishing.

Hardly anyone mentioned that there was a major difference between the 1930s and the 1980s and that it lay in the nature of the debts themselves. In the 1930s U.S. banks were allowed to act as brokers. They had underwritten a lot of Latin American bonds. The bonds had been sold to the public, however, and not retained by the bank. Thus the debtors were the same fifty years ago, but the creditors were not. When Brazil announced that it could not pay the interest on its bonds, investors were in a state of shock. There was panic selling of Latin American bonds and absolutely no chance of obtaining more money for Latin America through the sale of new bonds. In the 1930s the investing public, the crowd, acted as it always does. If the news is bad, the crowd assumes that it will stay bad or get worse. In the 1980s the U.S. government ran into a somewhat similar situation. In the late summer of 1984 it was popular to believe that interest rates would rise to new, record-high levels. In September, when the U.S. government tried to sell a large quantity of fixed-rate, long-term bonds, there was a virtual bond buyer's strike. For a short time there was the real risk of a panic-induced collapse in the U.S. government bond market. Fortunately British investors stepped in and bought several billion dollars' worth of U.S. long-term bonds, averting a potential disaster. If the public in 1984 could panic over U.S. government bonds, imagine the panic over the news in 1931 that Brazil could not pay the interest on its debts. The panic, of course, made matters worse. Without an inflow of new capital there was no chance of recovery in Latin America. Once the crowd panicked, the end of the story was guaranteed.

In the 1970s as international debts grew, the banks were not acting as brokers. They were making loans rather than selling bonds. This time the bankers themselves were on the line. When the problems surfaced, just as they had in the 1930s, the bankers did not run and hide. They negotiated and made new loans. Some called that throwing good money after bad. Few understood that the calmer, more reasonable approach by the banks acting for their own accounts meant that Latin American countries were not abruptly cut off in their hour of need.

Until very recently Americans had been spoiled. It was easy to get a long-term fixed-rate home mortgage. Without such loans most would never be able to afford to buy a home. The record high interest rates of the early 1980s have awakened us to the fact that long-term loans cannot be taken for granted. Many have been forced to accept variable-rate loans, and the risk of substantially higher future payments instead of the traditional fixed rate 20- or 30-year mortgage. Still, we seem to have too little understanding of the situation in Latin America. They are in the same position as an American who needs a long-term home loan but, because of high interest rates and other market conditions, is forced to borrow on a short-term note. Few Americans could pay the full principal on their home mortgages at any given time. But, when given the opportunity of paying in small installments over a long period of time most are able to make the payments on relatively large loans. Nations, like homeowners, also need long-term loans.

One of the theories that emerged as the long negotiating between Latin American debtors and U.S. banks progressed was that the people of Latin America would not be willing to make the sacrifices necessary to meet their end of the bargain. It was widely believed that when the economic consequences of negotiating on the debts hit home there would be "blood in the streets of Latin American cities."

One of the first countries to dig in and face the economic consequences was Argentina. Instead of blood in the streets there developed a spirit of national sacrifice. Shoeshine boys proudly posted signs indicating that they would not raise prices no matter how painful the immediate results. Argentina did the opposite of what the slick salesmen of the U.S. investment industry had expected. For weeks after the good news was evident there was little or nothing in the popular press. The papers continued to carry any bad news from Latin America but overlooked the goods news from Argentina. The fear-confidence cycle had moved so far in the fear direction that any good news was suspect and therefore required twice the scrutiny from the press before it could be published.

The U.S. crowd was so bent on developing the idea of the Latin American debt default that no one thought to ask the people of Latin America how they felt. After all, they had suffered the consequences of a debt default in the 1930s. In the 1980s Americans assumed that the consequences of a default would be more popular than the consequences of debt negotiation. The facts were that the people of Latin America had suffered terribly in the 1930s and did not care to relive those days if there was a way out. Negotiation offered a way out, so they negotiated.

All of this information was available to investors. The positive information, however, was not just brushed aside; it wasn't wanted at all. The crowd wanted a financial lynching, a disaster, and they were not about to listen to reason.

Thus another financial opportunity was created. The stocks in the big money-center banks doubled between 1982 and 1986. With a little common sense and digging into details, an investor could have discovered that the risks in those stocks were not so great as the market seemed to think.

A Great Irony: Investor's Delusions of Safety

Sometimes the answer is right there in front of our face, as plain as the light of day. Yet, somehow it eludes us. This was the situation with the pessimism of the early 1980s. The forecasts of gloom, doom, and disaster were compelling and convincing. At the same time, there was almost always a lingering, intuitive sense that things were not so bad as the experts claimed. The crowd was not on a lemming's rush to the sea of economic disaster. The crowd's investment activity was denying its own disaster predictions.

Why would anyone in his right mind buy U.S. treasury bills if he believed that the U.S. government was, one way or the other, headed for disaster? But as the warning cries increased, more and more money flowed into the "safety" of treasury bills.

By the early 1980s, tax-deferred, short-term, government-backed, and FDIC-guaranteed had become the popular financial buzzwords. Battered by volatile stock and bond markets, investors looked for safe havens. They bought tax shelters and insurance contracts of all sorts and invested heavily in U.S. government treasury bills. The common strategy was to invest for "safety," preferably with the highest possible income. Purchases that compounded at a high rate and were tax free were the ideal. Few people bothered to ask the obvious question, Who is paying and how long can they keep up the payments?

Alarm was often, almost daily, expressed at the federal deficit and the growing national debt. After expounding on that great danger, however, investors rushed happily to buy U.S. government treasury bills. Most were confident that their wealth would compound at high interest rates as they reinvested in more treasury bills year after year indefinitely. The source of that increasing wealth was to be the same debt-ridden U.S. government. This circuitous reasoning was readily embraced by well-educated, intelligent investors. The lure of the crowd and the pull of the fear-confidence cycle are powerful. Once you have joined a lynch mob, it is all but impossible to extricate yourself. The ideas that sweep across the investment field are just as potent and just as binding as the ideas that produced lynch mobs. Your best chance is not to join the mob in the first place. In the case of a lynch mob, that means staying home and not riding into town with the crowd. In the case of investments it means having a different point of view, one that gives you objectivity and keeps you apart, questioning all the popular ideas.

The government was borrowing to pay the interest on its debt. Neither the core national debt nor any of the new treasury bills being issued were backed by anything other than the "full faith and credit" of the U.S. government. The government's debts were a classic example of reverse compounding. Everyone wants his savings to compound at a high rate, but no one wants his debts to do so.

If the national debt kept growing at compound rates as high as they were in the early 1980s, a flash point would eventually be reached. The total debt would become so large that the economy could not support the interest payments. Soaring interest rates would run wild, the dollar would plunge, and the government would lose the confidence of the financial markets. That sort of catastrophe has occurred in other countries in the past. When it happens, the bonds of the bankrupt government become interesting wallpaper.

Something obviously was wrong with the markets in the early 1980s. Investors said one thing but did another. They found stocks too risky. Bonds, they said, were likely to go down when interest rates went up. Gold was dull because inflation was coming down. The government was swamped with deficits, the national debt was out of control, so the only "safe," investment was U.S. treasury bills. It sounds silly when the pieces of that investment puzzle are assembled. As late as 1985, however, those pieces were considered completely logical and sensible by thousands of intelligent investors.

Anyone who stopped and carefully considered the facts saw the inconsistency. The logic did not make sense. Something had to be wrong. Either the government was going to collapse or it wasn't. If, on the one hand, the economy and the entire United States were headed for economic catastrophe, then the only sensible investment would be gold (or silver). If, on the other hand, the U.S. was to survive, something had to change. In 1985 and 1986 something did change. Interest rates came down, reducing the cost of the government debt.

The only truly safe asset is gold. Gold holds its purchasing power through all economic changes. It bought food and shelter two hundred years ago, and it still does today. When you see the investment crowd trying to twist and distort the facts by declaring other assets such as treasury bills "safe", you know that something is wrong. With a little patient investigation and thought you might be able to profit from the crowd's misconceptions.

The crowd had been expressing confidence in the government that they were castigating with words. One rule that seems to work more often than not is to judge by what people do with their money rather than by what they say. The crowd was setting the stage for lower interest rates. Buying treasury bills not only made sure that the U.S. government had enough cash to finance the rising debt, it also created a growing surplus of cash in the short-term end of the credit markets. That cash flood would eventually force interest rates down. Buying bonds based on penetrating the circular reasoning of the crowd would have produced substantial profits.

Confusion over the Gold Standard

It was inevitable. Once President Nixon severed the connection between the dollar and gold, there would be arguments about the necessity of a gold standard. The roaring inflation of the 1970s added to the confusion. Proponents of the gold standard said, "See, we told you so. Without a gold standard, double-digit inflation is inevitable."

Surprisingly, those arguments lived on well into the 1980s, after inflation had fallen back to less than 4 percent a year. The gold-standard proponents should have stopped, looked, and reconsidered the basis for their position.

A gold standard is nothing more or less than a formal statement by a government as to the real, or gold, value of the currency. When the United States said that gold was worth $35 an ounce, it meant that for every thirty-five paper dollars the government will give one ounce of gold. The gold standard is a way of keeping a government more or less honest about the rate at which the value of paper currency is being eroded.

A gold standard is a useful monetary tool because it forms a basis for international understandings. Every nation understands the value of gold and is willing to settle payments and claims in gold. That is important to a country such as Saudi Arabia. Not every currency is traded on the open market. How can Saudi Arabia, whose paper currency is used only domestically, pay for goods, services, and materials from abroad? Payment can be in the form of gold or in the form of one of the actively traded world currencies such as the dollar. In years gone by, when paper currencies were tightly controlled and could be manipulated, gold gave nations assurance of continued independence. A small country with substantial gold holdings could pay for needed materials such as oil with gold. A small country holding German marks, for example, would easily have been crushed under Hitler's heel through manipulation by the German government of its own currency.

Today, however, a gold standard is not absolutely essential. It is conceivable that nations will be able to trade with one another based on paper currency rather than gold. Interlocking paper currencies may help to promote peace. They may be, along with nuclear weapons, a deterrent to war between the world's major trading powers. It is easier to go to war if you first sell the other country's paper currency and switch into gold. If you hold billions in paper Soviet rubles, it is far more difficult to start a war that might wipe out the value of your holdings.

At the end of World War I the victors set out to prevent World War II by means of economic oppression. Germany was cut off from credit and kept in a state of economic privation. From those financial ashes sprang the devastation of the 1940s. After World War II the victors did the opposite. The Marshal Plan was enacted to give money and support to the vanquished. Germany and Japan were rebuilt and allowed to become world-class trading competitors. The world after World War II became one of trade and economic interdependence instead of isolation. In this new era it may well be that moving away from the gold standard reduced the risk of war by fostering the continued integration of the world's financial markets.

In the 1930s the United States was on a gold standard, and we had a depression. We were on a modified gold standard when World War II began. The gold standard did not prevent those disasters. It was inevitable that gold would lose some of its official appeal in the post–World War II years. When the gold system began to put stress on the U.S. and British gold reserves in the late 1960s, it became clear that something had to give. The gold standard became the target. The United States and Britain were not going to stand by and do nothing while their currencies were being widely tendered in exchange for gold. If that continued for too long, confidence in the currency would be at risk as gold reserves plunged. The alternative was to change the official gold price. That too was risky, however. Once a change was made, there was no telling how high the gold price might have to go to stop the rush out of pounds and dollars. Better, President Nixon reasoned, to keep official U.S. gold reserves intact and let the markets sort out the right gold price.

On the one hand, Nixon was right. Through the 1970s, official U.S. gold reserves remained intact, even though the open-market price for gold soared to $850 before falling back to more reasonable levels. There is no telling how much of the U.S. official gold supply would have been lost had President Nixon tried to defend the dollar with a never-ending series of gold-price increases.

The proponents of the gold standard did not consider that possibility and kept insisting that the only way to keep money growth under control was through the gold standard. They may eventually be proven correct. In the short-run, however, they have lost credibility. The U.S. money supply did grow at accelerated rates in 1984 and 1985, but inflation remained subdued. Oil prices came down, and the gold supporters seemed out of touch with reality.

On the other hand, the gold supporters could be proven wrong. The Nixon move may turn out to be another step in the evolution of the world monetary system. A look back over the past few hundred years shows that there has been gradual change in the position of gold. At first gold was the currency. Then people began using paper money for convenience. The next step was for gold to become "official" for a government to hold. Then it became illegal for private citizens. In the 1970s the official and private positions were reversed. Gold became legal for private citizens but was cut out of the official realm. This might be a colossal mistake.

Then again, it might be another step on the road to a more efficient and sensible world monetary system.

At least, as investors, we should give governments a chance and not jump to conclusions about the long-term outlook for inflation, the dollar, and the entire monetary system. And we should take advantage of the crowd's misunderstandings whenever possible. We should be more concerned with remaining objective and open-minded about what is right or wrong with the monetary system. Personal profits are our goal.

Pursuing personal wealth is not a selfish, thoughtless, anarchist proposal. The Chinese have long known that society, like nature requires balance. Westerners, including Americans, too often look at social and economic issues as matters of choice. We assume that the individual goal of personal wealth is founded on greed and in conflict with society's goals of eliminating poverty and providing for the less fortunate. That is far from the truth. One of the important ways that society or governments discover the right method to use in moving closer to those noble objectives is through the financial markets. All we have to do is look beyond the Iron Curtain to see that, when it comes to economics, central planning without the benefit of free financial markets doesn't work. Under a communist economic system a few party leaders decide what is best for society. They issue decrees on how plants will be managed and how farms will be operated. In the United States we have the markets to tell the government what works and what doesn't work. Our government leaders, like the communist leaders, issue decrees in the form of taxes and laws. The difference is that in the United States the markets have a voice in the process. What can be easily forgotten is that the "markets" are the sum total of individual actions. Under a capitalist form of economics each individual is free to pursue his or her personal financial goals. Millions do. They are the "markets." Try to imagine what would happen if there were no risk takers, no one pursuing the personal goal of becoming rich. The financial markets would dry up, become meaningless and our entire society would lose much of its balance and vitality. Risk takers, willing to play by the system's rules in pursuit of personal wealth, play an important role in establishing the "right" fiscal and monetary policies. It may seem impossible, but one of the best ways to help an unknown, unseen neighbor in a distant part of the country is to honestly pursue your own personal interests.

The Outlook

By 1986 the tide of pessimism was ebbing. The stock market was up, interest rates were down, and investors had become more positive on the long-term outlook. This raises the questions, Is this new optimism as flawed as the old pessimism? Will the fear-confidence cycle be repeated? Will investors rush into the future with confidence, looking only at the good news and become overconfident, only to have their dreams of wealth shattered again?

Dealing with the Federal Deficit

The odds are good that the fear-confidence cycle has not been repealed. There are several currently visible possibilities that could lead to yet another cycle, a swing to overconfidence followed by a severe market correction.

The enormous trade deficit has two sides, imports and exports. There are two basic approaches to correcting a trade deficit. You can take steps to cut imports or you can stimulate exports. Cutting imports is a negative approach and can have undesirable consequences. Stimulating exports, as the Japanese did with such success over the years, is not without its problems, but it is a positive approach to a trade deficit and can lead to healthy international competition.

If the United States becomes impatient with world trade, as it did in the 1920s, and passes laws baring imports as the answer to saving U.S. jobs, the consequences could be another recession or worse. Protectionist laws are one way to deal world trade such a blow that economic activity slows and markets fall sharply. The U.S. Congress still has the power, as it always did, to precipitate a recession by a false move. In the 1980s one of the more serious false moves would be to pass into law too many of the hundreds of protectionist trade bills that circulate through congressional offices.

The federal deficit also holds possibilities for future difficulties. The only way to eliminate it is through growth. Recessions make deficits grow larger. When the economy slows, income tax collections fall while expenses for unemployment and welfare rise. This harsh fact is true today just as it was fifty years ago. If the United States decides to reduce the deficit in other ways—through either massive spending cuts or higher taxes—the economy will suffer.

Cuts in social spending reduce basic consumer demand by taking money out of the pockets of millions of Americans. According to official U.S. government figures, there were 34 million Americans, 14.4 percent of the population, living below the poverty line and in need of government aid in 1984. Like it or not, the figures make it clear that government aid is an important stimulus for the entire economy. Without that aid there would be as many as 34 million fewer consumers able to buy goods and services. The defense industry is a major force in the U.S. economy. There were many months in 1985 and early 1986 when the figures showed that without defense contracts U.S. factory production would have been down sharply. Right or wrong, defense spending is also a significant factor in supporting the economy. Cuts in defense spending would have a negative impact on the economy. This doesn't mean that spending can't be cut. It means that cuts must be made ever so slowly and then only as the private sector grows and more than makes up for the losses in government revenue. It may have been wrong to allow the federal government to grow so large in the 1970s. It would be equally wrong to cut it back suddenly in the name of balancing the federal budget.

If the government tries to reduce the deficit quickly by increasing taxes, they will reduce demand just as much as cuts in spending will. In the 1930s the tax increase of 1936 became the recession of 1938. The tax increase that was supposed to balance the budget created a recession, and the deficit grew larger. The stock market fell sharply in 1938. Taxes can be increased, but like spending cuts, that must be done slowly and only when there is *excess* economic growth.

The president and Congress have the power to produce another recession by being impatient and either raising taxes or cutting spending too quickly. They can also percipitate a recession through high interest rates. It is possible that the dollar will come under attack again and that the Federal Reserve will have to step in and defend the U.S. currency with high interest rates just as it did in 1979. Ironically, the huge federal deficit acts as insurance against higher interest rates. The huge deficits of 1984 and 1985 were the result more of the recession of 1982 than anything else. Another recession, while the deficit is large, is almost unthinkable.

After a few good years, however, when the deficit has been reduced through growth, it is possible that the Federal Reserve will feel free enough to deal the economy another blow.

A New Marshall Plan?

The next recession could be pushed off into the distant future. The result of the post–World War II Marshall Plan was twenty years of prosperity. We created export markets for our goods, and the U.S. economy grew. The national debt diminished as a percent of the economy, and American standards of living rose. We could repeat that process if we wish.

Latin America needs U.S. help. Those economies south of our borders represent opportunity. By providing financing, investment capital, and other support, we could assure ourselves of years of prosperity as we increase exports to Latin America.

Developing Latin America through a 1980s version of the Marshall plan may seem a pipe dream. It is tempting to look at a Mercedes Benz or Honda and conclude that the people of Latin America will never come up to that standard of industriousness. The temptation is all the more compelling when we remember Argentina's disastrous attempt to "defend" the Falkland Islands or when we see pictures of impoverished Mexicans scrambling for hope as illegal aliens. It is easy, and cheaper in the short-run, to conclude that Latin America in the 1980s and Germany and Japan in the 1940s are completely different situations.

We have forgotten that "made in Japan" was once an internationally recognized insult. It represented cheap, shoddy goods that didn't last and were not worth the price. In the 1940s and 1950s economic prospects for Japan looked far more like those of Latin America today than we care to admit. Japan, with the help of American capital, was able to develop a sound economy and become an international competitor. The more amazing fact is that as we helped, through the Marshall Plan, to improve the standards of living for the Japanese people we also improved our own standards of living.

Germany was a different situation. Before World War II Germany was a capable, industrialized nation. After the war, however, Germany had to do more than rebuild its industry. Germany was crushed by the war. The legacy of Hitler was a burden that for a long time seemed too great for Germany to bear. Germany had to develop into a respected, responsible world citizen. In 1946 no one in America, for example, would have taken a German car as a gift. Today we buy expensive German cars without a thought. We forget the painful, difficult steps that led from the Germany of the 1940s to the Germany of today. The process required not just money to rebuild but years of support and patience.

Can the same miracle be expected in Latin America? Can we develop markets for American goods? Can we improve our own standards of living while helping the economies of Latin America? We will never know unless we try.

There is a chance that we will follow that course. In the 1970s when we were waiting in line for gasoline, our national wish was that someone would do something to chastise OPEC. Someone did, Mexico. But Mexico didn't have the money to develop the oil fields. It had to borrow the money, and the U.S. banks provided the cash. For a short time in the early 1980s there was the risk that our national spirit would sink so low that Mexico would be thrown to the economic wolves. Many Americans looked on the loans to Mexico as foolish. They had forgotten their own wish in the 1970s.

Fortunately, by 1986 cooler heads were prevailing. Mexico was given support. There were faint signs of appreciation for what had happened, a realization that we might need Mexican oil again in the future, and there was even some talk of another Marshall Plan for Latin America. We might grow our way out of the 1980s through our own generosity, just as we did at the end of World War II. It is also possible that we will turn selfish or foolish or both. The outcome will depend on the national mood, the attitudes of millions of Americans. That will be determined again in the presidential election of 1988 and how we react to a full economic recovery.

There was a presidential election in 1936. The result was a tax increase to do something about the deficit. The consequence was the recession of 1938. This time the presidential election falls two years later in the decade, in 1988 rather than in 1966, or else we might have repeated the mistakes of the 1930s on exactly the same schedule. The election of 1988 will hold a major key to the future course of the economy and the financial markets.

We won't have to wait, however, for clues to what the future holds. It is normal for a national savings rate to dip in the early stages of an economic recovery. As people gain confidence, they will draw on savings or increase borrowing to replace a car or worn out household products. As a recovery matures, those savings patterns should change. People should be willing to put more aside for the future. The savings rate should recover. On the one hand, if that happens in the years just ahead, then there will be cash available to help our neighbors south of the border. On the other hand, if Americans go on a spending spree and the savings rate stays low, there may not be enough cash to help anyone. If we are too selfish and think only of our own immediate pleasure, we will have, in the savings rate figures, a clue as to what will happen in 1988 and beyond.

Whatever the outcome, don't you, as an investor, dwell on the politics. Don't blame the politicians for their often erroneous pronouncements. And don't wish for a better world. Be satisfied with the world you have. It is, after all, a world of opportunity.

Financial Markets and the Possibility of Stability

Can the financial markets go anywhere other than in a circle, when the primary fuel for their engine is alarm, hysteria, panic, or their opposites? When the dollar plunged, inflation rose to double digits, and the U.S. economy stopped multiplying citizens' wealth in the 1970s, Americans knew that something had gone wrong. Liberal social programs and their ideological roots took much of the blame. We said that massive social spending had bankrupted the government and made good-for-nothings out of the rest of us.

Naturally we didn't blame OPEC, rising oil prices, or anything else that was beyond our control. If the problem were beyond our reach, then we wouldn't be able to do anything about it. When there is a problem we feel compelled to do something to correct it. We haven't learned yet that there are problems beyond our control that are better left alone. We blamed Jimmy Carter for the problems of the 1970s and replaced him with a conservative president, Ronald Reagan. The nation swung from a liberal political position to a conservative attitude. The results seemed good for a while. The dollar recovered, inflation came down, and the economy began to grow in real terms again. Naturally, the conservatives got the credit. But all was not rosy under a conservative administration. There were federal and trade deficits, and much of the economy did not grow. Farmers were going bankrupt, and a record number of banks failed. Ironically, both the blame for the problems and the credit for the progress should have gone to Paul Volcker at the Federal Reserve. We didn't elect him. He was appointed by Carter and reappointed by Reagan.

The truth is that neither liberals nor conservatives have an answer to the riddles, mysteries, and challenges of economics. Extreme conservatives and extreme liberals may take different routes, but they end up in the same place, an economic mess.

The nation may swing from liberal to conservative in search of solutions, but until there is a balance, where both sides have genuine respect for the other, there is little chance of stability.

Don't chastise the liberals and don't be angry with the conservatives. Don't worry about what the nation should do; just be thankful that it is the way it is. The democratic system has produced free markets for all. You can buy stocks, bonds, currencies, or precious metals. You can pursue financial security in any way you wish. In addition, as if that weren't enough, this country has given us a political process volatile enough to create opportunities without destroying the basic foundations.

Don't change a thing. The defects, the flawed human reactions, the misconceptions, the wild markets are to be cherished. They assure a never-ending cornucopia of investment opportunity. Praise the political power brokers. Bless the errors of the Federal Reserve and the international misunderstandings.

You can beat these markets. You can stand apart from the crowd. You can make a fortune. But only if you try.

Your quest is for opportunity. Your challenge is to detect that point where you must change strategies or suffer a loss. Risk means periodic losses. Losses mean a temptation to blame the system. Don't. In fact, don't blame anyone. Losses are as much a part of the process of building wealth as gains. Accept them. Count on them. But don't let fear of losses or anything else stand in your way of pursuing the noble objective of personal wealth.

Index